'*The Likes of Us* brings the past to life . . . Michael Collins has woven an argument which has all the emotional impact of a well-wrought novel. If you want comparisons think Tom Wolfe and George Orwell' Michael Bracewell

'Unusual and provocative . . . a measured, well-researched and deftly written book. And to the extent that it forces us to confront our "acceptable" prejudices, it is most welcome' *Sunday Telegraph*

'Collins's account is enlivened by the telling local detail . . . He lines up some high-profile targets . . . and splatters them with well-deserved irony' *Times Educational Supplement* Book of the Week

'An often challenging polemic . . . one which poses some starkly necessary questions about class, identity and ethnicity' *Times* History Books of the Year

'A brilliant book . . . Refreshing, sharp and important. It deserves to be a documentary in itself' Garry Bushell, *The People*

'An important, moving polemic' Bryan Appleyard, *Sunday Times* Books of the Year

'Collins's own family history shows both adaptability and resilience, which Collins documents with an empathy and deftness of touch' *Times Literary Supplement*

'Collins is a sort of poetic hooligan' Laurie Taylor, *Independent*

'Southwark has produced a new kind of hooligan, one swinging his laptop like a bicycle chain around his head, if you are to believe the scandalised notices in some of the broadsheets.

Michael Collins has provoked a major breach of the peace'
Mark Simpson, *Independent on Sunday*

'Almost half a century after Richard Hoggart published his
pioneering insider's account of working-class culture, *The Uses
of Literacy*, the number of books giving a realistic view of life on
the other side of the great divide is still depressingly small. Better
late than never, Mr Hoggart has found an heir of sorts in
Michael Collins' *Washington Times*

'Thoughtful and provocative. Should be read by any fool eager
to dismiss whole swathes of society' *GQ Magazine*

'A resonant and affectionate picture of a vanished Walworth'
Michael Moorcock

'A masterpiece ... How this complex, brave and vital social
group went from being portrayed by their betters and their
wetters as the salt of the earth to the scum of the earth, and how
this view says far more about the thwarted desires and low
prejudices of the other classes than it does the actual decline of
the proletariat, are dealt with with staggering sass and style'
Julie Burchill, *Times*

'There are some wonderfully vivid and at times moving
passages ... compelling' *Financial Times Magazine*

'Fascinating, entertaining, personalized' *Time Out*

'What makes this book "a wonderful read" is his evocation of
the rich details of that milieu – from costermongers and
preachers to gin palaces and children's funerals' *The Week*

Michael Collins was born in Walworth, south-east London, in 1961. He has worked as a television producer and journalist. He has written for various publications including the *Observer*, *Guardian*, *Independent*, *Sunday Telegraph* and *Sunday Times*.

THE LIKES OF US

A Biography of the
White Working Class

Michael Collins

Granta Books
London

Granta Publications, 2/3 Hanover Yard, Noel Road, London N1 8BE

First published in Great Britain by Granta Books 2004
This edition published by Granta Books 2005

A CIP catalogue record for this book is
available from the British Library.

3 5 7 9 10 8 6 4

Typeset by M Rules
Printed and bound in Great Britain by Bookmarque Limited, Croydon, Surrey

Contents

CONTENTS

Acknowledgements

I would like to express my thanks to the following: the historian Stephen Humphrey, the staff of the Local Studies Library, Southwark. The counter staff of the British Library, the Family Records Centre, and London Metropolitan Archives. The Southwark historian Brian Green for allowing me access to his 2001 thesis: 'Social Reform and Social Change in Bermondsey and Southwark 1880–1930'. The essays of Chris Willis on the English social realists of the 1890s proved invaluable during the writing of Chapter 6, as did Rex Batten's *The Leysdowne Tragedy* for Chapter 8. A huge thank you to Sara Holloway and all at Granta, and the friends who cheered me on from the touchline. Finally, a very special thank you to my dad, Bill, and those who made this a story worth telling.

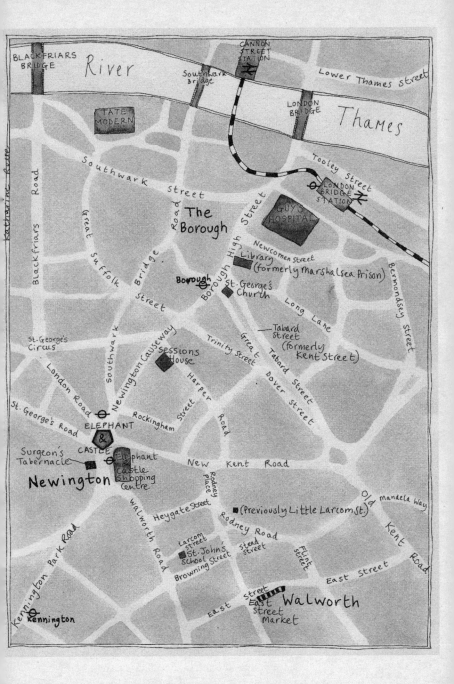

The good man is the builder, if he build what is good.
I will show you the things that are now being done,
And some of the things that were long ago done,
That you may take heart. Make perfect your will.
Let me show you the work of the humble. Listen.

T. S. Eliot, 'Choruses from "The Rock"'

Preface

EVERYBODY'S OBITUARY

He was young, black. Hair? Probably 0.5 on the clippers. Short goatee. Trousers with the seat at knee level, shirt worn with the neckline heading for the elbow, as though allowing freedom of movement for the scissors-cuts-paper-cuts-stone dance short-hand native to rap and hip-hop. It's as American as apple pie, yet certain social commentators pinpoint it as the national costume of black British youth, when illustrating how white kids are influenced by black culture. 'Excuse me', he said. 'Do you know when the murder of Stephen Lawrence happened?'

We were in a narrow room at the rear of a library in Southwark, south-east London, a room with two windows barely wider than wickets, where the past dominates. Outside, Borough High Street was alive with the local workforce, pausing for lunch and queuing for lattes. Close to the entrance of the main library, a plaque commemorates the day the people of Bermondsey fought back against Oswald Mosley and his black-shirts. The building stands on the very site that once housed the Marshalsea prison, where Dickens's father was incarcerated for debt. Next door is 'Little Dorrit's' church. That particular day I was immersed in tracing my ancestors, who lived on the street around the corner for much of the nineteenth century. I was doing research for this book which, coincidentally, I had decided would begin with the Lawrence inquiry.

There were people scanning microfiche, and people pulling out cuttings and photographs from cabinets. There were middle-aged and elderly white men and women, and younger black men and women, all engrossed in their own pursuit of history. There were several librarians on hand, but he had made a bee-line for me. *Do you know when the murder of Stephen Lawrence happened?* The reply stepped swiftly from my lips, like a line read from the wings, a prompt.

'April 1993.'

'Oh', he said.

'He was murdered in April 1993', I continued. 'The inquiry was in 1999.'

He delivered another 'Oh' and a 'Thanks'. Smiled, then disappeared to sift through rolls of microfilm and, amidst sighs and whispers to himself, scanned them on screen.

Why me? I wondered. Of all those present, particularly those seated closer to the entrance of the library, where he hovered for a while – why me? Why not the librarians? Or the man who arrived just after him, and asked a librarian: 'Is this the Commission for Racial Equality?', which had moved into premises above. Or the middle-aged white woman with two carrier bags and a soft 'r' – middle-class, cash-poor, at a guess – who in a conversation with one person, managed to address the library, informing us of her move here three years ago, and of the committees she had joined to bring more gardens to the area, and of her fear and loathing of 'Mr Blair'. Perhaps he singled me out as someone who oozed a certain self-conscious white middle-class liberal sensibility, as someone who'd know the date that Stephen Lawrence was murdered as surely as they'd know a good nanny; who'd know that 'middle England' is shorthand for evil; that politics, like olives and anchovies, can split a dinner party. Saw me, perhaps, as one of those journalists who actually live in a multiracial neighbourhood *and* send their kids to school within the catchment area.

'Excuse me. Are you sure of the date?' He'd returned.

'Eh?'

'The date – are you sure about the date of the murder?'

'Yep. April 1993.'

'I've looked right through into 1994 but can't find anything.'

'Well, you're looking at local papers for this area – Southwark. You'll definitely find it in a library that holds back-copies of broadsheets. Are you writing something on it?'

'Yes. I've been researching it for something I'm writing – a column.'

'What, for a newspaper?'

'Just something I'm writing', he said. 'I'm writing about black deaths. I want to look up someone else. Someone the police shot . . . they shot him because they thought he had a gun in his pocket. Derek Bent— er, Derek Bentley? *Not quite. That was the white boy hanged in the mid-Fifties. It was Derek Bennett he was reaching for.* But, um, you know what you said about the date when Stephen Lawrence was murdered?'

'Yeah.'

'I think it must be wrong.'

'It's not.'

'But, I'm sure the local newspapers would have covered it because he's – um, an ethnic member.'

It was an odd point to make. Local newspapers report on most violent crimes close to home, whatever the race of the victim, and particularly in Southwark, which is reported to have the highest number of violent crimes in the capital. During the year 2000 it witnessed what was described as a 'summer of violence': . . . *the north of the borough has seen several violent attacks, including a racist attack by a gang of black youths on a white teenager last week. The sixteen-year-old, from Bermondsey, was pursued through the streets of Borough and beaten with a baseball bat. He was left with severe head injuries, while his mother suffered broken ribs as she tried to defend him.*

'The local papers wouldn't necessarily cover the murder, because it was outside Southwark', I suggest.

'Oh.' A beat, and then: 'Where?'

Everyone knows where Stephen Lawrence was murdered – not much need for research. There have been TV documentaries and TV dramas and TV discussions materialising on each of the five terrestrial channels. There have been radio programmes and books and a stage play. There was a high-profile inquiry into the murder and the subsequent investigation. There have been features, articles, headlines and columns in broadsheets and tabloids alike, highlighting every aspect of the story and its reporting, written from Clapham town houses, the kitchens of upmarket north London eyries, and the Olympian heights of West Kensington mansion blocks, by those far removed from the scene of the tragedy. And here was another, from someone without a grasp on the essentials. But at least this was a work-in-progress.

'Eltham', I answered.

'Eltham, oh.'

'Like I say, you'll find what you need in a library that stocks national broadsheets.'

'Do you know where there is one?'

'Colindale's your best bet.'

'But that's too far.'

'Well, if you want to get your research right you'll have to travel.'

'Maybe I'll stay here, and look up the inquiry. That was local – wasn't it?'

*

The inquiry was staged minutes down the road at the Elephant & Castle, in the imposing Hannibal House above the shopping centre. It had been painted Schiaparelli pink at some point in the 1980s, and was like a comical pantomime backdrop when juxtaposed with the riotous scenes that occurred outside. At the heart of the proceedings was a tragedy, the senseless murder of a teenager, and the subsequent attempts by his grieving parents to see the perpetrators of the crime brought to justice. This followed a police investigation which was overshadowed by allegations of incompetence and racism. The erstwhile suspects had officially become 'witnesses' by the time of the inquiry, but unofficially, according to the media, would never be anything but murderers, and – even worse – 'racist' murderers, and if not murderers or racist murderers, then on the video evidence depicting them simulating the stabbing of a black man, potential racist murderers, or at least confirmed racists.

Daily a crowd gathered at the Elephant & Castle for the duration of the inquiry. They arrived to take on a gang of racists. There was a large black presence. Among the white faces were those to be found on 'anti-Nazi' marches, who made strange bedfellows with the troop of representatives from the Nation of Islam who showed up and sat in on the inquiry. Their uniform suits were reminiscent of Mosley's men in black, with whom they had things in common, notably their views on Jews.

The atmosphere that permeated the crowd became like that once found at public executions. It was a mood translated as righteous anger in some quarters. One reporter present at the scene described how a white teacher present shouted a repetitive chant in which she listed various violent activities the crowd should carry out on the gang of suspects, including slowly chopping them into pieces. The opinion appeared to be echoed by other white middle-class professionals and students.

These characters are usually vehemently opposed to capital

punishment, and the imprisonment of individuals without air-tight evidence. They have a preference for reform rather than incarceration, and believe that social environment is likely to be the real culprit in a majority of crimes. However, at the Stephen Lawrence inquiry there was a complete about-turn. Suddenly the very people traditionally identified with such liberal views began to express the knee-jerk opinions and rabid rhetoric of those they despised on the right. From the mouths of middle-class professionals in the crowd, and from the pens of journalists and columnists noteworthy for their liberal sensibilities, came the argument that we should hang 'em high, or at least lock 'em up and throw away the key. Failing that, we should reform the law on double jeopardy: those acquitted of murder *should* be retried if fresh evidence of guilt emerges. It was a term new to most of us. It was the kind of stance given an airing from the right after Winston Silcott was cleared of the murder of PC Blakelock during the Broadwater Farm riots. Had this been taken up at the time, some of those now calling for this reform would have challenged the idea that a person could be charged for the same murder again and again, until the state got the result it desired, as a flagrant annihilation of a civil liberty. Paradoxically, those notorious for making their feelings known about false convictions had shifted the focus to false acquittals. But for one case only.

At the inquiry, the fantasies of the chanting teacher baying for blood were soon echoed by the rest of the crowd, so much so that it was as though a lynching might ensue when the group of men left the building via a ramp leading from the shopping centre onto the street. Eggs, flour, missiles were hurled from the crowd, amidst a shrill chorus of verbal abuse, and they were caught on camera retaliating. It was the kind of behaviour identified with those small crowds of largely white working-class women who sometimes gather when a child murderer within their neighbourhood has been convicted, to pelt the police van that protects the killer with eggs, and scream abuse. The same journalists who frown on such illiberal behaviour, who dismiss such activities as worthy of 'the mob', failed to apply such disdain to the unruly crowd outside the Lawrence inquiry, where apparently the public opinion of the crowd rather than the populism of the mob was making itself heard.

The image too, of that little set of 'witnesses' caught in freeze frame, in combat, and emblazoned across the front pages was imbued with a potent significance that again brought to mind the reporting of the Winston Silcott story, and the infamous image of Silcott, bleary-eyed and dishevelled, taken after being held for hours in police custody. But the very newspapers that justifiably condemned the implicit racial stereotyping of Silcott, and the emphasis put on the famous mugshot, which like that of Myra Hindley was regularly trailed by the tabloids as an icon of pure evil, were now applying the same approach to the suspects at the Lawrence inquiry.

Unlike Silcott, it was not their colour – or at least not just their colour – but their class, that assisted in this stereotyping. Suzanne Moore was one of a number to write of the 'white trash' suspects. In the USA, the term had previously been described by film director John Waters as the last racist phrase that you can get away with. Yet it refers both to colour and to class. This became apparent when references to the illiteracy of the men – the spelling and grammar within their handwritten press release – and to their lack of education – 'they didn't have an "O" level between them' – were cited as though further evidence of guilt. Meanwhile much was made of the fact that their mothers were neither non-smokers nor natural blondes. It wasn't simply the suspects, their families, that were on trial but the neighbourhoods in which the tragedy was played out. Some journalists even traced the story further, to the streets of Southwark, birthplace of some of the parents of the suspects. The moral panic that ensued, around racism and white working-class youths, had echoes of the past – from the 'hooliganism' of the 1890s, to the cosh boys and Teddy boys of the 1950s and the 'mugging' phenomenon first documented in the 1970s. But what became apparent in the aftermath of the inquiry was that reports on racism had segued into a demonisation of the white working class.

Historically, the right harboured desires to keep the white working class below stairs. There they could use the wrong knives and drop their aitches to their hearts' content, until trenches needed manning and flags waving in the name of patriotism. Now, middle-class progressives who had traditionally come out fighting these underdogs' corner, or reporting their condition as missionaries or journalists, were keen to silence them, or bury them without an obituary. They were reputedly more obese than their equivalent throughout Europe. They loved Gucci; loathed the Euro. More important, to their pall-bearers in the press they were racist, xenophobic, thick, illiterate, parochial. They survived on the distant memory of winning one world cup and two world wars, and were still tuning in to the ailing soap that is the House of Windsor. All they represent and hold dear was reportedly redundant in modern, multicultural Britain. It was dead. Over. Otiose.

It was this representation, which ignored both the detailed experience and the wider history of the white working class, and simply reduced them to a caricature similar to that in which they were cast centuries before, that encouraged me to write this book. And it was the research for this book that brought me to the library that day, where I became immersed in ancestry and local history, along with my fellow travellers to the past.

For generations, both sides of my family had lived in Southwark. The history of the family, and of the class itself, was exemplified by my mother's mother, Nell Hall (née Larter), who died in 1991, months before her centenary. Not long before her death – at which point she could remember the Relief of Mafeking but not where she had put her keys – I slipped a 90-minute cassette tape into a machine and began recording her story. Her voice is intermittently drowned out by a tumble dryer rumbling in the background; her concentration drifting in the direction of the muted television and *The Chart Show*. There are pauses in the recording; she stared at the tape as though waiting for it to talk back, like Beckett's old man Krapp playing a recording of his younger self.

Her memory had served her well. The remembered fragments of her story provided me with her potted biography; just enough to place her in the context of a bigger story – that of a class and the evolution of the landscape in which they carved out their lives. For the rest I would one day need to refer to local history, and the accounts and descriptions of working-class life in Southwark that remain from the nineteenth century onwards. Like the East End, Southwark was fertile soil for those from other classes who slipped into the missionary position and embarked on expeditions to discover and understand the working class by social investigation, social anthropology, or simply slumming it. Almost all were well-intentioned, many were deluded, many more were patronising, some changed lives for the better, and collectively they attempted to familiarise the working class with – for starters – God, sobriety, reform, revolution and utopianism.

Nell Hall was among the last of that generation born in the 1890s, just as a post-industrial, urban working-class culture established itself. It was a culture that thrived until the 1950s, and survived in a more disparate and diluted manner until the 1970s. But much of contemporary British culture has its origins in the working-class counterculture of the late nineteenth century.

Days before my brother died in his late thirties in the early 1990s, he described the street in which we had grown up as 'the last outpost': an uncharacteristically poetic line, but apt, as his first love was Westerns. It was a reference to the exodus from urban working-class neighbourhoods like Walworth, Bermondsey and Rotherhithe in Southwark to the satellite suburbs of south-east London: Eltham, Welling, Bexleyheath. It began slowly in the late Seventies and swelled to a diaspora the following decade. He was part of it, and so were my parents. The day they moved, Morrissey murmured into my Walkman: '"goodbye house – forever!"'

Our generation was perhaps the last unbroken link to that original colony, in a setting that, like its inhabitants, was characterised by a history of neglect and exile. 'For centuries the settlement on the south bank was not known as London, and even today the appearance of homogeneity is superficial,'[1] wrote the historian Harry Williams in 1949. 'The southerners are "foreigners", still, and the threadbare town is almost unknown to the vast majority of visitors to London.' Outside the City and Westminster, Southwark is the capital's most ancient borough, but historically it has soldiered on as the poor whore across the water, housing the smells, the produce, the noise, the prisons and leper hospitals those two boroughs wouldn't harbour. In his 1945 novel *London Belongs to Me,* Norman Collins writes: 'Strange, isn't it, how much of the real London still lies south of the river, just as it did in Shakespeare's day, and in Chaucer's day before him? It is as though across the Thames – in London's Deep South – times and manners haven't changed so much as in the Parliamentary North.'[2]

Today, the area is in the throes of significant change – as is the tribe with which it is historically identified, and its number elsewhere. The white urban working class that dominated the area for so long is being succeeded by different races and nationalities, as well as a new middle class that is beginning to colonise this area south of the river, as it becomes defined by Tate Moderns, lofts, lattes and multiculturalism. This book is therefore a native attempt to take an audit of the area and its inhabitants, including my family, from the early nineteenth century to the beginning of the twenty-first century, and to cast an eye over the works of those aforementioned missionaries who attempted to bring about change. It focuses not just on the people who have inhabited this area, but the changes that have occurred within the physical landscape. It would be impossible to attempt a biography of the urban working class without focusing on a particular landscape, as this class more than any other is inextricably linked with the concept of home, a street, a neighbourhood, a community. Yet historically, the landscape of the urban working class has been subject to more change than elsewhere because of redevelopment, the arrival of migrants en masse, and incessant attempts to accommodate its dense population. This is therefore by no means the definitive story of the white working class, but one of many – hence the 'A' of the subtitle. At best it uses the personal and the local as a cue to a more general picture of the urban white working class, past and present. At the least it is the inside story of a tribe on a particular reservation and during a particular period, as told by an erstwhile native son.

PART ONE

AN EXCAVATION

1

SOMETHING OUT OF DICKENS

In 1814 the prophetess Joanna Southcott died of a brain tumour in her mid-sixties, having convinced the followers from her 'House of God' at the Elephant & Castle that she was pregnant with the next Messiah. Two years later my great-great-great grandfather Thomas Francis Larter was born in the same neighbourhood, but without the fuss and the fanfare that greeted the phantom pregnancy of the elderly prophetess. Tom's father, William, was a rope spinner, and the figure who begins the Larter family line on the south side of the river. He was born in Whitechapel and moved across the water – possibly to find work at the riverside at London Bridge – where he married a local girl, Martha. A first child, Tom, was born in January 1816. His arrival was followed three years later by a brother, William, and soon two sisters, Martha and Mathilda. Martha died in infancy and a third daughter was given her name. Christopher was born in 1830, and their final child Robert arrived a year later. He died at twenty months. By the year of his birth, William and Martha had lived in Kent Street since at least the time of their marriage almost twenty years earlier, along with other relatives from the extended Larter family. I pieced together their skeletal story from parish records, censuses and electoral records. According to the 1831 census, the household consisted of 5 males and 11 females.

Kent Street, the road that connected Borough High Street to Old Kent Road, was made famous by Chaucer's pilgrims. The Larters lived and worked at number 130. In those days the boundaries of Southwark were essentially those now associated with the 'Borough', beginning south of London Bridge, and stretching to the Elephant & Castle.* London Bridge, which led onto Borough High Street was the only thoroughfare across the Thames to the south until the eighteenth century. Paths from Westminster, Blackfriars, Vauxhall, Waterloo and Southwark converged at the Elephant & Castle. Dickens had referred to it as 'that ganglion of roads from Kent and Surrey and of streets from the bridges of London centring in the far-famed Elephant'. Although the area was built up at the riverside, further inland, and beyond Kent Street, it was dominated by St George's Fields, north-west of the Elephant & Castle; and Lock's Fields, which extended to Walworth. This was previously the home of the Lock Hospital for lepers, which had been erected because the northern shore wouldn't house such an establishment within its city walls.

Kent Street remained the main route to London from the south, and one of which the City was ashamed. It had become a built-up working-class neighbourhood with a bad reputation even in the 1830s. A newspaper report described it as 'a byword and reproach, inhabited by a squalid gang of vagrants'. Its residential pockets were tiny, dingy, broken-down dwellings, with

---

*In 1900 Walworth was incorporated into the Metropolitan Borough of Southwark, and in 1965 Bermondsey and Rotherhithe were added to what was now known as the London Borough of Southwark.

shutters at the windows instead of glass. The main trade amongst the more respectable residents was brush-making, but the neighbourhood was dominated by prostitutes, thieves and pickpockets in the habit of knocking doorways between the houses they occupied to give them boltholes when the police arrived. Tenants were subjected to the 'Kent Street ejectment', described in Brewer's dictionary as: 'Taking away the street-door; a method devised by the landlords of Kent Street, Southwark, when their tenants were more than a fortnight in arrears'.

The year his youngest sibling was born Tom Larter was fifteen years old. It's unlikely he had any education, as less than half the children of Southwark of the relevant age attended school. At the time, the wealthier local ratepayers of Southwark and Walworth were reported to be so grievously 'burdened with numerous and expensive poor' that local children were sent to the cotton and woollen mills of northern England. The wealthy industrialist and socialist Robert Owen, who had worked in Southwark, had written: 'it is common for parents to send their children of both sexes at seven or eight years of age, in winter as well as summer, at six o'clock in the morning, sometimes of course in the dark, and occasionally amidst frost and snow, to enter the manufactories, which are often heated to a high temperature, and contain an atmosphere far from being the most favourable to human life . . .'[3] The reformer William Cobbett claimed it was 'to be a despicable hypocrite, to pretend to believe that the slaves in the West Indies are not better off than the slaves in these manufactories'. Those working fourteen hours each day, in a heat of over eighty degrees, were subjected to rules he believed 'no negroes were ever subjected to'.[4]

By the time Tom Larter was a teenager, parliament had passed the 1833 Factory Act reducing the working hours for children, and had set about abolishing slavery throughout the British Empire, a move that led to home-grown radicals criticising the conscience of a ruling class that 'showed itself so tender for black slaves overseas but so tough for white "free" labourers at home, in cotton mill and coal-mine'.[5]

Tom Larter – like something out of Dickens: the name perfect for a cameo in the tales of Oliver Twist, Nicholas Nickleby, Pip, or David Copperfield. The streets he grew up in were those in which Charles Dickens – Tom's senior by four years – found his muse. As an adult Dickens returned regularly to wander the neighbourhood where his father had been incarcerated in a debtors' prison, the Marshalsea, on Borough High Street, and he fictionalised John Dickens's experience in the stories of William Dorrit and Mr Micawber. In *Little Dorrit*, published in 1857, he writes: 'Thirty years ago there stood, a few doors short of the church of Saint George, in the Borough of Southwark, on the left hand side of the way going southward, the Marshalsea Prison. It had stood there many years before, and it remained there some years afterwards; but it is gone now, and the world is none the worse without it.' Charles occupied a nearby attic room, overlooking a lumber yard, during his father's imprisonment. David Copperfield sold his waistcoat to Mr Dolloby on Kent Street. Little Dorrit was christened and married in the parish church of St George (where in 1819 Tom Larter was the first of the Larter siblings to be baptised, where the funeral for his sister Martha took place, and where he was to marry).

Dickens, the first, or at least the most successful chronicler of London slum life, converted to the page much of what he witnessed in the lives of the labouring classes of Southwark, and particularly the criminal element: 'to show them as they really were, forever skulking uneasily through the dirtiest paths of life, with the great, black ghastly gallows closing up their prospect'.[6]

His stories as 'Boz' appeared from 1833, often in the *Morning Chronicle*. At the end of the 1830s he was becoming the most popular author in England, but how many literate Southwarkians would have read him? He himself believed the English working class were 'as hardworked as any people upon whom the sun shines. Be content if in their wretched intervals of leisure they read for amusement and do no worse. They are born at the oar, and they live and die at it.'[7]

By the time of the 1841 census, Tom is married with a young son, Will, born four years earlier in the month of Queen Victoria's accession to the throne. Unlike his father and his two brothers, Tom no longer lived on Kent Street, but like them his work was that of a rope spinner. His home was close to the rope walk – where he may have carried out his trade – overshadowed by Horsemonger Lane gaol, between Kent Street and the Elephant & Castle. The family occupied dwellings in a blind alley behind the gaol. In 1848 and 1849, the neighbourhood attracted the attention of the press with events and developments that proved more newsworthy than the story, years before, about Joanna Southcott and the next Messiah.

Throughout the early decades of the nineteenth century, revivalists and radicals each attempted to convert the working class to their cause. While the latter were inspired by the utopian visions of Robert Owen, or the writings of William Cobbett, the former were influenced by the self-penned pamphlets that transformed the domestic servant Joanna Southcott into a national figure. These characters had a greater impact in the north than in the south, but Southcott carved out a substantial following in Southwark. After the first Reform Act (1832), support shifted from the Southcott cult to the Chartist campaign for universal suffrage.

Chartism has been described as the first working-class

movement, even though its leaders were predominantly middle-class. It reached its pinnacle in 1848 with a meeting which its organisers claimed was attended by 300,000. The actual figure was reputed to be closer to 40,000. The meeting at Kennington Common on 10 April 1848 was the culmination of widespread frustration at the failure of the Reform Act to bring greater democracy.* This was the southern shore versus the City, the poor versus the rich, almost as though Southwark itself was attempting to settle an old score for being cold-shouldered by the City for so long. The decaying portrait in the attic: *leper hospitals . . . prisons*. The government prepared for the event as though for a revolution. The Duke of Wellington treated it as a sequel to Waterloo: a force of special constables overwhelmed the crowd, from parliament to the Elephant & Castle and Kennington. Shops in Southwark were closed; streets deserted. Delegates were transported by a horse-drawn cart emblazoned with the words: 'Who would be a slave that could be free? Onward, we conquer; backward we fall.' Heavy rain dampened the ardour of the crowd, and a large number of the signatures on the petition presented to parliament were exposed as forgeries, which dampened the credibility of Chartism and marked the movement's decline from that day forward. Still, the campaign for reform continued, and the expected rebellion had made Queen Victoria jittery. Days later she summoned Lord Shaftesbury, who recalled how the monarch 'was anxious to know, in view of the disturbed conditions of the country, which were the best ways to show royal interest in the working class'.

Dickens and the Chartist meeting had raised awareness of the

---

*The People's Charter, which laid down the six main objectives of Chartism, was first published ten years earlier. Its aims were annual parliaments, universal manhood suffrage, equal electoral districts, the removal of the property qualification for membership of parliament, a secret ballot, and payment for members.

urban working class. The year after the march, the cholera epidemic in the summer of 1849 had the same effect. The disease took 13,000 lives in the metropolis. On the southern shore it was particularly devastating in Bermondsey, and the area where the Larters lived. 'The land of death in which it dealt was Newington, hemmed in by Lambeth, Southwark, Bermondsey, and other gloomy parishes through which the pestilence stalked like a destroying angel.'[8] In September, Henry Mayhew, cofounder of *Punch*, visited Bermondsey to report on the epidemic for the *Morning Chronicle*. Of one street he noted:

> along the reeking banks of the sewer the sun shone upon a narrow slip of the water. In the bright light it appeared the colour of strong green tea, and positively looked as solid as black marble in the shadow – indeed it was more like watery mud than muddy water; and yet we were assured this was the only water the wretched inhabitants had to drink.

The neighbourhood in which Tom Larter lived was dominated by Rockingham Street, a road that had suffered minor floods throughout its recent history. Until the end of the eighteenth century it had been bounded all around by a common sewer and was partly under water for nine months of the year. The trustees of the land had no desire to raise and drain the ground until the influx of immigrants increased the demand for working-class housing, ensuring that this would be a profitable course to take. Both Newington and Walworth had remained damp, and without decent drainage and sanitation. Despite this Tom Larter and his family survived the epidemic. He was now the father to three sons: Will, my great-great grandfather, Henry and Alfred.

Henry Mayhew, meanwhile, convinced his editor that the newspaper should investigate the plight of the labouring classes, and the impact of bad housing, disease and poverty. Like Dickens, he saw there was a story to tell. It was Mayhew's intention to record it, in weekly reports in the *Morning Chronicle*. Other journalists were recruited for the task, and dispatched throughout England and Wales for their investigations. Mayhew concentrated on the working class of the metropolis, producing two articles each week from October 1849 and throughout the following year. Each instalment was published in the style of a letter, and the content featured in the first volume of *London Labour and the London Poor*, edited and largely written by Mayhew, and originally published in 1851. This was the first expedition by a middle-class journalist into the world of the working class in the name of sociological observation and analysis. It would be the first of many. It supplied information on 'a large body of persons, of whom the public had less knowledge than of the most distant tribes of the earth – the government population returns not even numbering them among the inhabitants of the kingdom'. With illiteracy dominant, and so few prominent spokespeople emerging from their ranks, it was left to sympathetic middle-class journalists to speak on behalf of the poor. Before Mayhew, working-class culture had remained, according to J. F. C. Harrison, 'virtually terra incognita for the first half of the nineteenth century'.[9]

Here was a sociological survey that reproduced the words of the thousands of its subjects verbatim, without shaping the original idiom, syntax and slang to standards of literary convention. There was no previous work to which it could be compared, and it provided the only major oral history of the urban working class of the period – the first documentary journalism of the nineteenth century. 'It surely may be considered curious as being the first attempt to publish the history of a people', Mayhew writes in the book's introduction, 'from the lips of the people themselves – giving a literal description of their labour, their earnings, their trials, and their sufferings, in their own "unvarnished" language.' It is these authentic interviews with working-class characters that mark the special brilliance of Mayhew's work. Setting aside the occasional patronising generalisation and the sometimes sketchy social anthropology, it is the voices of the subjects themselves that reach out, touch us, and give a real insight into those hearts and minds. Here is a young coster* interviewed:

On a Sunday I goes out selling, and all I yarns I keeps. As for going to church, why, I can't afford it, besides, to tell the truth, I don't like it well enough. Plays, too, ain't in my line much; I'd sooner go to a dance – it is more livelier. The 'penny gaffs' is rather more in my style; the songs are out and out, and makes our gals laugh. The smuttier the better, I thinks; bless you! the gals likes it as much as we do. If we lads ever has a quarrel, why, we fights for it.

I'd precious soon see a henemy of mine shot afore I'd forgive him, – where's the use? Do I understand what behaving to your neighbour is? – In coorse I do. If a feller as lives next me wanted a basket of mine as I wasn't using, why, he might have it; if I was working it though, I'd see him further! I can understand that all as lives in a court is neighbours; but as for policemen, they're nothing to me, and I should like to pay 'em all off well. No; I never heerd about this here creation you speaks about. In coorse God Almighty made the world, and the poor bricklayers' labourers built the houses arterwards – that's my opinion; but I can't say, for I've never been in no schools, only always hard at work, and knows nothing about it. Before father died, I used

---

*'Coster' is an abbreviation of 'costermonger' – originally a fruit-seller selling their wares by hawking a barrow through a market. The costard was the large English apple that was their speciality.

sometimes to say my prayers, but after that mother was too busy getting a living to mind about my praying.

Mayhew maintained that he had made every attempt to avoid exaggeration and never exceed the truth. He revealed that there was not simply the working class, but the working classes, which he divided into subgroups: those who work, those who don't work, those who can't work, and those who don't need to work. This final category referred to a criminal class that thrived within a culture of vice that ultimately distinguished it from the poor and the 'respectable' working class. Oddly, cabmen, a large category of men within Southwark, were lumped with prostitutes, pickpockets and street performers. In describing them, Mayhew took the anthropology theme to an extreme: 'there is a greater development of the animal than of the intellectual or moral nature of man, and that they are all more or less distinguished for their high cheekbones and protruding jaws . . . for their use of slang language . . . their love of cruelty . . . their pugnacity . . . and their utter want of religion'.[10]

It seems that costermongers loved their dogs almost as much as they loved making them fight. Those who could read rarely did, but enjoyed illustrations and were familiar with the drawings of Cruikshank. Mayhew's informants revealed that a number of costers considered themselves Chartists, yet knew nothing of the six points of the charter. Many were pigeon 'fanciers', and kept them in cages on the roofs of their houses. The beer-shop was their focal point, where landlords provided gloves for sparring between punters. 'The costers boast', wrote Mayhew, 'that they stick more together in any "row" than any other class.'[11] This was equally true with regard to other aspects of their lives, as all the costers in a court or a street would visit a sick coster in hospital on a Sunday, and none would steal from each other's stalls. Thefts that occurred on street markets were those carried out by regular thieves.

About a fortieth of the population of the metropolis earned their money selling on the streets. Within this group the coster-mongers were not the most dominant in number, but at the time of Mayhew's survey they were increasing rapidly, as those traditionally employed elsewhere found themselves unemployed or their trade redundant in the wake of further industrialisation. Down the road from the borough at this time, in Walworth, its market on East Street – which connected the area's two main thoroughfares, Old Kent Road and Walworth Road – had come into being. Here, my father's ancestors became the first of generations of Collinses that would trade there, largely selling fruit and veg.

Mayhew wrote of how the 'thoroughbred' costermonger was one within a family of costers that went back generations, or at least worked a regular stall or pitch. These frowned on 'the illegitimates' who did the rounds selling oranges and tea and peasoup, rather than the fruit, fish and veg with which the coster had become identified, and who included a growing percentage of Irish and Jews. As if to emphasise their membership, the coster fraternity – who reputedly became irritable, even aggressive, when confronted with foreign words they didn't understand – were linked by a language of their own.

> The slang language of the costermongers is not very remarkable for originality of construction; it possesses no humour: but they boast that it is known only to themselves; it is far beyond the Irish, they say, and puzzles the Jews. The root of the costermonger tongue, so to speak, is to give the words spelt backward, or rather pronounced rudely backward ... With this backward pronunciation, which is very arbitrary, are mixed words reducible to no rule and seldom referable to any origin, thus complicating the mystery of this unwritten tongue; while any syllable is added to a proper slang word, at the discretion of the speaker.

One of the conclusions that Mayhew drew from his expeditions was that the labouring classes were in need of wholesome amusements rather than the 'dry abstract truths and dogmas' that 'serious' people attempted to impose upon the poor in order to educate them, or the low-priced amusements peddled by 'venal' traders that 'seek only to gratify their audience'. Within the weeks that followed his first instalments to the *Morning Chronicle*, the class he had set out to investigate were enthralled by one particular amusement staged in Southwark. There's no way of telling if Tom Larter or those who he knew took part in the Kennington Common Chartist meeting, just as there is no way of knowing if he ever read Dickens, or passed him in the street as a boy. But it's almost certain that he was in the crowd for the execution of the Mannings in November 1849, as it was literally on his doorstep. Dickens definitely was.

The rear of Horsemonger Lane gaol occupied much of the road adjacent to Rockingham Street. Mayhew described the building as 'enclosed within a dingy brick wall, which almost screens it from the public eye'. The Mannings were a married couple found guilty of murder, and their execution drew a crowd of thirty to fifty thousand spectators that day, surrounding the gaol, the rope walk to its side, and spilling into Rockingham Street. Tom Larter had no hand in creating the hangman's noose; that was the job of Edginton's, the ropemakers on the Old Kent Road. Days before, rooms had been rented by reporters chronicling the event. Well-off spectators arrived early, setting themselves up with seats in the gardens opposite the entrance to the gaol. Each had paid one guinea to the residents for their seat, whilst Dickens had paid ten guineas for the use of a nearby roof so as to have a perfect view of the crowd, rather than the macabre spectacle on the roof of the gaol. Both before and after the execution, policemen used ropes to pull individuals free of the mob, to prevent them from being crushed. Several were hospitalised with fractures and broken bones, and days later a woman died in Guy's Hospital from her injuries. Traders stationed at the barricades that penned in the crowd sold 'Manning Biscuits' and 'Maria Manning peppermints'.

Silence fell just as the clock struck nine, with the final, fatal toll from the prison chapel. Mrs Manning, for ever after known as the 'black satin murderess' because of the clothes she had chosen for her execution, seized her husband's hand as the cap was drawn over her face and the rope adjusted. Her struggle was reported to be longer than that of Mr Manning, whose death came after a couple of convulsive jerks. It was only an hour later, when the bodies were finally taken down, that the crowd began to disperse, leaving the nearby roads littered with shoes, bonnets and shawls that had become detached from their owners during the crush. On this very patch in the twentieth century there would be other mob scenes, from Teddy boys rioting to those that occurred outside the Lawrence inquiry, but nothing that would match this particular spectacle.

Following the Mannings' execution, Dickens wrote in a letter to *The Times* that kindled a campaign to abolish public executions: 'I do not believe that any community can prosper where such a scene of horror, as was enacted outside Horsemonger Lane Gaol, is permitted. The horrors of the gibbet and the crime which bought the wretched murderers to it faded in my mind before the atrocious bearing, looks and language of the assembled spectators'.[12] Some of the leading London Chartists had suggested that the working class of the mid-nineteenth century were more educated, well-mannered and disciplined than the mob of the previous century, who would turn out in the name of anti-Catholicism or in support of an imprisoned MP, simply to participate in a riot. But even in 1849 a public execution was still by far a greater pull than a protest for a parliamentary vote.

2

IT'S A SMALL WORLD

When William Larter senior died in 1857, aged sixty-five, he was living at the same Kent Street address, and still working as a ropemaker. On that site a decade after his death* his two younger sons began to establish a thriving business, listed in the street directories as 'Larter Wm & Christopher, rope manufacturer'. When William Jnr died in 1883, he had a wife thirty years younger, a young son, and a servant. They lived in a house off the Old Kent Road. Christopher died three years later. His address was the same as that of the business.

At the probate office in Holborn in 2003, I discover that Christopher's personal estate, of which his sister Martha is named as executor, was an incredible £2,968 4s 9d. It's a colossal amount for the period, and I can't but wonder where or who it eventually went to. Certainly, there's no indication that his elder brother Tom received any of it. More than twenty

---

*By which time Kent Street had been renamed Tabard Street in recognition of its part in Chaucer's travels (the name is a reference to the nearby Tabard Inn from where the pilgrims set out).

years earlier, in 1860, Tom Larter had moved south to East Street in Walworth just as the market had become established, where in the 1970s I would earn a part-time adolescent living at various shoe stalls, record shops and boutiques between the death of glam and the birth of punk. Tom's work was less varied but more skilled. He was employed as a wheelwright, working on market barrows, which were increasingly in demand with the growth of the local costermonger class.

Like Southwark and Newington, Walworth was changing, with more terraced streets, mainly of two up, two downs, springing up to house an increasingly working-class population drifting inland from the river. The growth stemmed mainly from the surplus of births over deaths, the continual flow of immigrants from rural areas and, since the potato famine of the mid-1840s, a steady influx of Irish immigrants. Because of the rise in the number of streets and families, there was, in 1860, a major exodus of Walworth's middle class, who moved further afield to Peckham, Brixton and Clapham.

In the summer of 1860, Will Larter – Tom's eldest son – married Harriet Hackett. He was one of that pugnacious breed of men that Mayhew had distinguished by their high cheekbones, protruding jaw, mouthful of slang and utter want of religion: a cabman. His young wife was pregnant with their first child, born that same year and christened Harriet Henrietta. Two years later the couple produced another daughter, Rosina, and by the end of the decade three sons had been added to the fold: Francis, Henry and Charles.

Henry Larter, my great-grandfather, was born in July 1867. It was the year of the second Reform Act, one of a number of developments that would lead slowly and circuitously to a better deal and greater representation for the working class. Trade unions were finally legally recognised, and an Education Act was introduced to ensure that all children had the option of some form of elementary schooling. Previously, the Ragged School Union had been created to establish institutions 'for destitute and depraved children in the location, courts and alleys where they abound'. A ragged school in Walworth was started in a loft over a disused cowshed. Now the children of Henry Larter's generation were the first to – at least in theory – attend the board schools that began to appear on a number of local streets; education was paid for by all except the most poverty-stricken parents. But even two years after the 1870 Act, the chief inspector of schools described Southwark and its environs as 'an educational desert'.

Tighter laws regulated children's working hours in factories, and after the Chartist and Christian socialist Charles Kingsley highlighted the plight of working children in *The Water Babies* there was a ban on using children as chimney sweeps. However, the treatment of minors that fell foul of the law remained extreme, as Will's son Henry was to find to his cost. In 1881 he was presented at the Sessions House in Southwark accused of stealing sherbet from a shop at the Elephant & Castle. Another local boy, William Henry Bramwell, also aged thirteen, was charged with 'unlawfully obtaining a silver watch with intent to cheat and fraud'. The court was built on a site near Horsemonger Lane gaol, demolished the previous year following the outlawing of public hangings. Ironically, the land was transformed into a children's playground, officially opened by the wife of the prime minister, William Gladstone.

Earlier in the century a crime like Henry's would have led to the scaffold, or at least the 'Parish Cage' – a local building where delinquents were incarcerated, and from which only the dangling dirty legs of the chained youngsters were on view to passers-by. At thirteen, Henry's punishment, despite the slightly more enlightened times, and the whispers of reform, seemed no less barbaric. The London Metropolitan Archives in Farringdon contain an index of industrial and reformatory cases of the time, which gives details of juveniles bought before the court. My great-grandfather is listed as being sentenced on 26 February 1881. There is a column adjacent to his name entitled 'How dealt with'. He was plucked from his family, and placed on a industrial training ship, *The Shaftesbury*, that provided discipline for youths in need of 'assistance'. In the census of 1881, taken the following month, I discover that Henry is described as a 'scholar', with the ship – docked at East Ham – as his address. There is no record to be found of the length of his sentence, but *The Shaftesbury*, managed by the School Board, is described elsewhere as accommodating 'London boys under legal detention to the age of 16 years according to the Industrial Schools Act of 1866'.

When Henry returned to the southern shore, after serving his time, Southwark and Walworth were undergoing change. The sporadic regeneration that occurred within the borough throughout the decades that followed prompted the historian and social reformer Walter Besant to describe Southwark as the 'city of transformations'. George Peabody (1795–1869), an American banker living in London, remembered as 'the founder of modern philanthropy', had donated £500,000 to 'ameliorate the condition and provide for the poor and needy of London'. The terracotta tenements erected in Peabody's name were revolutionary; they housed families in units, in blocks with communal sinks and lavatories, built around a courtyard to maximise air circulation. It was argued in some quarters that this 'block system' was something locals would reject: 'It does not commend itself unreservedly to the English mind so far as residence is concerned, and the possession of a home separate and distinct from another, and free as possible from any interference.'[13] Yet it became the blueprint for the 'model dwellings' that emerged throughout Southwark and Walworth on what remained of the former fields and commons, and land where prisons once stood.

Many of the local tenements were run by private landlords who let them descend into disrepair, and often inhabited by tenants who used the wooden banisters for firewood. The stairwells were dark throughout the day, and the rooms at basement level barely got light at all. The landscape was still dominated by housing that was dilapidated and often rat-infested, while the population continued to increase far beyond the availability of suitable homes. Once again, the area became a favoured territory for expeditions from middle-class journalists, among them James Greenwood, the son of a coach-builder, notable for his regular contributions to the *Pall Mall Gazette*, and later the *Daily Telegraph*, about conditions in the city's working-class neighbourhoods.

Greenwood was also a novelist and, in the 1860s, a writer of books that took the anthropological approach to understanding the 'manners, customs, habits and recreation, peaceful and warlike, of the uncivilised world'. His subjects included Bushukulompo hairdressing and Samoan modes of punishment. Much of what remains of his collected journalism (published as *Low-Life Deeps: An Account of the Strange Fish to be Found There*; *Unsentimental Journeys: Byways of the Modern Babylon*; and *The Wilds of London*) is preoccupied with the rites and ceremonies of urban tribes. Here he finds the 'costers' carnival' that occurs annually at Barnet Fair, and the gypsies that park their yellow and green painted caravans ('bedecked, chilled, and blistered by the sun') on the waste ground of Lock's Fields each winter, as curious as rain making in savage lands. In an attempt to understand that 'ruffianly, blackguardly, bullying race'[14] of which Will Larter was a native, Greenwood spends the night accompanying a cabman as he goes about his 'peculiar line' of business:

'You'll excuse my incredulity', said I; 'but you must admit that being eat up with rheumatism is not commonly made grounds for preferring to pass the night out of doors rather than in one's warm bed at home.'

'Well, it do seem strange to them as has the enjoyment of their limbs, I dessay. When you're brought to hate your bed, to cuss it cos of its warmth, and you gets no more comfort out of sheets and blankets than if they was harsh and raspy as soleskins, it makes a difference. That's just my case. And my old woman, she works a ropery up Bermondsey way – on her legs from morning till night, poor old creeter, and coming home as tired as a dawg. Well, nat'rally she wants sleep, and how's she goin' to get it with me alongside of her rilin' and groanin' with rheumatics? That's how the bed serves me; d'ye see, sir? Soon as I get warm it gets at my bones like rats a gnawing at a wainscot.'[15]

Unlike Mayhew, Greenwood was preoccupied with the gypsies, tramps and thieves that existed as a minority within the general working class, and who fitted into that criminal fraternity alluded to by Mayhew. He is the roving correspondent, 'the amateur casual', as he refers to himself, dipping into these worlds with no attempt at disguise. For *A Night in the Workhouse* he made an exception. Published in the *Pall Mall Gazette*, and reprinted in book form, it would become the work with which he was most identified, one for which he both dressed and played the part in 'what had once been a snuff-brown coat, but which had faded to the hue of bricks imperfectly baked'.[16] Much had been written about the issue of workhouses on *behalf* of those forced to lodge in them, but 'nothing by any one who, with no motive but to learn and make known the truth, had ventured the experiment of passing a night in a workhouse, and trying what it actually is to be a "casual"'. Greenwood writes that: 'No language with which

I am acquainted is capable of conveying an adequate conception of the spectacle I then encountered.' Describing the sleeping arrangements of his fellow inmates, he notes: 'Some were stretched out at full length; some lay nose and knees together; some with an arm or a leg showing through the coverlet. It was like the result of a railway accident: these ghastly figures were awaiting the coroner.' In the final lines of the piece, he points out that he has 'avoided the detail of horrors infinitely more revolting than anything that appears in these papers'.[17]

Greenwood's technique marked the beginnings of a tradition that continues today. In the recently published *Hard Work*, the columnist Polly Toynbee documents how she left her Clapham town house to spend some time living on a council estate and doing low-paid jobs. The journalist Fran Abrams, commissioned by the *Guardian* to work as a night cleaner at the Savoy, used the experience as the basis for the book *Below the Breadline: Living on a minimum wage*.

Back in the 1860s, Greenwood's adventure inspired the journalist Richard Whiteing, whose father worked for the Inland Revenue, and whose family had lived on the Strand. The year 'the town was startled by Mr Greenwood's account of "A Night In The Workhouse"', as Whiteing described it, he began writing a series of columns in the character of 'Josef Sprouts'. The collection was published in 1867 as *Mr Sprouts His Opinions*. In the preface 'Sprouts' reveals how an editor encouraged him to reverse Greenwood's original concept: 'middle-class had been to see low class, low class should return the visit'.[18] It was decided that Mr Sprouts should be a costermonger, and the subject of the first of his of columns – each one written as a letter – was 'A Night in Belgrave Square'. Soon Mr Sprouts was sharing his thoughts on Derby Day, and offering his opinions on reform and manhood suffrage.

Apart from inspiring Whiteing's mocking of the cockney character, Greenwood's *A Night in the Workhouse* inspired a brand of newspaper reporting that came into play years later. Greenwood's style, with the cliffhanger ending – implying that there was something out there so savage, so alien, that the Grand Guignol within a newspaper report could only tentatively hint at the real horror – became essential to the later slum journalism of the 1880s, although it was not Greenwood but another writer, George R. Sims, who would be credited as the pioneer of the form. Sims's grandfather had been a leading figure in the Chartist movement, and was present at the mass meeting at Kennington Common, while Sims himself become one of the most famous journalists of the day. His face was a familiar one. He was questioned as a possible suspect in the Jack the Ripper case after being spotted by a passer-by in a London street who turned out to have recognised the author's features from the prominent ads for a cure for baldness – one that Sims had invented.

George R. Sims made the transition from journalist to author by highlighting the plight of the urban working class. He can therefore be credited with pioneering not merely the slum journalism of the 1880s but the slum fiction movement of the following decade. It was while lecturing on the issue of reform, in Southwark, that he took up the invitation to explore the district with a local school board officer. He suggested to a newspaper editor – at the new *Daily Pictorial* – that he write an authentic account of the experience of the working class in Southwark and elsewhere. The essay was eventually published in book form as *How the Poor Live*. Sims prepares the readers for the territory as though a missionary destined for the forbidden reaches of the Empire. He begins: 'This continent will, I hope be found interesting as any of those newly-explored lands which engage the attention of the Royal Geographical Society –

the wild races who inhabit it will, I trust, gain public sympathy as easily as those savage tribes for whose benefit the Missionary Societies never cease to appeal for funds.'[19] These funds, the author believed, should be delivered by 'Dr State', urgently, and particularly in relation to housing. Sims seemed to be threatening his middle-class readers: if this issue wasn't addressed, the savages from the dark, depressed continent of Southwark might rise up and revolt. 'This mighty mob of famished, diseased, and filthy helots is getting dangerous, physically, morally, politically dangerous. The barriers that have kept it back are rotten and giving way, and it may do the State a mischief if it be not looked to in time and its filth may spread to homes of the wealthy . . .'[20]

The method was similar to that employed by those writing more recently about the 'mobs' that took to the streets when paedophiles were in their midst, or the reports by journalists that descended on Eltham in the wake of the Lawrence inquiry. Unlike Sims's dispatches, these were simply attempts to shock the educated middle-class reader by revealing that there was something wicked in this particular woodshed, perhaps a potentially dangerous mighty mob. All of which was implicit in such apparently horrific revelations as the news that: 'Because of the local authority's "sons and daughters" tenancy policy, the area has remained almost exclusively white working class' (David Pallister, *Guardian*).[21]

Sims's impassioned reports inspired a congregationalist, Andrew Mearns, to take up his own mission to this newly explored land. Mearns's pamphlet *The Bitter Cry of Outcast London*, published in 1883, inspired a number of editorials in the *Pall Mall Gazette* that referred to a people 'brutalised into worse than beasts by condition of their environment'. Mearns stressed that nothing he described was fiction. He recalls a visit to Bermondsey:

Entering a doorway you go up six or seven steps into a long passage, so dark that you have to grope your way by the clammy, dirt-encrusted wall, and then you find a wooden stair, some of the steps of which are broken through. Ascending as best you can, you gain admission to one of the rooms. You find that although the front and back of the house are of brick, the rooms are separated only by partitions of boards, some of which are an inch apart. There are no locks on the doors, and it would seem that they can only be fastened on the outside by padlock. In this room to which we have come an old bed, on which are some evil-smelling rags, is, with the exception of a broken chair, the only article of furniture.[22]

When the author asks the room's inhabitant if she intends to sell some rags at the pawn shop because she's poor, the response is indignant: 'Call me poor? I have got a half a loaf of bread in the house, and a little milk.'

Mearns understood that the situation of the poor could not be improved by conversion, prayer, and the handing out of shelter and soup to the few. He recommended the assistance of Sims's 'Dr State', but also the establishment of mission halls within working-class areas, to carry out work that would be greater and more effective than anything attempted in the name of a single denomination. The aim, he declared, was to rescue, not proselytise. 'There is no room for sectarianism', he said.[23] The view was echoed by the founder of the Salvation Army, General William Booth, who published his own account of expeditions into the deprived continent of the urban working class, *Darkest England and the Way Out*: 'all through my career I have keenly felt the remedial measures usually enunciated in Christian programs and ordinarily employed by Christian philanthropy to be lamentably inadequate for any effectual dealing with the despairing miseries of these outcast classes'.[24]

Mearns revealed that in the borough where the Larters lived the landlord of a number of houses that were verminous and beyond human habitation was the Church of England. Its commissioners swiftly enlisted the services of housing reformer Octavia Hill to advise and act on regenerating their properties within Southwark. Once again the physical environment surrounding the working class was in the throes of change. Hill supervised the building of cottage-style homes with conical roofs, outside of which borders were left for plants. There were communal halls and gardens, in order to create a villagey neighbourhood. Both Hill and those working for the Peabody Trust strove to ensure that the working-class tenants under their jurisdiction should begin to conform to the 'respectable' values of the middle class. Hill encouraged tea parties and the growing of crocuses. Like Mayhew, the reformers and the philanthropists believed that the working classes could be sorted into specific subgroups. Mearns had written of ideal dwellings that might separate the 'incorrigible' classes from 'the well intentioned poor'. The Peabody Trust insisted that tenants were selected 'upon the principle of excluding the workshy and others of known intemperate habits'. The concept of state housing would not be realised until the beginning of the following century, but Sims's work and, more significantly, that of Mearns brought the plight of the people on the southern shore and elsewhere into the newspapers and onto the agenda.

Despite his crime, it is difficult to ascertain which category the young Henry Larter may have fallen into. Those cast as the 'respectable' working class, who were neither criminal, workshy, nor the slaves of 'intemperate habits', still lived under the conditions that Mayhew, Sims and Greenwood had described, and the poor laws and workhouses remained from the days of Dickens. At the age of fifty-seven, Tom Larter died of the consumptive disease phthisis, according to his death certificate. It was a disease that would later be attributed to living in squalid, densely-packed neighbourhoods. His home had remained close to the market, on the fringes of Lock's Fields. Here there was now, in the words of James Greenwood, 'nothing more suggestive of cows than the heels and paunches of the animals in question exposed for sale in the grimy little shops that plentifully dot the neighbourhood; whilst as for grass, not a solitary blade would meet the eye except in the form of those saucerised bits of turf retailed at a penny each, and which imprisoned larks speedily convert into the frowsiest of hay with their hot feet'.[25]

A cousin of Will's, Henry, would end his days in the workhouse. In the ledger – splintered and crumbling at the spine, and tied and knotted like a parcel from the past – that contains records from the year of his admission and death (1891) the Larter name is one of a number recorded by a neat and steady hand in ink now the colour of rust. Another relative was sent to the greener pastures of Caterham and to a hospital to which many of the mentally ill from the district were consigned. As for the young Henry Larter, he was employed as a carman, transporting goods between factories in Southwark and Bermondsey. Born in 1867 he reached eighteen in 1885 when the fortunes of the family seemed set to improve for the better.

3

FROM LOCK'S FIELDS TO GOLDFIELDS

Throughout the nineteenth century the middle classes not only reported on the urban working class, they also embarked on missions to mould or rally them, offering a path to equality and opportunity. Radicals, reformers and progressives touted utopian socialism, manhood suffrage or revolution. The religious revivalists and Tractarians chipped in with education, sobriety and redemption, whilst the Christian socialists straddled both camps. But nothing provided a quicker shortcut to heaven on earth than gold. The little word that was big in the dreams of the poor had encouraged many to migrate in search of their fortune. In 1885 gold was discovered in the Transvaal. Prospectors and miners from across the globe descended on the goldfields and diamond mines. Among them were members of the Larter family, taking shore leave from Southwark.

According to Peter Clarke 'opportunities for new settlement in rich new lands under the dear old flag, were surely one benefit of Empire which the working-class electorate could be brought to appreciate',[26] and South Africa was 'a gilt-edge opportunity for the British race to go forth and multiply their wealth'. It was a moment in history when the term 'Little Englander' was bandied about the letters pages of British newspapers to deride those antagonistic to the expansion of the Empire (long before it metamorphosed into a label to dismiss those opposed to a single European currency). The English working class had no wealth to multiply at home, and little to lose by emigrating to South Africa, where the colonial immigrant had a better chance of picking up work, land, and food.

It is difficult to establish exactly which members of the Larter household migrated to South Africa in pursuit of their fortune, as few records remain, and the full story, as relayed to Nell Hall, passed with her death almost a century later. She always maintained 'there was once money in my family' and that this had come from relatives who struck lucky 'in a diamond mine in South Africa'. It may have been her father's brother, Francis – known as Frank – whom she recalled meeting on his return from the Boer War in 1900: 'We met him at Waterloo Station. He had a navy blue kit bag.' It may have been her grandfather Will, and his wife Harriet. There is no record of a death to match Will's details in Family Records Centre, which suggests that he may have died abroad. Whichever of the Larters had in fact migrated did so in the mid-1880s, and their faith in a windfall was great enough for my great-grandfather Henry, his parents, and his siblings to change their name. By the time Henry married Kate Harris in 1889, at the age of twenty-two, he had become Henry Diamond Larter. Ironically, theirs was one of a number of 'penny weddings' at St John's, the 'costers' church' – where Henry's parents had married – in which up to forty couples were married in a single ceremony. The press referred to these occasions as 'batch-weddings'. The *Pall Mall Gazette* wrote of the churches that 'the match-making democracy in the thickly-populated eastern and southern quarters of the metropolis are wont to regard them as temples of Hymen on Easter Sunday and Monday'.

This was a time when working-class men were forever relocating their families to temporary homes in pursuit of brief spells of employment. Henry found work in Shoreditch, and moved with his pregnant wife to Hoxton, in the second year of their marriage. Generally, families seldom moved beyond the borough for work, let alone 'over the water', as they called it. However, some of the Larters had left before Henry of course – for the goldfields and diamond mines of the Transvaal, or the green fields and asylums of Caterham. Henry and Kate had their first child, Harry, in 1891. Their second arrived the following year: Nell Hall, born Caroline Larter. The surname came with marriage; the Christian name she purloined in her mid-twenties. Whilst waiting for employment in a crowd on a factory forecourt, she heard the foreman call out her surname, and that of 'Nell', as one of those picked for work. No one answered. She raised her hand, took the job and became known by that name ever afterwards. Soon after his daughter's birth, Henry decided to resettle the family in the south to be closer to factories he knew, and available work. He had found employment with a coal merchant at the Elephant & Castle. When she was a few weeks old her mother wheeled Caroline across London Bridge and back into Southwark, where her father had found lodgings.

Library photographs exist of Borough High Street from 1892. In these, the profiles of its shops rise and bow, are puffed up and sucked in, each forehead attempting to nudge ahead of the one in front. Above the window of W. Straker's stationery agent, four lamps rise from thin metal stems. The toy shop next to Chatfield's the boot maker has its sign obscured by small wooden carts and a hobby horse. On the right-hand side, pans and colanders hang from a baker's, alongside 'bath chair tyres' at Chaplin's. Towards 'Little Dorrit's' church, the shops become smaller, thinner, some as dark as a cavity, concealed beneath charcoal shutters as dusty and grazed as school blackboards. Some are pasted with the same solitary poster: TO BE LET Field & Sons. The area's main surveyors, Field & Sons has the face of a gold metal sun above its entrance, and a funereal façade – as polished and plain as a coffin. It is as though it is in mourning for another time; perhaps the past when Bankside was famous for theatres, making the neighbourhood a prime location to visit, or the future. Gold had been discovered in the Transvaal, but for Southwark the gold rush would not begin until more than a century later, at the end of the 1990s.

There is barely a pane of glass in the windows above these boarded shops. From hollows, rag curtains flop on the window sills, waiting for a breeze to waft them back inside. Here was Tabard Street, the former Kent Street, where the rope business of William and Christopher Larter remained until 1895. This was the poorest part of the area, where gas lamps burned all day to bring light to rooms below ground level. The calls to demolish and regenerate this neighbourhood had gone unheard for decades. In photographs, the buildings along Borough High Street are taller, as the road hands over to Newington Causeway, leading to the Elephant & Castle. The Causeway was in decline by the 1890s, with the final exodus of the middle class. As the population increased the tenements began to dominate the district. On the right-hand side approaching the junction at the Elephant & Castle, a Turkish Bath advertises itself with 'forget your prejudices'. Much of the opposite side of the road is taken up with Tarn's department store. On this corner is the Rockingham Arms pub, with the Alfred's Head on the opposite corner to its right. Unlike the stores that queue behind them, these were the main port of call for locals. And the scene these buildings created was like a stage set, the very tallness and width of each business concealing the greyness and grime of the streets in the shadows behind them. The entrance to that world was a break in the chain, before the department store began; a street whose opening was in the shadows beneath the railway bridge. Here was the Larters' new home.

By the time Henry settled into Rockingham Street with Kate, there was still no sign of the windfall, and judging from their daughter's birth certificate the 'Diamond' name appears to have been discarded. The family rented number 76. Before reaching the house you passed the huge coal depot next to the railway bridge, where Henry now worked, stables, a basket works, a glass works and a dilapidated block of dwellings referred to as 'the buildings'. A currier's was opposite. On Sunday lunchtimes when the railway was silent, the sound of a Salvation Army brass band could be heard on the Causeway. For Henry, the louder the sound, the closer he knew he was to a drink and a bet at the Rockingham Arms. Like the Alfred's Head, this was one of the larger, more elaborate local gin palaces, decked with ornate glass and polished brass fittings. There was a plushness within the gin palaces that was absent from the small pubs on the corner of slimmer streets, where the floors were strewn with sawdust. And there were as many pubs on the corners of the streets of Newington and Walworth as there were bookies later.

Despite the docks helping Britain create an empire that had made England 'the workshop of the world', 68 per cent of Southwark was below the poverty line,[27] and Bermondsey was cited as one of the worst slum areas in Britain. Working-class adults in the 1890s, the descendants of the 'white "free" labourers' at home who helped build England into the country on which 'the sun never sets', were living in homes on which 'the sun had never risen' according to an apparatchik[28] of the

Independent Labour Party. Men were employed in the tanneries, as carmen and draymen in the breweries, on the railway and the wharves, in factories and workshops. Many of the women worked in the jam, biscuit or gelatine factories. Nationally, around one hundred factory employees lost an arm each year, and some two thousand fingers went missing. Nell Hall said factory women held on to their engagement finger, whilst a lot of factory men lost theirs. And despite the changes in the law, child labour persisted.

There was a board school at a corner of Rockingham Street facing the wall of the former gaol, which Nell Hall attended between the age of three and six years. In the 1890s an editor of *Pall Mall Magazine*, Charles Morley, embarked on an expedition to the area to gauge the success of these schools. His dispatches first appeared in the *Daily News*, and were amongst those collected in his *Studies in Board Schools*, published in 1897. Both the book and Morley's journey begin with the essay 'The Wild-Boys of Walworth':

> All roads lead to 'The Elephant' in this part of London; but after making polite enquiries for the famous landmark from a butcher, a baker, a greengrocer, and a young lady of five, who was picking a winkle out of a shell with a crooked hairpin, I still found myself groping in the wilderness, when I suddenly stumbled into the middle of a miserable street full of the wildest ruffians.

The wild-boys he discovers use 'sulphurous words' as shocking as those he later hears nearby, where even the 'Borough sparrow has a minatory tone about it'. One child is spotted snatching the stock of the cat's-meat man and swallowing it. A mother bemoans her efforts at keeping her son in school: 'I wish he were dead – God forgive me, sir, but I do. I've buried ten, and only this and another one's left, but I wish he were dead, I do. He's fast breaking our 'ome up he is. His father's lost two days work a-lookin' for him.'

The streets that Morley writes about are those that Dickens wandered, and the characters he stumbles upon have a touch of the stock caricature about them. Both their names, and the words that he puts in their mouths, lean more towards the comic novel than a journalistic document. Reading the study now, I am transported not to the Southwark of the 1890s, but a Lionel Bart songbook and the voice of Jack Wild. Morley happens upon Rufus Rainbow, the red-haired son of a scavenger who refuses to go to school. Tom Tipping has 'a pair of roving black eyes, a curly nose, a nice fringe dropping over his forehead, and a mobile laughing mouth, his chief garment being a long overcoat which reached nearly to his ankles. On the whole he rather reminded me of the artful dodger without his guile.' There's the full-time truant Tommy Musselwhite who excuses his behaviour with: 'I atto go out seling [*sic*] matches, and after a few howers I became hill, and then I atto go home and go to bead.'

Ultimately, Morley's original fears for the wild-boys of Walworth are allayed when he returns to the board school months later, and notes a marked improvement Those who, unlike Tommy Musselwhite, have become regulars have undergone a transition. 'Take Tom Tipping's case', Morley enthuses. 'Tom lifted his cap politely, bowed and sirred me till I was quite abashed. Never did he say "guv'nor", nor let fall a D, big or little, nor use such words as bloke or cop (which are not to be found in any dictionary you know), and even when he was taken with a severe fit of sneezing in the middle of our conversation he produced a handkerchief. To be sure, it was only the leg of a stocking, but he did his best.'

4

OVER THE WATER

The new year was heralded by the traditional chimes and cheers as well as an uncharacteristic frost, the worst for eighty years. It arrived on the eve of 1895 and lingered until the following March. In January, after a week of respite in which the weather became comparatively mild, more characteristic of an English winter, the frost returned, but fiercer. During its stay, an arc like a rainbow, but as pure a white as housewives with lace curtains dreamed of, stretched itself across the upper sky. Although its presence was at first a talking point, diverting conversations in trams and cabs from the subject of the frozen river, it quickly became, like other fantastic sights in those months, just another unbelievable image in an unbelievable winter.

Shortly before sunset on 30 January, Londoners looked to the sky and saw a vision that was even more extraordinary. The sun, brilliantly luminous, had taken the form of a comet. On the wealthier parts of the northern shore, skaters paused on frozen lakes and gazed upwards. In the poorer parts of the south, aspiring visionaries, the easily led, and certain devotees of the evangelism practised in Spurgeon's Tabernacle at the Elephant

& Castle, saw in it the hand of divine intervention. One devotee described it as 'a visitation from God'. Across the road, shop girls living above Tarn's stretched skyward from the windows of their lodgings. In rooms next door, above the Rockingham Arms, drinkers jostled for a glimpse of the sun. The pub's turret obscured their view, along with the iron sunflowers – with petals encased in grime and soot – that sprouted above the eaves. Locals returning from factories, or traipsing to pubs, or settling their young down in rooms as damp as the houses and alleys that surrounded them, continued to look to the sky, sporadically checking for more lights, more visions, after darkness had fallen.

Nell Hall was not yet three years old, yet the images from that season stayed, and became the first she was able to recall in her old age. The Thames had frozen over, and she remembered 'men with buckets on their feet wading through Walworth'. A crowd of seagulls appeared on the southern side of London Bridge one day in February, returning daily for the duration of the winter. As a notably sociable species bred in colonies they were perfectly placed, as could also be said of Southwarkians. The spot where they settled proved an impeccable choice. Because of the weather, the ships and boats in the docks of Rotherhithe, and the river traffic that flowed by the wharves of Bermondsey, were icebound for days at a time. With no boats to circle and scavenge for food scraps thrown overboard, the seagulls relied on the kindness of strangers. Commuters arriving at London Bridge station brought scraps of food and tossed them to the foot of the bridge as they passed. Mothers from nearby streets, relishing a brief but welcome break in their arduous routine, brought their infants to the bridgehead. Crumbs were sprinkled into the chilled palms of children, as their elders nudged them in the direction of the gulls. This was Nell Hall's first memory. She approached the bird, tentative, afraid, with hand outstretched. The white of the gulls' backs, the clay grey of their wings, even the dusky coats of their young, seemed to blend with the wider setting of snow, ice and sleet.

As the weeks passed, the Thames developed islands of snow and ice that were whipped into fluffy peaks. These soon froze into various shapes too shapely to be lumps, yet too amorphous to be statues. For as far west as you could see (Westminster Bridge) to as far southeast as you might venture (Woolwich), the length and breadth of the river was paved in white. The formations on its surface resembled the ghostly shapes concealed beneath the dust sheets of a house, awaiting another season and the arrival of guests.

In March the ice began to thaw rapidly. Activity returned to the surface of the river. The wharves and the warehouses came back to life, but gentle breezes and slight rains continued. Within weeks there was a heatwave, and Londoners were rewarded with a season that was almost tropical. Throughout the frost of 1895, soothsayers and the superstitious had a field day. The brief belief that the white rainbow was a 'visitation from God' appealed to the more fervent followers of Spurgeon's evangelism and to the few locals who remained faithful to Joanna Southcott.

The impact of the weather on the young and old led to many deaths from respiratory diseases. Water pipes froze in Southwark. Households went without water for nearly ten weeks. Efforts were made by the churches and Poor Law Unions to deal with an increase in unemployment, arising from the adverse conditions. When the frost thawed, water pipes burst and Rockingham Street and the neighbouring streets were affected by floods. Nell Hall witnessed her father and the other local men wading along the street and across the New Kent Road, with buckets, bins and other makeshift contraptions on the lower half of their legs. By the end of the month, when the waters had cleared and the Thames had become its old self, her family were among the many who headed to the riverside at London Bridge, almost by way of a celebration. The event seemed as ritualistic as anything practised in the name of religion, and to a child, the stuff of which miracles were made. They joined the crowd to watch a man walk on water.

A music-hall performer named Wallace Ross walked along the Thames from Vauxhall Bridge to London Bridge, equipped with a small canoe-like contraption attached to each foot. The prank was to publicise his performances at the South London Music Hall – later the South London Palace of Varieties – at the Elephant & Castle, where his routine was of a less precarious nature. His forte was to cut a horizontal broomstick in half while it was supported on two rings of paper suspended from the edge of two razors – without cutting the paper itself.

The stunts that performers carried out at the music hall capitalised on the local love of spectacle. The arrival of the hypnotist Professor Dale frequently drew crowds. He materialised via a horse-drawn hearse with a couple of passengers as prostrate and lifeless as corpses. These two assistants were carried into the venue and brought to 'life' by the power of hypnotism. Other turns included Professor Wingfield and his performing and vaulting dogs and Professor Carl Hermann, who produced live rabbits 'from nowhere in particular'. There were exotic acts: The 'Indian Princess Zenobia and her aerial fantastique flight', Professor Desmonti & Nubar Hassan with an 'Anglo-Indian pot pourri'. It was the place where men became female caricatures, and women became male caricatures. Music hall was also the British home of 'black-face' cockney performers such as Black Cookey – the champion spade and stilt walker, with hoops of white greasepaint circling his eyes, and lips made up in white. One newspaper referred to these characters as persons 'of colour (acquired)'. To the white working class the sight of a 'person of colour' that had not been acquired was rare, but not quite as rare as a white rainbow, a sixty-four-year-old woman pregnant with the next Messiah, or a hypnotist in a hearse. It was perhaps for this reason that 'touching a black man' was meant to bring luck.

The resident chairman at the South London Music Hall was an eccentric character. Nell Hall remembered seeing Bob 'The Baron' Courtney dressed in a a shirt studded with fake diamonds. When presiding over the events at the South London, according to a newspaper review, 'his air is youthful, almost juvenile, and his abundant hair is as black as the wing of a many-wintered crow . . . He can be backed to discharge his functions with punctuality and dispatch on a mixture of Pomery Greno, bottled stout, Old Tom, the dew of Ben Nevis, sherry, zoedone, and ginger wine'. Newspaper critics often descended on the area to slum it for a night of authentic working-class entertainment. One critic wrote of how the language spoken by the 'Aborigines' queuing outside the Roman entrance of the South London was 'racy, of the pavement, which it in some respects resembles'. The wall facing the stage of the auditorium was dominated by a huge mirror in which the performers could see themselves above the audience in the pit and the stage had a permanent backdrop depicting a scene within a Flemish market. An aesthete from Grub Street suggested that: '[Oscar Wilde] the poet of languor and lilies and La Langtry should be allowed an opportunity of gloating over that resplendent interior. Then he might be removed to the nearest hospital'.

As theatre critic for *The Saturday Review*, Max Beerbohm wrote: 'The mass of people, when it seeks pleasure does not want to be elevated: it wants to laugh at something beneath its own level. Just as I used to go to Music Halls that I might feel my superiority to the audience, so does the audience go so that it might compare itself favourably with the debased rapscallions of the songs.'[29] The attitude of the working class to music hall was in fact the antithesis of this argument. These musical acts touched the parts of the audience the authors of slum journalism and slum fiction had no hopes of reaching. The songs used their language and drew on the wit, pathos and sentiment that especially appealed to this audience.

Here was a genre created largely by working-class performers, and those most relevant to the crowd at the South London were the 'coster comics'. Yet the master of the art, the 'Costers' Laureate', was one of the few performers from a middle-class background. Albert Chevalier's influence was such that he is credited with creating the original Pearly King image. He was often accused of 'idealising the coster', as some of the songs were outrageously sentimental. 'Jeerusalem's Dead' is an ode to the coster's love of his donkey. Chevalier immortalised the area surrounding the South London with his composition 'Knocked 'em in the Old Kent Road'. He was famous for performing his 'My Old Dutch' before a backdrop of a workhouse, depicting the two entrances that broke up husbands and wives as they entered.

When the South London opened on the site of a Roman Catholic chapel, its most vociferous opponent was the Reverend Charles Spurgeon – 'the prince of preachers', whose Tabernacle had been built at the Elephant & Castle in the 1860s – because the music hall was built on consecrated ground. Later on there was a more pressing concern for the preacher: the South London was frequently packed to capacity, its audience as large as the congregation at the Tabernacle. And it was the music hall that was described in the press as 'the shrine of south London'. On Saturday and Sunday nights the crowd outside extended to the surrounding streets, and people packed the pubs, restaurants and coffee rooms at the intersection at the Elephant & Castle. When cash could stretch to a place in the gallery Henry Larter, accompanied by his wife, headed for the South for a big

Saturday night out. His favourite turn was Bessie Bellwood, the daughter of a Bermondsey rabbit-puller.* Kate Larter favoured Marie Lloyd, who, like her daughter, was born in Hoxton. In 1886, Charlie Chaplin's mother made her debut on the stage of the South London. Her son was born in the same street as Henry Larter, and his family lived in and around the market in Walworth.

The management of the South reserved the right to turn away those with 'children in arms'. Nell Hall's initial experience of the venue was therefore from the window of Palmer's opposite: an establishment that sold 'eels, pea soup, tripe & onions'. Within its sage-green walls, and those of the area's two gin palaces, frequented by Henry Larter, the stories of the South had become the stuff of legend. Henry Larter told his daughter a tale heard in his youth, which regulars to the music hall continued to believe in the 1890s. The mirror that dominated the rear wall of the venue was said to be haunted by nuns, who resented the existence of this establishment on the site of the former chapel. According to numerous witnesses, during one night each year the reflections of the theatre lights blurred in the mirror, and its surface turned to mist. When this cleared, it revealed the image of three crucifixes that remained for an hour or two. Anyone who tried to remove the mirror reputedly met their death. One employee at the venue who attempted to dismantle the mirror died on his first day in the job. Another stayed to remove it during the night, and was found dead the next morning. After a major blaze at the venue, a fireman attempted to move the mirror to the cellar. He was rumoured to have been discovered hours later, hanging from the remaining beams in the gallery.

There was a regular at the Rockingham Arms, a local man,

---

*The job of skinning rabbits.

who claimed to remember the apparition that appeared in the mirror, before the legend around the crucifixes materialised. He had been in the pit, watching a female dancer on stage, when she stopped her act, screamed, and told the audience to look in the direction of the mirror. 'Everyone turned and saw a dim shape steadily grow, until it took the form of a tall lady in black', he told the *South London Press* years later, when the South closed its doors in 1934. 'Women fainted. People fell to their knees and prayed. She had her back to us, but in the mirror we could see her face. She raised her finger to the mirror and said "They have placed you on consecrated ground. Let no one remove you."'

The pattern of urban working-class life and culture that was in place by the 1890s was one with which the tribe would be associated throughout the first half of the following century, with its pub, popular songs, football, fish and chips, elaborate funerals, good neighbours and street markets. It was a culture created in isolation, distinct from the official culture of the country. Generally England was manacled by the rituals and ceremonies of offices, guilds, clubs, institutes, colleges and regiments that were anathema to the working-class experience. Elements of this urban working-class culture would eventually move into the mainstream as part of that dominant popular culture that kicked in during the 1950s. The birth of popular music owes a debt to British music hall, which even Kipling believed supplied 'a gap in the national history, and people haven't yet realised how much that had to do with the national life'. Popular drama can be traced to the same period, as can the entertainment presented at the few theatres within working-class areas that supplanted the 'penny gaffs' that had enthralled Mayhew's young costermonger.

In a part of London so identified with Shakespeare,

Southwark offered a form of stage drama that earned it, rather disparagingly, the adjective 'transpontine'. The term came to describe the 'cheap melodrama' of productions on the south side of the Thames, such as *Sweeney Todd the Demon Barber*. The Elephant & Castle theatre, opposite Tarn's department store on the New Kent Road, staged this form of entertainment.[30] The narrow frontage of the theatre, where Nell Hall saw *Uncle Tom's Cabin* as a child, was finished in polished marble, with a small statue above its doorway depicting an elephant with a castle emerging from the rise in its back. Within the auditorium, a band of amber satin was suspended from the dress circle, and there was an ornate proscenium arch along which rats were seen scurrying throughout the performance. The smell from the fish and chipped potatoes in the punter's lap merged with the odour of horses and leather from the London Horse Repository next door. The venue was managed by the impresario John East, who 'understood the warm-hearted transpontine audiences who gave hisses for villainy, applause for heroism, and tears for sentiment. It was to this public that he directed his efforts – not to the sophisticate who went down nightly to see how the poor lived, and were only intent on mocking when they paid a visit to the Elephant & Castle'.[31]

But what was to become most identified with working-class men from the middle of the nineteenth century was football. Fifty years later it was the one national sport that was representative of the masses. The seeds of its popularity were sown in the city streets when the working week ended at Saturday lunchtime. Teams sprang up within schools, factories and pubs. When leagues were established with professional football teams, fans put the relatively new railway system to good use by travelling to matches. Working-class men became regulars in the crowd at local games, as a show of grass-roots patriotism. Henry Larter was a supporter of the local team, Millwall, and like most of football's devotees he and his eldest son began to focus on the fixtures like converts taking to prayer.

Queen Victoria's Diamond Jubilee in June 1897 transformed Southwark. Even Wallace Ross walking on water had not brought out such crowds. It was reported that the sun 'shone gloriously', glinting off the metal armaments of the troops and regiments of the Empire as they led a procession and the monarch herself through Borough High Street towards the Elephant & Castle. The tyres, the toys and the meats usually to be found dangling from the shop fronts on Borough High Street's main stretch were absent. Now there were floral festoons suspended from Venetian masts, and part of the street was set up with grandstands. Everything in view along this historic road was dressed up, spiced up, spruced up to conceal the stark reality from the gaze of the monarch. Nell Hall, raised aloft on her father's shoulders above the crowds outside the Alfred's Head, was dazzled by the colour of the velvet trim spilling from Queen Victoria's state carriage. It was a shade between 'Parma violets and varicose veins'. Streams of sightseers had flowed into Southwark early and set themselves up with a good view. Those with a guinea to spare secured a place in the grandstands. 'Out of the courts and alleys trooped the denizens of dwellings which require constant sanitary supervision',[32] commented a newspaper on the day.

The golden jubilee ten years earlier had been less of a spectacle and a crowd-puller, but it had proved a turning point in the monarch's relations with her subjects, following the rise of a republican movement that raised questions in parliament concerning the cost of the civil list. Even the death of Prince Albert in 1861 had not evoked a groundswell of royalist sentiment. During those years when the monarch was out of favour, the urban working class were largely as silent and sullen as those peoples that Kipling had written of in the far reaches of the Empire. This apathy was attributed to the dissolution of Chartism, the advent of the second Reform Act, and the wider acceptance and legal recognition of trade unionism: 'Affluence – or what men used to starvation regarded as comfort – had extinguished the fire in hungry bellies.'[33] The promise of redemption couldn't pull them en masse into church; the prospect of a revolution couldn't get them out on the street, even at a time when the monarchy was at its lowest ebb. But a number of events – perfectly timed, as it turned out – helped to win over her subjects: the Prince of Wales was seriously ill, but had a miraculous recovery; there was an attempt on the monarch's life; and Victoria's role and job description expanded as she became Empress of India, and the linchpin of the Empire. It was the beginning of a modernised, more accountable monarchy, whose makeover was complete by 1897.

Those subjects also took to the streets three years after the Diamond Jubilee, on 18 May 1900, following the relief of Mafeking during the Boer War. In Southwark, a newspaper mused on a future when 'those young patriots in their perambulators grow up and innocently ask their fathers "Did you wave union jacks and sing in restaurants when Mafeking was relieved?"' All over the borough 'the streets, the theatres, all places of refreshment and resort, abandoned themselves to a carnival . . . and sombre streets were lighted up with rapture'.[34] The celebrations at large, and the jubilant, jingoistic hysteria that greeted the relief of Mafeking, both on the streets and on the stages of music halls, inspired the invention of a spanking new verb as shorthand for the patriotic fervour of the English: to maffick was to 'exult riotously'.

The working class of Southwark were also known to exult riotously at what was locally referred to as the 'Steve', a kind of impromptu party that spilled into homes when the pubs were turned out, after an organised 'spread' for family and friends: 'there is a superstition abroad that the English are not a musical race, but that can scarcely be accepted without qualification of the cockney. For him, music is the concomitant of almost every occasion. Three instruments that he has made his own, concertina, mouth organ and piano, are essential to every well-equipped 'Steve".'[35]

In the final decades of the nineteenth century, fish and chips had emerged as a staple of working-class life. Before then fish had been cured in alleys, courtyards and backyards, engulfing the immediate neighbourhood with its stench. The beginning of the fried fish trade dates from the middle of the nineteenth century, when costermongers sold on fishmongers' leftovers. Like music hall emerging from the pubs, the fish and chipped potato trade was something that grew underground and was sneered at and ridiculed from above, but by the end of the nineteenth century it had few rivals as a cheap and convenient meal.

That pattern of working-class life that had become established and would persist until the 1950s, and in a less apparent form afterwards, was not entirely based around work and leisurely pursuits like football and music hall. Despite an absence from church, a spiritualism of sorts persisted among the urban working class, alongside a belief in superstitions and strange cures. Rooms above shops on the Walworth Road, and on stalls within its market in East Street, were occupied by quack doctors selling their wares. Homemade 'cures' would be passed down to each new generation along with a range of superstitions, some of which were heard from the lips of relatives and neighbours as late as the 1970s. Never put new shoes on a table . . . Never whistle or put an umbrella up indoors . . . Never begin a journey on a Friday . . . Never put a newborn baby in front of a looking glass . . . Pick up a dropped knife and pick up strife . . . Never have the colour green in the house . . . Never cross anyone on the stairs. Having a child photographed at an early age was considered a bad omen. Crossed knives and forks and cross-eyes were bad luck, as was receiving a penknife or a pair of scissors as a gift. Some turned around three times at seeing a black cat, others spat on the ground when passing a white horse. If a picture fell from the wall a death was imminent, whilst an elephant charm, like a rabbit's foot, was carried for luck.

It was believed that a child's whooping cough might be cured by cutting a lock of its hair, placing it between two slices of bread, and feeding it to a passing dog. More commonly practised cures included applying saffron to measles, and curing coughs with onions and vinegar. When Nell Hall and her siblings appeared to be catching a cold, Kate sewed them into brown paper vests smeared with lard. Many of these beliefs were still being voiced by grandparents and parents, even when those of my generation were growing up. When a family moved into a new home – as when the Larters arrived in Rockingham Street – a neighbour or a family member brought a tiny parcel containing grains of salt, a chip of coal, and some breadcrumbs. This was kept and stored as a talisman to bring luck, warmth and food into the home. Luck was a theme of many of the ornaments found in working-class interiors. There would always be a horseshoe hanging somewhere.

Just as the poverty of the urban working class provided the impetus for slum authors, this belief in superstition, like a love of music hall, pubs, fish and chips, aroused the curiosity of certain journalists in the 1890s. A historian living in Camberwell named William Harnett Blanch, who wrote a weekly column for the *South London Press* as Peter Pickup, was so intrigued that he established a club as an antidote to superstition. The London Thirteen Club was created in a spirit of mockery of the working classes. The first meeting was on 13 January at a Holborn restaurant, with subsequent gatherings on the thirteenth day of the following months. There were thirteen dinner tables each with thirteen settings, awaiting diners who wore green ties, and with toy skeletons in their buttonholes. Meals were served by two cross-eyed waiters who announced dinner by each smashing a mirror. The guests then proceeded into the dining room under a ladder, and were seated before a centrepiece that was a cornucopia of bad luck: black cat, peacock feathers, witch's cauldron. Each spilled salt before eating, and received a present of a penknife before leaving. The London Thirteen Club listed members of parliament and journalists among its coterie. George R. Sims was a board member, but never attended a meeting as he believed it might bring him an early death and leave his dog without a master. Oscar Wilde rejected the offer of membership. 'I love superstitions', he wrote in his reply. 'They are the opponents of common sense. Common sense is the enemy of romance. The realm of your society seems dreadful. Leave us some unreality.' Behind the mockery of the club lay an altruistic motive: the proceeds collected from membership fees contributed to keeping the elderly poor of Southwark out of the workhouse. According to a copy of the club's rule book, still in existence in a Southwark library: 'a fund for the benefit of those, who in life's battle have fallen by the way – having outlived friends and relatives and the means of earning a daily bread'.

5

THE MISSIONARY POSITION

In Blewett Street, Walworth, on the hot and humid afternoon of 28 June 1899, the street doors of dwarfish houses were slung open, along with those leading to back yards, where sometimes a pony or a donkey could be seen. This was the image that greeted George Duckworth as he passed by with a local police-man, Sergeant Wyatt, who was helping him with his inquiry. Duckworth was a researcher on a lengthy and extensive survey into the lives of the poor and working class in London, and on this day his rounds took him to the cluster of streets around the market on East Street, known locally as 'The Lane'. Henry Larter had recently moved his family here. The windfall he had hoped for – from that 'diamond mine' – had materialised, according to Nell Hall, and the sum was enough for him to open a tiny shop at 13 Blewett Street, selling coal. Duckworth described it as the 'coster colony', using the Empire metaphor that George R. Sims had rarely strayed from.

In Mayhew's day stallholders and costermongers were found side by side on many of the main thoroughfares. However, the increased traffic, and the arrival of tramways, led to dealers being siphoned off the main roads and into the one market street within a district. Outside her father's shop, Nell Hall saw people selling 'medals, clothes-pegs, old reading glasses, blacking, stewed eels, sarsaparilla, lucifer matches. And there was a quack doctor on the corner who cut corns and pulled out teeth while you waited.' The street was a pitch for makeshift stalls created from 'trestle tables, the frames of old prams with crates slotted in between that held sugarcubes before'. On the pavements throughout the market the very poor attempted to sell tobacco dried from collected dog ends. Others made a clearing near the kerb and fixed bicycles or sharpened knives.

Beyond Blewett Street were two imposing buildings, one of which was Walworth's workhouse, hovering like a threat. R. Whites, the second building, was the main local factory, where women were employed to bottle lemonade and ginger beer. During Nell Hall's childhood, the front gardens of many of the bigger houses on the main roads were replaced by shops, with the gardens to the rear disappearing beneath sheds, stables, garages and cab yards. The houses themselves, after the exodus of the better-off inhabitants to suburbs further afield, were stacked with three and more families. The newer houses built within the longer streets by eager property developers falsely anticipating an influx of middle-class tenants had lapsed into makeshift factories. Nell Hall's mother Kate Larter was a trousermaker by trade. Most of her six sisters worked in men's tailoring. Some women were able to buy a sewing machine, which, like a piano, was something that could be paid for by instalments. A sewing machine transformed the home into a sweatshop with a staff of one. On many local streets of two-up, two-down houses the windows, shut tight and smelling of old rain throughout winter and spring, were wide open in summer, rickety and rattling, as sewing machines surged at full throttle inside as if competing with the noise and speed of the trains on the railway above.

In Blewett Street, Duckworth discovered 'labourers and costers: dirty children: rough women . . . broken windows'.[36] The children seemed happy but 'dirty: hatless: ill-booted'. Nell Hall was six at this time. Had she been playing on Blewett Street on that summer day, she and her mother might have wondered who the well-dressed man was, strolling along accompanied by a policeman.

George Herbert Duckworth was the half-brother of Virginia Woolf. She herself later made trips to South London to teach evening classes to 'anaemic shop girls'[37] at Morley College. In *A Room of One's Own* Woolf cites this area as the perfect place for a life of anonymity and thwarted talent as epitomised by her fictional Shakespeare's sister, who 'killed herself one winter's night and lies buried at some crossroads where the omnibuses now stop outside the Elephant & Castle'.[38]

Duckworth was among the team of researchers enlisted to compile the evidence for a project that began in 1886, the brain-child of Charles Booth. Under the title *Life and Labour of the People in London* it was published in full in 1902 and compiled from seventeen volumes condensed from 392 notebooks. Within its small group of researchers, along with Duckworth, were the Fabians Beatrice and Sidney Webb, who founded the London School of Economics, and it is there the original archive is stored.

Booth was not unlike Robert Owen early in the century in being an unlikely candidate as a social reformer. Like Owen, he was wealthy: he owned a shipping fleet in Liverpool. But Booth was not a socialist. The survey was defined by its author as a social inquiry rather than social work. Booth used maps of the metropolis which, through a crude but effective method of colour-coding, highlighted the social groupings within the areas covered. On average, the increase in the population on the south side of the river was 26,000 each year, compared with 14,000 on the northern shore. Booth's survey was an attempt to reveal the kind of lives led by those who occupied these streets: their work, their leisure, their religious activity, their production, their consumption. The maps classified the streets by colours according to poverty levels and social class:

BLACK: Lowest class. Vicious, semi-criminal.
DARK BLUE: Very poor, casual. Chronic want.
LIGHT BLUE: Poor. 18s. to 21s. a week for a moderate family.
PURPLE: Mixed. Some comfortable, others poor.
PINK: Fairly comfortable. Good ordinary earnings.
RED: Middle class. Well-to-do.
YELLOW: Upper-middle and Upper classes. Wealthy.

Walworth was predominantly purple, with chunks of light and dark blue, and some black. Blewett Street was light blue. The neighbourhood had fewer open spaces for the size of its population than anywhere in the capital. 'The area of the entire parish is slightly less than one square mile, but on this small patch of earth there were crowded together no fewer than 120,939 human beings. In the whole of the vast dominions of the Tsar there are only one thousand times the number of those who dwell in less than one square mile'.[39] These were the words of one Reverend W. Stead, who worked in the Robert Browning settlement in the neighbourhood where the Larters lived (the poet had worshipped in Walworth as a child). As warden of the settlement, Stead believed that the relief of Walworth, at the heart of the Empire, mattered more than the relief of Mafeking. A local newspaper, writing of the mission, observed: 'Within the last six months, the government has sent 100,000 soldiers into South Africa. During the next six months how many "soldiers of the cross" will move into Southwark to relieve its distressed population . . . ?'[40]

*

The settlement movement of the 1890s took its inspiration from Andrew Mearns's *The Bitter Cry of Outcast London*. Unlike previous missionaries, their plan was to return some of the middle class that had benefited from greater social advantages back into the neighbourhoods, and settle them in working-class colonies. Among the key settlements in Walworth and Bermondsey in the final decade of the nineteenth century were those managed by the 'political priests': W. H. Stead, warden of the Robert Browning Settlement; the Reverend John Scott Lidgett (born in Lewisham, educated at University College), co-founder of Bermondsey Settlement; A. W. Jephson, the vicar at St John's Church and founder of the St John's Institute. Stead believed these communities should 'no longer be raided or merely invaded, they must be occupied with garrisons of culture and religion, they must be secured by the planting of colonies of help'. It was an approach commended by Walter Besant, who had founded the charitable mission the People's Palace in the East End in 1887. He wrote that Stead desired 'to plant a settlement house in every poor street; a house which shall be inhabited by the workers, men and women, and shall serve as a model for the other people in the street'.[41] Although the scheme had a touch of Octavia Hill's crocuses and tea parties, Stead maintained that settlement workers should not exist as 'missionaries' or 'superior persons' but as neighbours.

Just as the municipal authorities were concerned with their schooling, sanitation and public health, with inspectors shaping the environment of the urban working class, missions were intent on having an impact on their cultural lives. A major concern of the settlements in these early years was the welfare of wayward urban youth. Since the opening of the original missions in the nineteenth century, there had been an effort to impose a muscular Christianity on local boys. The Reverend A. W. Jephson had continued the trend by organising boxing bouts, as, along with football, boxing was the dominant sport in the area. They were staged at the swimming baths, with contenders, boys and men, bringing a supportive fan base affiliated to specific local pubs. Some of the first teenage football teams were created by local missions, even though the players were more likely to turn up for matches than for Bible readings.

The settlements attempted to cure the young of the disease of hooliganism. Like consumption it appeared to be a plague peculiar to urban working-class areas. The very word 'hooligan', which came into circulation via a music hall song, was said to have originated in Southwark – a derivative of 'Houlihan', the name of a notoriously troublesome Irish family that had lived in the borough. A teenager from Southwark named Patrick Hooligan, a part-time bouncer in a pub on Borough High Street, had made headlines for the brutal murder of a policeman. It was the youth of the assailant that proved the most shocking aspect of the crime for the press.

Overnight, the younger generation of the borough came under the scrutiny of newspaper scribes. The disorder within the area, almost entirely attributed to excessive drinking, reached its peak on Saturday evenings, and brought in more outsiders keen to write about this trend among the working class. The goal was to meet a hooligan. 'On this occasion we met by appointment at the Elephant & Castle', begins the journalist Clarence Rook in his book *The Hooligan Nights* in 1899. 'He had a kip in the vicinity. That is there was a bed, which was little better than a board, in one of these places where your welcome extends from sunset to sunrise.' The book, a non-fiction account of the life and crimes of a local thief called 'Alf', caused an outcry when extracts were published in the *Daily Chronicle*, because it appeared to portray the criminal life as appealing and alluring.

An article in *Surrey Magazine* reported of the hooligan epidemic in Southwark: 'Our estimable person, our watches, our purse are in danger. This is a serious matter; it must be dealt with promptly. We rub our eyes, hoping the ugly thing is a passing nightmare, and discover to our chagrin that the Hooligan is no phantom but a very stubborn fact, and the conditions that breed him fruitful soil for the germs of revolution.'[42] As though in a nod to the legacy of Robert Owen and William Cobbett, who adhered to the doctrine that social behaviour was determined by environment, the missions argued that culpability did not solely rest with the hooligans. 'The people are of the same make and maker that they always were; the land is the same, the climate the same, the language and religion the same', wrote William Cobbett, in the wake of riots and machine-breaking in the early nineteenth century. 'There must, therefore, be some *other cause*, or causes, to produce these dreadful acts in a people the most just, the most good-natured, and the most patient in the world.'[43] Meanwhile, a local member of the London school board, the Reverend W. Copeland Bowie, voiced a contrary opinion to that expressed in the press: he felt safer after dark walking the streets and 'slums' of Southwark with his wife and daughter than he would in Pall Mall or Piccadilly. 'What is the terror which the year gone, 1898, had brought so vividly before the minds of the people of London?' he asked in a speech at the time. 'Too much has been made of the hooligans.'[44]

The little schooling that had come the way of this younger generation provided them with a greater insight into society, and the world outside their own. Less likely to accept parental knowledge and opinions as absolute, they were also alert to the minimal creature comforts that might be within reach if their ready cash increased. Gambling and crime were shortcuts to this goal. Drinking was on the increase among the young. Football was an even more major interest in their lives than it was for previous generations. The phenomenon of hooliganism also attached itself to the beautiful game, with occasional tales of vandalism and rowdyism chewing up column-inches in the local press. And the pastime itself became, like other aspects of working-class culture, cause for concern for the educators, the churchmen, the missionaries, just as today the white working class have been portrayed as couch potatoes with satellite dishes sprouting like fungi from the walls of their homes.

There was a fear that leisure time might turn too many of the masses into hooligans, what with the saturnalian Saturday of football, sing-alongs and alcohol. (This echoed the old fear of the Victorian establishment that bringing democracy by way of suffrage to the working class would inevitably lead to socialism.) The aim was to introduce recreational activities that were educational. The Robert Browning settlement opened a coffee tavern, as a way of coaxing local men like Henry Larter from the pubs. It offered billiards and a gym amongst other things, and was opened by Charles Booth. The settlement also held weekly events entitled the Pleasant Sunday Afternoon for men, and a Pleasant Tuesday Afternoon for women. There was an attempt to encourage reading at the men's club, where it emerged that the most popular author was Charles Dickens. The existence of these weekly rendezvous, along with the opening of the nearby Walworth Library in the 1890s, mostly made books more widely available to those that wanted them, though perhaps it also enticed a percentage of the local population that were previously non-readers.

Even in this decade the English poor may have been the hardest-worked people on whom the sun shines, as Dickens once described them: Be content if in their wretched intervals of leisure they read for amusement and do no worse.[45] But even if a majority of the urban working class did not read books, they themselves became a subject for authors in the 1890s, much more so than when the works of Dickens and Mayhew first reached the shelves.

6

SLUM FICTION

In the south London suburb of Norwood during 1898 and 1899, Emile Zola was holed up in the Queen's Hotel, exiled from France during the Dreyfus affair. Ten years earlier the author's oeuvre had been described as 'corrupt' by England's National Vigilance Society. In the House of Commons an MP tabled a motion deploring 'the rapid spread of demoralising literature', citing Zola as the culprit. Consequently his publisher, Vizetelly, was imprisoned for three months. The excitement had diminished sufficiently by the mid-1890s for Zola to be guest of honour at a Crystal Palace dinner, organised by the Institute of Journalists, where his name and image were the centrepiece of a huge firework display. Throughout his next visit – his year's exile in nearby Norwood – he maintained a low profile, distancing himself from other writers, and dabbling in the new technology of photography. Having created an authentic picture of the working life of his homeland in words, he was documenting that of London and the suburbs with his camera. Meanwhile a group of English writers, inspired by Zola's works and the journalistic methods of Sims, and with a cursory nod to

Dickens, had cornered the market in the novel of social realism. Chief among these budding Zolas was Arthur Morrison, author of the novel that would become synonymous with 'slum fiction' – as it was termed by the cynical – *A Child of the Jago*.

Like other crusading writers of this new wave, Morrison had made his print debut in the press. A number of his short stories from the *Daily Observer* contributed to his book *Tales of Mean Streets*, published in 1894. His description of the setting for the tales is similar to George Duckworth's impression of the neighbourhood in which the Larters lived. Morrison describes streets where: '"Mangling done here"[46] stares from windows, and where doors are left carelessly open; others where squalid women sit on doorsteps, and girls go to factories in white aprons'. The author could be describing a number of urban working-class neighbourhoods, but Morrison's patch is the East End, and the choice was not an arbitrary one. He was born in Poplar, where his father worked as an engineer fitter. But in the little that Morrison was to reveal of his past to the press, it's apparent that he was something of a snob, claiming Kent for his birthplace and distancing himself from the people and the postcode that inspired his novels. Even the claim that he was a civil servant before embarking on a journalistic career may have been an embellishment.

An undisputable biographical fact is that the younger Morrison assisted in the running of the East End settlement established by Walter Besant, the People's Palace. It was this experience that provided the material for *A Child of the Jago* in 1896, a novel that aroused an anger among its critics not witnessed since Zola was first published in England. Set in the fictional quarter in Shoreditch known as the Jago, it is the story of Dicky Perrott, 'a boy who, but for his environment would have become a good citizen'. That environment encroaches upon his development. His father is hanged for murder, amid gang wars within the mean streets of the Jago that divide young and old onto the sides of two rival families, the Learys and the Ranns. Dicky's mother Hannah is set apart from other women in the neighbourhood because she is never drunk, never quarrels, is rarely beaten by her husband, and never with the chair or the poker: 'Justly irritated by such superiorities as these, the women of the Jago were ill-disposed to brook another: which was, that Hannah Perrott had been married in church.'[47]

The passage in which Dicky sees his mother become the victim of the champion female fighter of the neighbourhood, Sally Green, is one of the book's most brutal episodes:

Thus Dicky saw it in a flash, and in an instant he had flung himself on Sally Green, kicking, striking, biting, and crying, for he had seen his mother and Looey.

The kicks wasted themselves among the woman's petticoats and the blows were feeble; but the sharp teeth were meeting in the shoulder-flesh, when help came. Norah Walsh, vanquished champion, now somewhat recovered, looked from a window, saw her enemy vulnerable, and ran out armed with a bottle. She stopped at the kerb to knock the bottom off the bottle, and then, with an exultant shout, seized Sally Green by the hair and stabbed her about the face with the jagged points. Blinded with blood, Sally released her hold on Mrs. Perrott, and rolled on her back, struggling fiercely; but to no end, for Norah Walsh, kneeling on her breast, stabbed and stabbed again, till pieces of the bottle broke away.[48]

The only note of hope in the novel is the boy's relationship with the parish vicar and the East End Elevation Mission, which along with the Panosophical Institute offers lectures and clubs, similar to the 'garrisons of culture' established by the political priests in the settlements of Walworth and Bermondsey, and Besant's People's Palace. The mission may have helped Morrison, but Father Stutt cannot save Dicky Perrott. He meets a typically tragic end by the blade of a knife in a street brawl.

Children feature heavily in the slum novels from 'the Cockney school', as it was known – Dicky Perrott in Morrison's *A Child of the Jago* and Stephen in *Hole in the Wall*, Edwin Pugh's Tony Drum, William Pett Ridge's Mord Em'ly, William Somerset Maugham's Liza of Lambeth. Almost all lack the great expectations and happy ending that rescue the likes of Pip and Oliver Twist in Dickens. Perrott and his ilk are tragic Candides forced to endure the worst of all possible worlds. The descriptions of these worlds created a shudder in Morrison's readers. 'It is exactly the same thing in a lesser degree for us to sit down and deliberately to read these books, as it was for the much-blamed crowds of sightseers to flock to bullfights at Boulogne', opined the author J. H. Findlater, in an essay on the slum movement in fiction.[49]

Edwin Pugh was a slum novelist who attempted to insert a layer of sympathy between the hooliganism and the hangings. A former city clerk, Pugh was notable for lighting up the nether worlds of which he wrote with pathos and humour, even when the subject is a child with a hunched body, rickety legs, a flute-playing, philosopher father who seldom works, and a mother who drinks herself into oblivion, or at least the nearest kerb. Such is the content of *Tony Drum, A Cockney Boy* (1898). There is a greater scope for the aspirant working-class boy to free himself from the shackles of his circumstances and his class than in the work of Arthur Morrison. Tony Drum is 'the pet of the Garden Row Mission Hall. He attended all the services held there, led the children's singing, and was cock of his class in Sunday school'. Yet still, in the worst of all possible worlds, he dies young, and the day before fulfilling his dream of seeing the sea. Pugh maintained that the writer should 'observe life as a highly-sensitized photographic plate and receive and record impressions without bias'.

Like George Gissing's *The Nether World*, Morrison's novels portrayed slum life solely in terms of its brutality, despair and squalor. And both writers, like Mayhew and Sims, claimed there was no hint of exaggeration. James Greenwood had stated some years before: 'No language with which I am acquainted is capable of conveying an adequate conception of the spectacle I then encountered.'[50] Gissing elaborated upon this. 'The vituperative vernacular of the nether world', he wrote, 'has never yet been exhibited by typography, and presumably never will be.'[51] Morrison believed *A Child of the Jago* had succeeded in this. His aim had been to write a different story of working-class life than that which had gone before, told with austerity and frankness, and without sentimentality: 'I felt that the writer must never impose himself between his subject and his reader. I could best bring in real life by keeping myself and my moralizings out of it.'[52] It was the absence of a moral that distinguished most of these writers from Dickens, even though they were essentially treading the same territory. And unlike those by other authors, these particular novels by Gissing and Morrison were narrated by fictional working-class characters who inhabited these neighbourhoods, instead of factory owners, middle-class missionaries and flâneurs arriving from outside and reporting back.

If Morrison's novel was the most controversial to arise from the slum fiction movement, Richard Whiteing's best-selling *No. 5 John Street*, from 1899, was the most commercially successful. Both the style and the content of Whiteing's writing had moved on since he produced *Mr Sprouts His Opinions* in the 1860s. Whiteing acknowledged that this latest novel was inspired by the approach of *A Night in the Workhouse*. The narrator of *No. 5 John Street* is a wealthy upper-class man who embarks upon a charitable pilgrimage to explore the conditions of the working class. Having jettisoned his manservant, and kept his accent, he temporarily trades in his West End lifestyle for a tenement and a factory job:

> I had been invited to join a University Settlement at the East End, I went down to look at it, but it proved to be a mere peep-hole into the life I wanted to see, with the Peeping Tom still a little too much on the safe side. The inmate did not live the life, he observed it merely from all the comforts of home.[53]

Two novels set on the south side of the river completed the most memorable works in the slum movement: *Liza of Lambeth* and *Mord Em'ly*. Maugham, like Morrison, had based the story on first-hand experience, gained when he studied medicine at St Thomas's Hospital and visited the homes of expectant mothers in the courts and alleys of Lambeth. In the evenings he applied himself to writing a novel inspired by his observations, with the fictional Vere Street as the setting. Respite, hope and aspiration have no place in Maugham's novel any more than in Morrison's, but his hours of chatting to expectant fathers provided him with the details he used to depict working-class interiors. He writes of Mrs Kemp's home:

> At either end of the mantelpiece were pink jars with blue flowers on the front; round the top in Gothic letters of gold was inscribed: 'A Present from a Friend' – these were products of a later, but not less artistic age. The intervening spaces were taken up with little jars and cups and saucers – gold inside, with a view of a town outside, and surrounding them, 'A Present from Clacton-on-Sea', or, alliteratively, 'A Memento of Margate'. Of those many were broken but they had been mended with glue . . .[54]

At thirteen, the protagonist of William Pett Ridge's *Mord Em'ly* (1898) was a few years older than Nell Hall, and her capers throughout the novel occur in the streets of Walworth, and the 'coster colony' around East Street. Home is a flat within one of the model dwellings erected in the recent decades. Pandora Buildings,

> despite its bare passages and blank, asphalted yard and draughty balconies, all suggesting that it was a place where people were sent for some infraction of the law, was nevertheless, for its inhabitants sufficiently cheerful, and there were very few of them who were not happy. To understand this fact, it was necessary to become an inhabitant in Pandora, and not merely to come down on a hurried visit, as lady philanthopists did, and sniff, and look sympathetic, and tell each other that it was all quite dreadful.[55]

The idea that some of the inhabitants of the neighbourhood might have interludes of happiness, and a loyal attachment to their environment, despite the air of destitution that permeated it, was absent from other novels of 'the cockney school'.

William Pett Ridge, like Pugh a former clerk, had been a writer of comic sketches for the *St James's Gazette*. The story begins with a confrontation between the Gilliken gang, whose members included older girls who, like their real-life counterparts in Walworth, work in R. Whites factory, and a Bermondsey gang. Mord Em'ly is a gang member, and the confrontation is her last adventure before she is forced to support her mother by going into domestic service in nearby Camberwell. As close as she is to the family home during her 'service', Mord Em'ly is filled with a sentimental longing for the environment with which she is familiar, which again sets her apart from similar characters in slum fiction who long to escape. She dreams of Tarn's at the Elephant & Castle, the music hall with 'the four white globes'[56] over its entrance, where 'You paid twopence to an old lady seated in a little sentry-box'. She longs for the Walworth Road, with 'the barrows stacked with yellow Lent lilies and scented violets, and giant bundles of wallflowers tied with twigs round their thick waists; pyramids of oranges, too, and huge cliffs of sweets'. Ironically, Mord Em'ly proves to be the one young character within the novels of the slum fiction movement who actually leaves the class and the neighbourhood, by making a new start in Australia.

In his history of *The Cockney* published in the 1950s, author Julian Franklyn writes of Arthur Morrison: 'His mean streets are mere ditches between banks of dismal brick; channels of vice, crime, brutality and misery. In his tales the heroes are clergymen and doctors; and there is no denying it, clergymen and doctors, in those days, and in those districts, were invariably heroes; but Morrison missed the point that costers and dockers are also heroes.'[57] But by far the most fierce critic of the genre was the journalist G. K. Chesterton, who believed that the man of letters who took up the missionary position was worse than the man of the cloth. In his eyes artistic slumming was far more despicable than religious, political and social slumming:

> The religious teacher is at least supposed to be interested in the costermonger because he is a man; the politician is in some dim and perverted sense interested in the costermonger because he is a citizen; it is only the wretched writer who is interested in the costermonger merely because he is a costermonger . . . He has far less psychological authority even than the foolish missionary. For he is in the literal and derivative sense a journalist, while the missionary is an eternalist. The

missionary at least pretends to have a version of the man's lot for all time; the journalist only pretends to have a version of it from day to day. The missionary comes to tell the poor man that he is in the same condition with all men. The journalist comes to tell other people how different the poor man is from everybody else.[58]

Within the work of the slum novelist, according to Chesterton:

The chiaroscuro of the life is inevitably lost; for to us the high lights and the shadows are a light grey. But the high lights and the shadows are not a light grey in that life any more than in any other. The kind of man who could really express the pleasures of the poor would be also the kind of man who could share them. In short, these books are not a record of the psychology of poverty. They are a record of the psychology of wealth and culture when brought in contact with poverty. They are not a description of the state of the slums. They are only a very dark and dreadful description of the state of the slummers.[59]

These books were also not generally read by the class that featured in them. In an essay on the English realist movement published in 1965, author and broadcaster Vincent Brome wrote: 'Such was the social guilt of many well-to-do readers of the middle classes that they read with avidity any novel whose heroine cunningly and with considerable humour outwitted the worst the fates could bring her, and Mord Em'ly was no exception'.[60] Chesterton claimed that there were a number of reasons why these novels would fail to appeal to a working-class readership, in particular the fact that these writers were realistic. Rather like Oscar Wilde demanding that the London Thirteen Club leave him some 'unreality', the poor according to

77

Chesterton were 'melodramatic and romantic in grain, and never realistic'.

Nell Hall said that her parents could barely read or write. There was only one member of the family interested in books – Henry Larter's sister, Rosina. Her niece remembered she always referred to them as 'nobels', and she named her sons, born throughout the 1890s, after characters from the books she read. They were names more likely to be found in the epic heroism and romance of melodrama than tales of slum life: Horace, Clarence, Claude. According to the 1901 census, Rosina was a widow within a decade of her marriage, with five children, the youngest barely a year old. Like those women that Morrison described in the Jago she worked at home. Her occupation – 'mangler'. She, like many a working-class reader, preferred the melodrama of the 'shilling shocker', the late nineteenth-century equivalent of the 'penny dreadful' from the Dickens era. They revelled in the transpontine drama staged at the Elephant & Castle theatre, which the Larters had been known to visit. It was here, rather than in the works of Arthur Morrison, that good defeated evil and the hero emerged triumphant. 'We have stopped writing stories to that effect', wrote J. H. Findlater, 'and the pendulum has of course swung too far in the opposite direction. Still the public taste holds firmly to the old convention, as you may see exemplified at the theatres every night. The villain is always hissed; the audience has nothing but applause when the virtuous hero is successful; it is only in our books that we reverse this law of taste.'[61]

In *Across the Bridges*, published in 1911, Alexander Paterson wrote:

There is a great genius for watching among Londoners. They are happy to look on at any scene that accidentally or by design may stimulate emotion. A funeral may be seen any day at any cost, and appeals to all. This and a fire-engine, an arrest in the street, an epileptic in a fit, the short quick appearance of friends at the police-court, are scenes in melo-drama not a bit less moving than the sensations pumped up for sixpence at a theatre.[62]

The Oxford-educated Paterson had moved to Bermondsey to teach in an elementary school, live in a tenement, and work for the district's settlement. *Across the Bridges* is his account of life as he experienced it on the south side of the river, relayed not as a novel or an autobiographical account, but as a sympathetic, personal observation of the habits, rituals and culture in the lives of those native to Southwark, Bermondsey and Walworth.

The scene might well open on a Saturday night, when the streets will seem full of every happiness that is known to tired people in their leisure hours. Every road and every public-house and shop is full of busy people. Gramophones and costermongers fill the air with their noise. There is much to buy and see and talk about. A score of different pleasures, that may be obtained for twopence, assail the passer-by.[63]

The Bishop of Southwark wrote of how the book was 'the material out of which romances of street and slum might be made, but it is served up to us without the flavourings and com-binations which romances need, but which spoil them as documents of life'.[64] It was also without the Grand Guignol or the idiosyncratic characters identifiable in the slum fiction canon, and therefore a more sober, typical and realistic view of the 'chiaroscuro of life' that Chesterton had mentioned. Paterson's book, like others written and published by those involved in the London settlements and the institutes, offered a more representative portrait of urban working-class life, in all its quotidian glory, than the English social realists. These were books that touched on but did not dwell on squalor, hooliganism and crime. Paterson's was by far the most significant work, with chapters covering family life, work, education, eating habits, clothes, marriage, birth, and even the homeless.

Across the Bridges documents the existence of an urban working class dominated by work and family, rather than by gang warfare, murder and flute-playing philosophers. And it concludes by making a point that is absent from the work of Morrison et al.: The riches to be found within these districts lie in the 'natural goodness' of most of the inhabitants:

> here, born of the struggle of life, unfold those lives of love and perseverance, that are to the traveller that has eyes to see as the golden furze on the bleakest slope of the mountainside. Generosity touches a point reached nowhere else, and does so by the prompting of instinct, rather than as the result of exhortation and conscious virtue. The family may consist of ten very different people, who have little to say to each other, and are never demonstrative; yet one member of it will support by his own wages all the others for many months, and will see nothing unselfish in the surrender of all his pocket-money. For he has only done an ordinary and expected thing, and does not look for gratitude or applause. The father or mother will go without the food the children want; the elder brother will abstain that the younger one may eat; for it is an unwritten law that first the children must be fed.[65]

7

DR STATE

Evidently Alexander Paterson was an example of one of those middle-class people Stead hoped would find their way to the settlements to become neither a missionary, nor 'a superior person' – like the philanthropists on a day trip to Pandora Buildings – but a neighbour. Writing of those who might follow in his footsteps, Paterson hoped they 'will find the way across the river if they come, natural and unassuming with a pure heart and a ready hand, anxious to only serve and learn'.[66]

A year before the publication of *Across the Bridges*, Arthur W. Jephson, a man with the figure of a baritone and a walrus moustache that swept over his lips, had written of his efforts in Walworth in *My Work in London*. Not in the league of Paterson's book, this was a plain and simple account of what he had achieved since his arrival at St John's, the church where Nell Hall's parents had married. On moving to Walworth he found that 'The church was dilapidated, the schools almost given up and the mission room almost over run with rats'.[67] Although he presided over services that were High Anglican, politically and socially Jephson considered himself a 'progressive'. The same was true of the other local 'political priests', the Methodists Lidgett and Stead.

Generally, it seems that lectures, classes and politics at the settlements were attractive to a specific type of working-class man. Perhaps those who attended the Elevation Mission and the Panosophical Institute in Dicky Perrott's neighbourhood: 'tradesmen's sons, small shopkeepers and their families, and neat clerks, with here and there a smart young artisan of one of the especially respectable trades'.[68] Plus those daytrippers from other classes whom Morrison described as being 'astonished at the wonderful effects of Panosophic Elevation on the degraded classes, their aspect and their habits. Perhaps it was a concert where nobody was drunk: perhaps a little dance where nobody howled a chorus, nor wore his hat, nor punched his partner in the eye'.[69]

The institute and the settlements did attract the wider population in their efforts to provide assistance for the elderly, the sick and the unemployed, and help and advice with the health of children. Before the welfare state, the settlements offered some financial support. The area immediately surrounding the Robert Browning Settlement contained the largest proportion of pauperism of any Poor Law union in the country, and the workhouse was the only option for the elderly poor. Under the aegis of W. H. Stead, the settlement became the centre of a campaign that would ultimately lead to developments that had an impact beyond the local streets, and benefit the working class on a national level. He began preaching at the head of a brass band in East Street market every Sunday. But this was not a sermon on the demon drink, but a campaign for a pension scheme that would benefit 'respectable, sober, honest, hardworking men and women who have brought up families but in old age find themselves destitute. The moment someone ceases to be of value as an economic tool, they are flung aside as worthless . . . in place of that which should accompany old age – honour, love, obedience, troops of friends, was offered – Newington workhouse, where old folks had to sit on benches without backs'.[70] When the Old Age Pensions Act became law in 1908, it was the first step toward the creation of the welfare state. Like his contemporaries, Stead documented his experience in book form, with the story of the success of the pension campaign: 'It happened not with the bursting of bombs, not with the click of the guillotine, but with the quiet handing over in innumerable post offices of a weekly couple of half-crowns had the English revolution of the twentieth century begun.'[71]

Reform was in the air, from the major wards of Bedlam Hospital,* each identified by a letter which collectively spelt R-E-F-O-R-M, to parliament itself. The main political parties were becoming aware that the working class was an increasingly prominent part of the electorate. Trade unionism membership was rising and an embryonic Labour Party taking shape out in the wings. In 1900 there were over 1,300 trade unions with a total of 2 million members. Both the press and politicians were drawing attention to poor urban areas. Since the 1890s, red-brick municipal buildings had sprouted in Walworth, housing infirmaries, a library, a new vestry hall, and a wash house and swimming baths. 'For a population like ours, which is justly proud of its supremacy of the seas', said the chairman of the school board at the opening, 'it would literally be a shame if we did not give our children every opportunity to learn to swim.'[72] It was declared that Walworth's new building, with its terracotta columns, cornices and turrets, would look at home in areas over the water, as select and opulent 'as Paddington or Kensington'.

---

*The original Bedlam hospital was moved from the northern shore to Lambeth, where it opened in 1815.

Just across the road Jephson had declared his ambition to create a school in south London 'which should be equal to any in the suburbs or west end'. There was talk of regenerating the Elephant & Castle, and stemming the flow of traffic that clogged its arteries. Would Southwark finally begin to mirror the wealthier parts of the northern shore?

The English working class were no longer seen as an amorphous mass but a body with form, known to exult riotously at football matches, and national victories in battle. They looked like a different race. Bandy legs and rickets distinguished many from the ranks of the upper classes, but stunted growth distinguished all. A medical officer from the London County Council noted that 'the worst average physique is to be found in the low-lying areas along the Thames'. The average height was below that of the English middle and upper class, due to malnutrition and the impact of the still-persistent child labour.

Nell Hall worked in various jobs during her brief schooling, either before the school day began or at its close. At the age of ten her mother found her work in the house next to St John's school. She arrived at 6.45 each morning to clean and 'black' the grate in the kitchen. With the job finished she had minutes to get to the nearby board school she attended, where daily she would be caned because of the soot on her hands.

If the entire working class were one day to receive the vote it was worthwhile to fatten them up, and educate them in order that they might know who and what to vote for. In 1902 a new Education Act gave working-class pupils the opportunity to obtain qualifications and be educated beyond elementary level.

Boys were taught a 'practical knowledge of reading, writing, arithmetic, and a grounding in geography, history as may enable [them] to read a newspaper or give a vote'.[73] The girls were largely schooled in domestic duties, which would prove useful when they married. When it came to the teaching of standard

English, the local dialect, native to the working-class Londoner, and particularly in an area like Walworth dominated by the hubbub of its market, was ruled out. A national report on education argued that there was an element of loss when schoolchildren of Devonshire, Lincolnshire or Yorkshire were forced to forsake their native dialect for the King's English. 'But with the pupil in the London elementary school this is not the case. There is no London dialect of reputable antecedents and origin which is a heritage for him to surrender in school. The cockney mode of speech, with its unpleasant twang, is a modern corruption with legitimate credentials, and is unworthy of being the speech of any person in the capital city of the empire.'[74] It wasn't until the 1930s that a native working-class Londoner, who had crossed the class divide to join the ranks of the teaching profession, wrote the first book putting the case for the defence: '[cockney] has been by far the most important of all non-standard forms of English for its influence upon accepted speech ever since speech emerged. In the early modern period the vulgar speech of London served as the model for accepted speech, and later when standard was formulated, vulgar London speech served as a criterion of error by which correct speech should be measured. Accepted speech has bitten the hand that fed it'.[75]

Despite the vilification of her native brogue, Nell Hall excelled at English. In the last year of her schooling she wrote an essay entitled 'A Day in the Life of Big Ben', in which London's old timer recorded all that it witnessed on the streets, bridge and river beneath it. The day it was pinned on the classroom wall was the day she got a scholarship.

The year after Kate Larter gave birth to her second daughter, Nell Hall returned home on what was to be the final day of her education, with dreams of the school she might attend and the uniform she might get to wear. Her thoughts settled on, amongst other things, 'a straw hat with a ribbon'. Immediately her mother informed her that now was the time to put to good use the things she had learned: the domestic duties that girls of her generation and station had been taught in class. At twelve years old, her role was to be in the home, keeping the wheels of the household routine in motion so that her mother could go out to work. She was responsible for 'scouring the house, whitewashing the window sills, colour-stoning the doorstep, washing clothes in an iron tub, scrubbing stone, polishing fire-irons and furniture – well, what furniture there was'. Often the paltry inventory within the house slimmed down by Monday, as the more precious items were sent to the pawnbroker's, who was referred to as 'Uncle'.

When her sister was old enough to attend school, Nell Hall began work. She was employed in the washrooms at the municipal baths, from 8 in the morning until 7.30 at night, and on Saturday mornings. 'I kept a potato in my pocket, because this was supposed to stop you getting rheumatism', she said. 'All the old girls there had rheumatism because of having their hands in water for years, and all that scrubbing.' She later worked at Pink's jam factory, on the street where Tom Larter was raised. Like the workhouse, it was known as 'The Bastille'. According to Charles Booth it was a place of 'low class work for low class pay'. Nell Hall said: 'There was chains of girls. Directly we got there, we had to ladle hot jam into stoneware jars. You could never get rid of the smell. So everyone knew if you was a Pink's girl. And there was no shortage of girls to take your place.'

A few days after her nineteenth birthday, Nell left home after an argument with her mother. She started sharing a room with another girl at the Old Kent Road end of East Street market. On 14 August 1911, the women of Pink's left the heat of the factory, which was heightened by the intense heat of that summer, and took to the streets to protest at low pay. Those who returned did so to stand at the factory gates with placards declaring: 'We are not white slaves we are Pink's.' Women from nearby factories walked out over the same conditions. 'Most of them saw it as a bit of a laugh', she said. 'They was all having a sing-song. I came home, me. Well, I didn't see the point. It was a baking hot day. I walked back to the Old Kent Road and packed me clothes. Not that I had much. That was the day I moved back in with my mother, because my dad weren't well. Mind you, I shouldn't have done because they thought it was consumption.'

The strike itself had enough impact to ensure that Pink's raised the wages and allowed staff to form a union. When the upheavals of that long hot summer had settled, Nell Hall left to work as a packer at another factory on Southwark's riverside: 'I got a job working for Oxo, wrapping individual Oxo cubes – they'd just brought them out. Shorter hours. I had to help my mother more, she couldn't abide me 'cos I was independent, but what with my dad being laid up. I'd just starting courting Bill.'

Bill Hall was born in 1891, the year before his future wife, and two streets away, into a large family. His mother and father were Suffolk-born, but the couple moved to the borough in the 1880s, after the birth of their first child. Bill's father, James, died when his son was in his teens. Like Arthur Morrison's father he had been an engineer fitter. Bill's grandfather on his mother's side was Jewish. His name was Emmanuel Rainbird. Like the Larters the Halls moved further into Walworth and closer to the market.

Henry Larter's passion for horses only extended as far as betting on them, but his future son-in-law had a deep affinity and attachment to the animal that was uncharacteristic for someone raised in an urban landscape. Throughout his early adulthood he worked with horses as a carman, before getting the job of driving those at the head of local funeral processions. Despite the lack of money in Southwark, cash would somehow be found in order to provide a decent, elaborate funeral. The elegance, opulence and comfort absent from these lives was present in death. Even at the workhouse money was found under mattresses, belonging to inmates who didn't want a pauper's burial. The working class, as families, as a network of neighbours, and as a community, came together to ensure that each of them would not have a poor man's funeral.

'Everyone in the street or the block put in for a wreath', said Nell Hall. 'All the men in the street used to wear a black diamond, cut and sewn on the sleeve of their coat, as a sign of respect. On Sundays, if there was a funeral, the mourners used to stop halfway to the church for a drink.' Death was the greatest call to unity, according to Alexander Paterson in *Across the Bridges*. 'At all costs, there must be black clothes; at any risk, work must be abandoned, in order that the family may in a body drive together to the funeral. At such times of death, or illness, or disgrace, the cord is tightened, and ideals are found to be true in these dark days which in brighter ones are almost lost to sight.'[76] This was never more true than in the wake of a local funeral held at Jephson's church, the year after Paterson's book was published.

8

THEY SHALL GROW NOT OLD

The Thames had not been this still, this silent, since the winter of the great frost three decades before. All activity in the wharves had ceased, and any movement on its surface, as the destroyer appeared on the horizon. Cranes ceased to rattle. On the boats men stood to attention, like guardsmen, with oars planted upright before them. Every ship flew its flag at half-mast. There was no bellowing from ships; no hooting from the tugboats; no clatter in the barge yards. Much of the machinery in the factories and wharves ceased its whirring and whining, and no officials in these workplaces dared to object. The bodies of eight boy scouts, drowned at sea, were being brought along the Thames, returning home to Walworth. They belonged to a local troop formed shortly after the movement was founded by Robert Baden-Powell, in 1908. It was whilst serving in Mafeking that he was inspired to lay the game plan for the scouting organisation. A boy scout was to be a brother to all scouts no matter what his country or creed. A scout should smile and whistle under difficulties. And while performing his duties, being a patriot and earning his badges of honour from doing good deeds daily, he should adhere to the motto: Be prepared.

After the Boer War it became apparent that if the men of the working class were called upon in great numbers to defend the Empire they would not pass the physical. This was perhaps pivotal to Baden-Powell's venture, in which nothing would be overlooked in the efforts to preserve a form of pure, muscular and masculine Christianity. Girls were anathema, masturbation an evil brought on by rich food and warm beds with too many blankets. For the boys of Walworth, in the neighbourhood containing the church, the institute and the market, among the 20,000 youths living on an acre or two of asphalt, scouting brought the promise of adventures close to home.

The adventure for the boy scouts in 1912 was to be a camping expedition to Leysdown in Kent, on the Isle of Sheppey, by dinghy along the Thames. They were waved off from the St John's Institute on Larcom Street. A crowd of locals gathered to see them off, as often happened when neighbours took off to the hop fields, or adults left for a beano. Around sunset, two hours into their journey along the river, an unexpected wind arrived. The abrupt change in the weather caught the boy scouts and their scoutmasters unaware. Within minutes the vessel carrying them capsized, just when it was about to reach the shore, and the passengers were thrown into the water. All the scouts had learnt to swim at municipal baths, but the boys were small and undernourished, and the Thames pulled them down. They lost their struggle very quickly, despite the efforts of the adults present, who attempted to keep as many boys afloat as they could. One of the adults was helpless as his two sons drowned.

News of the deaths united the inhabitants of Walworth in grief. It made national headlines, and was a lead story until after the funeral at St John's church, where the scouts had worshipped. It put Walworth in the national consciousness, and brought in crowds not seen since the Relief of Mafeking and the Diamond Jubilee. The sense of loss within the community was far greater than that which followed the death of the Queen herself. One newspaper reported: 'Never again would the nation mourn, as it did on Saturday 10th August 1912'.

The *Daily Mirror* published a special memorial edition. It was as though the boys in the troop, with their code of honour to Queen and country, were being celebrated as young soldiers lost at sea in war. From Westminster, the Lord of the Admiralty, Winston Churchill, commanded that the destroyer *Fervent* bring the bodies back along the Thames in a display of public honour. On the eve of the funeral, the doors of the church remained open all day.

Along the Thames, people had begun to gather early on. As the *Fervent* came into view on the horizon, factory workers hurried out and headed for the Thames. Nell Hall was now employed at Hartley's jam factory further into Bermondsey. The night the news of the deaths had reached Walworth, she was celebrating her engagement with her family and her future in-laws: 'We'd walked down to have a drink at the Elephant, before going over the road afterwards to meet me mother and father in the Alfred's Head. I remember my Bill's mother coming into the bar at the Elephant, saying she had bad news. I thought my dad had died, because he'd been bad on and off. But he was back at work. Back working as a coalie on Rockingham Street, where he worked when I was a baby.'

The coffins were small with gilt facing, small enough to be concealed by the Union Jack draped over each one. Later in Walworth, Nell Hall, along with her sister and mother, was among the 100,000 who passed through the church to pay tribute to the scouts, many of them finding their way to the district for the first time. Nell's future husband went along, and like a number of local workmen turned up early, before beginning work. All of them laid their tools at the entrance to the church. Draymen turned up in their lunch hours, clad in their leather aprons. Cabmen, carmen, railway men and coal porters queued, heads bowed and caps held at chest level. Children and women prayed before the altar. The stillness and silence of those milling in and out of the church was sometimes broken by the sound of mothers crying. 'It was like a dream', one reporter claimed. 'This lily-scented church and the endless procession of men and women who came and went like phantom-figures.'[77]

Any funeral for the working class was an event that could draw a small crowd, with those the hearse passed on the street pausing, bowing their head, or simply removing their hats and caps. Although the funerals of local characters familiar from the market had often taken on the local spectacle of a state occasion, nothing that had happened before in these streets compared to the mood, the mourning and the procession that marked the farewell to these eight young boys. The crowds and the clouds gathered early on in the day itself. The rain did not stop people queuing along the streets. They stood in silence throughout, even as the queues formed into crowds that were eight rows deep, until a figure reputed to be close to a million had formed from the church along Walworth Road, and along the route to the cemetery.

The English working class knew how to maffick, and they knew how to mourn. Everyone appeared to be wearing some sign of mourning. Kate Larter had cut black triangles from old material she had collected for work, and sewed them on her husband's coat, and Bill Hall's. In front of the crowd there was a small fence of khaki made of boy scouts, each standing to attention, not turning as the procession passed, but keeping their eyes ahead, as though to the future (a future in which some of these boys, and their older siblings, would become part of the lost generation of the Great War). In the wake of the funeral of the scouts, a collection was made for a memorial, in the form of a silent scout, to watch over the eight graves. The owner of Pink's made a generous contribution, but 'the bulk of the money came from scouts and working-class people', said the press.

Certain hawkers arrived early and capitalised on the mood of the event. They sold milk chocolate, and Nell Hall bought a memorial handkerchief created of paper tissue, with the boys' names and scout troop printed on it: 'What struck me was how bad the weather was. It poured down. But it didn't deter people from turning up.' Rain was the prelude to a major thunderstorm that erupted an hour before the service. Like the deaths and mourning for the young of the neighbourhood, the rattle and hum of the thunder in the skies that day appeared, in hindsight, to be an omen of what was to come. Chopin's funeral march competed with the crash and rattle of the thunder above the church during a service in which candles burned above the small white coffins, each with a lifebuoy created from white and purple asters, and with the words 'In remembrance' and 'Be prepared'. Outside, the traffic had been diverted from Walworth Road, and so the silence and the stillness that had enclosed the Thames the day before now captured Walworth's main thoroughfare, and the crowds that coiled into the distance. It was broken by the sound of bugles, as six scouts played the Last Post.

Within two or three years, the young men of the area were being recruited by another veteran of the Boer War. The eyes of Lord Kitchener peered down from posters plastered throughout Walworth, between those offering the melodrama of the Elephant & Castle theatre and those promoting foods that locals could not afford. His gaze seemed to follow its able-bodied men, and he pointed them out with an extended accusatory finger thrust from beneath a handlebar moustache. Your country needs YOU.

Horatio Herbert Kitchener was Secretary of State for War. His role was to mobilise the British forces and assemble new British armies. By the summer of 1915, the War Office had requested that the local borough councils take up the business of organising volunteer battalions. Soldiers were stationed at particular points within Walworth, as part of an initial fifteen-day recruitment campaign. Trafalgar Street, adjacent to Blewett Street, found itself newsworthy and in the national press, for sending more of its men to war than any other street in the city. 'They went without being fetched', proclaimed the *Daily Herald*. Elsewhere it was reported of Southwark that 'it has to a great extent been depleted of its manhood to a far greater degree than the richer boroughs'. In keeping with the superstition prevalent within the local folklore, wives and mothers sent them off with lucky mascots: a farthing sewn into the left brace just above the heart, or a golliwog pinned under their tunics. Nell Hall's older brother was among those who signed up from the Larter family. Bill Hall also volunteered, as did his brothers, and he was soon adhering to a regimen that included physical exercise and instruction in military drill ceremonies, musketry, signalling and elementary engineering.

Bill and Nell decided to marry before he went away. The ceremony took place one month after the recruitment campaign was launched. She was twenty-two. The wedding was a brief affair, with most of the guests from the groom's side, as he had the bigger family – his widowed mother, her six children, and their offspring. The day was marred by a minor conflict within the family: one of the groom's sister's six daughters had left home in the morning because her mother had worn her stockings! The wedding took place at St John's, and the couple moved into one room at the top of a house on the same street as the church. 'We was kept awake at night by all the mice between the walls.' When she later saw her husband off as part of the

Southwark battalion, she had been a wife for just a few months and was pregnant with their first child.

William Emmanuel Hall, named after his father, was born 1 March 1916, and called Billy from that day. Nell had moved in with her parents before his birth. She had been lucky to go the full term with her first child, as the local rate of miscarriages and babies stillborn remained high throughout this decade and the next. The year that war broke out, 693 children born in Southwark died under the age of two years, which amounted to 123 deaths out of 1,000 babies born, and there was a high number of children born with deformities.

Now, in the midst of war, came the news that some of the local men would not be returning. The Deputy Mayor of Southwark received news of one of the Southwark battalions, which had lost 400 of its men. According to the government they had 'distinguished themselves in Flanders by capturing and holding against many counter attacks, some German trenches which on previous occasions have been assaulted without success'. The loss of local men was the impetus for three days of anti-German riots in the area. A German butcher's on the Old Kent Road had its shutters pulled down and its windows broken by a crowd reputed to be several thousand strong. Later they aimed pease pudding at the shutters protecting a German greengrocer's nearby. The German owner of another shop had pinned a notice outside which declared that he had taken an oath of allegiance to England in 1909. Still the crowd broke all the windows on the premises. One of Nell Hall's uncles was interned at the beginning of the war: 'His name was Lensburg. He was married to one of my mother's sisters, my Aunt Ria. They lived above a tailor's where she worked on Lambeth Palace Road.'

The call went up for more men for Southwark's volunteer

regiment. Now it was not merely Lord Kitchener but the King himself who was campaigning for recruitment. Notices were attached to walls around Walworth in January 1917:

> I am confident that all who are now prevented from under-taking active service abroad WILL JOIN THE VOLUNTEERS and show to our enemies that my SUBJECTS OF ALL AGES are ready to serve in the defence of our beloved country.

With so many of those young and eligible absent, the manpower targeted in this new campaign was older men, those between forty-two and fifty-five years, with the promise that the instruc-tion and training would put 'ten years on your life'. Henry Larter, still working as a 'coalie', was not fit enough to sign up and win the promise of those extra years. He died of consump-tion three months later at the age of fifty.

Just as Kitchener and the King had spoken from the upper echelons of the social hierarchy to remind a tribe of undernour-ished workmen whose hours were long and whose lives would be short that now was the time for them to do their duty, now the Food Controller – a figure as omnipotent and remote as the Kaiser himself – commanded that working-class wives and mothers of Southwark do the same. He authorised local councils to direct and enforce rationing within their boroughs. Suddenly, with emphasis on recruitment and rationing, war had suppos-edly rendered class divisions redundant: the women in the munitions factories, the women doing the jobs previously car-ried out by men, the working-class men who were expected to fight for a country in which they were not allowed a vote – all were conveniently being informed that they were on the same side as their social betters, and eating at the same table, so to speak. On the walls of Southwark the words of Kitchener, urging the menfolk that their country needed them, were replaced in 1917 by those of the Food Controller: With regard to food there are no rich people.

The 1914–18 war was the first in history in which a civilian population was bombarded from the air. Despite the claims that England was suddenly one nation, undivided by class, the Kaiser himself had issued explicit instructions that Buckingham Palace, Westminster Abbey and the museums of London should not be bombed. All in all there were 27 air raids on the capital during the war, and Southwark was to suffer damage and endure casualties in 14 of them. It was in September 1915, during the third raid on London, that Southwark was first hit, when two bombs damaged houses in Bermondsey. One of those injured was a woman the same age as Nell Hall. She too was not long married when her husband was called up as a reservist, and had moved in with a relative for the duration of his absence. Within weeks of leaving hospital, suffering from injury and shock, she was the victim of another raid. This time she was blinded.

The first aerial torpedo ever fired over London demolished a row of houses in Walworth, and warranted a royal visit from the King the following day. On almost the same spot, months later, 158 people were killed and 24 injured in what was the heaviest bout of casualties reported in one single raid on the capital. A bomb dropped onto the roof of Pink's, killing three workmen. In what was to become the final air raid of the war on London, on Whit Sunday in 1918, six bombs were scattered over Rotherhithe and the Old Kent Road. When Nell Hall and her parents were warned of air raids, they made their way on foot to the tube station at the Elephant & Castle which was being used as a shelter. Mothers attempted to reach it by packing themselves into trams, cradling babies, with their frightened children clutching their skirts. The public health committee later reported that there were more deaths of young children and babies from infectious diseases and pneumonia picked up by exposure in air-raid shelters, than from the impact of the bomb attacks.

Billy Hall died of pneumonia when he was two years old. He had survived to an age that many babies in Southwark failed to reach. Nell Hall had taken heed of the superstition subscribed to by her mother and many other women locally, that it was a bad omen to have a child photographed at too early an age. Her husband never got to see his son.

The choice of reading at the funeral service at St John's came from the Book of Luke; the same passage that was delivered at the service for the boy scouts six years earlier: 'Suffer little children to come unto me.'

Armistice arrived on 11 November 1918, a month after the locals of Walworth had set about creating their own memorial for those who had died by purchasing an aeroplane named after the borough, which was to be used, according to the *South London Press*, in 'bringing the Hun to heel'. The RAF had requested the sum of £100,000 to build *Southwark*, but the appeal raised £163,000.

As the fatalities of war mounted, and it emerged that so many young men of Southwark were part of that 'lost generation', the services, the congregation and often the crowds around St John's church grew. For the latter part of the war, and immediately afterwards, the church became the spiritual centre that it was intended to be when it was consecrated more than half a century earlier. For those few years locals visited for reasons other than the usual family events, or 'to change their luck' as A. W. Jephson once put it. At a particular remembrance service at St John's one Sunday evening, the vicar spoke of 'the waste of human life in this awful war. Men in the prime of their life, not soldiers by profession, but mostly drawn from the peaceful occupations were being killed by thousands'.[78] One of those being commemorated lived in Larcom Street, a neighbour of the Halls. Bill Hall was home on compassionate leave from France, to mourn the loss of his child. Neither he nor his wife were churchgoers, but they both turned up for the service for the neighbour. The soldier's body had been returned, along with a diary he had kept, with the final hurried entry written two days before his death. His words recorded an attendance at a service at the Front where, in the midst of singing a hymn, he began thinking of home and 'thoughts of Joe and Reg, in the choir at St John's'.

9

ASPHALT AND THE ASPIDISTRA

At some point in the 1860s when the journalist James Greenwood was doing his Southwark rounds, he proposed the following idea: 'For humanity's sake, it would be well, were it possible, to cut away a good sized block out of an acre of fair average of London squalor, and carry it out somewhere into Hyde Park, say, where it might be safely and conveniently exhibited. There is a broad field for selection. In the south, between London Bridge and the Elephant & Castle . . .'[79] By the 1920s, a pamphlet issued by the Robert Browning settlement, speculating on the same issue, suggested a variation on this: 'Why not bring Hyde Park to Walworth? In order not to create a suspicion that we are appropriating too much of the Empire we will be modest and ask for 10 acres. Mark off a strip of 10 acres in Hyde Park and sell it for building; and with the money buy 10 acres in Walworth for the making of open space.'[80] This space it was suggested would provide a park in the district, as within Southwark there were 12 acres of open space to every 100,000 of the population, compared with 161 elsewhere in 'the county of London'. A report on the conditions in the area in the same decade revealed that 'the whole residential conditions of the borough point to its being the most overcrowded part of London, and as compared with its population it is sadly lacking in open spaces serving as "lungs".'[81] Hyde Park stayed put, and four acres of Southwark were given over to 'lungs' in the form of gardens.

The call for further reform at the beginning of the century had been put on hold because of the Great War, but came back onto the agenda in its aftermath. After more than a hundred years, universal manhood suffrage had been achieved following the Representation of the People Act of 1918, and votes would be extended to all women over the age of twenty-one by 1928. There were promises of reconstruction and a land fit for heroes, and a home for each and every one of them. More than 40,000 of the residents of Southwark were living in a condition of indefensible overcrowding in the 1920s. Those without homes included ex-servicemen, like the soldier living with his wife and four children in Walworth in a shack made from an old army ground sheet.

The state had been brought in to administer the housing problem. A Housing and Town Planning Act was passed in 1919, allocating government subsidies for local authorities to build low-rent accommodation. Southwark became the centre of a vigorous redevelopment programme. Throughout the century there had been tentative attempts at slum clearance in the borough. Before the war a site in Walworth had been earmarked for the biggest slum clearance campaign ever undertaken in the capital.

For more than a century, Southwark's bad reputation had persisted. But by the end of the 1920s a redevelopment scheme that had taken almost twenty years was nearing completion. The street where Tom Larter once lived was soon dominated by an expansive red-brick housing development – the Tabard

Gardens Estate – that, like a number of others, was made up of self-contained flats, built close to small playgrounds that went some way to providing the much needed 'lungs' in the neighbourhood. Bankside, described as 'insanitary' at the beginning of the century, was finally to be built on.

The Surrey Gardens Estate in Walworth, built on the site occupied a century before by Surrey Gardens Music Hall, lawns, terraces, and a zoo famous for its glasshouse menageries, had been one of the first of the new estates in the area. Built towards the close of the nineteenth century, it now consisted of self-contained maisonettes and flats. Henry and Kate Larter had lived there for the last sixteen years of Henry's life. Streets that had played a part in the history of the Larters since the beginning of the nineteenth century when William and Martha married were in the throes of slum clearance and regeneration, and replaced with new housing estates. Many of these adhered to the blueprint of the 'block' system, even though it was thought to be anathema to the English way. They were equipped with lavatories on each landing, and sometimes with a coal box and scullery for each flat. (There had previously been comments in the press that the working class might use baths as wardrobes, beds, or a place to keep chickens.) These new estates were a vast improvement on some of the original model dwellings, of which Alexander Paterson had written:

The evening visitor will sigh many times before he reaches the fifth flight. He may have fallen over the cube-sugar box on wheels of a bygone trolley which stands outside No. 131 and serves as a perambulator and a barro [sic]. He will have guessed the menu of some fifteen dinners or teas, and wondered why philanthropists are so opposed to light.[82]

It was argued that many of the new, attractive council buildings were only affordable to artisans. 'Many of them are
immigrants to the district', wrote the Methodist minister John
Martin in the book of his time in Southwark, *A Corner of
England*, 'for only a tithe of our own people can afford such
rents.' This is an echo of a current concern within Southwark, as
the area begins to attract new settlers and undergoes
redevelopment.

It was not Dr State but philanthropy in the shape of the Earl
of Iveagh that helped improve the housing condition of the
Halls. In 1890 he had provided £200,000 to build dwellings 'for
the poor and needy' of the metropolis by creating the Guinness
Trust. One of the first of the charity's developments had been
erected at the end of the nineteenth century on Lock's Fields,
opposite where the Halls lived. The couple moved into the flats
after the birth of their second child Rose, in 1922. Nell Hall had
already had two miscarriages and would lose twins before the
birth of her second daughter, Eileen. Her last-born, Harry,
would arrive at the end of the decade. 'Everyone had to share
the laundries, sinks and lavatories', she said. 'Everyone had to
take turn cleaning the toilets, passages and landings. They
expected you to sweep the stairs every day and wash them on
Saturdays before ten o'clock in the morning.' The one incon-
venience was that 'for funerals you couldn't have the body at
home because they couldn't get the coffins up the stairs and
along the balconies'. There was a ban on the beating of carpets
after 11 a.m., except on Saturdays. Clothes were not to be hung
in the courtyards of the estate after Thursday, and noisy and dis-
orderly tenants were swiftly threatened with eviction.

Despite all these developments, the housing situation in
Southwark remained particularly dire, with a quarter of its res-
idences said to be unfit for human habitation even in 1938. But
by the end of the 1920s the landscape of the borough had

altered from that of forty years earlier, when Nell Hall was a child. 'To the eye, apart from the new council flats,' wrote John Martin, 'the factories and the churches – mostly these last in disrepair – the great army of public houses and cinemas alone breaks the depressing monotony of Victorian industrial dwellings. Laughter and tears are both as common as orange-peel on the pavements. Saints and heroes are to be found, but ascetics from choice are rare.'[83]

10

NOSTALGIA FOR THE MUD

Lenin's line that cinema was the most significant art form for revolutionary socialism was lost on the English working class, who were always more likely to opt for Ealing than Eisenstein. When cinema was big, really big, with at least one weekly visit from 40 per cent of the population, there was only one person with the potential to link revolutionary socialism to cinema, and that was Charlie Chaplin: 'It is precisely because Chaplin portrays a kind of primitive proletarian, still outside Revolution, that the representative force of the latter is immense.'[84] His forlorn tramp, oscillating between slapstick and pathos, emerged from his music hall routine and was inspired by childhood memories of the men he witnessed entering the pubs in Walworth, and during his time in the workhouse. His 1917 film *Easy Street* was a reference to his place of birth, East Street, and featured a tramp who is taken under the wing of a local missionary to be 'reformed'.

Chaplin had revolutionised cinema by snatching audiences from music halls, and pulling them to picture houses like those that sprouted in Walworth such as the Montpelier and the

Purple Palace – where, according to Nell Hall, 'you sat on wooden forms as hard as them at the workhouse'. The doors of the South London Palace remained open until 1934, by which time there were ten cinemas in the borough. In 1928, academics from the London School of Economics followed in the footsteps of Charles Booth forty years on, updating his survey under the title of *The New Survey of London Life and Labour*. Among the changes was the fact that cinema has 'driven out of existence the public-house "free-and-easies" of Charles Booth's day'.

When Chaplin returned to England in 1921, his first visit since emigrating to America in 1914, he made a pilgrimage to the birthplace that inspired his screen persona. And when he returned to the capital in 1931 for the premier of *City Lights*, London crowds came out to welcome him, during a depression and an economic crisis in the West which was manifested on a local level by high unemployment and a halt to the financing of further reconstruction. Chaplin was invited to dine at Downing Street, and there were rumours of a knighthood. Such events in the life of a product of poor working-class stock would have seemed unimaginable before the war. But now the prime minister himself, Ramsay MacDonald, like several of his ministers, was from humble origins. The home secretary J. R. Clynes later recalled: 'I could not help marvelling at the strange turn of Fortune's wheel, which had brought MacDonald, the starveling clerk, Thomas the engine-driver, Henderson the foundry labourer and Clynes, the mill-hand to this pinnacle.'[85]

Despite the economic gloom, luxury came to the Elephant & Castle, at the site that Tarn's once occupied beside the Rockingham Arms. The Trocadero was opened in 1931. *City Lights* was screened here, in what was designed to be the biggest cinema in Europe. It was the brainchild of two East End brothers who had previously built its older, smaller sibling, the Trocette, on nearby Tower Bridge Road. At the Trocadero there was a carpeted lounge, an orchestra, tea rooms and an athletic club. It was a piece of paradise in this postcode. In his novel *London Belongs to Me*, which begins in the late Thirties and concerns the inhabitants of a nearby boarding house, Norman Collins recast the Elephant's art deco oasis as the Toledo:

> It was a huge ferro-concrete refuge from the cares and troubles of life, complete with a marble fountain in the forecourt, carpets like bogmoss, the largest organ in south London, attendants like chorus-girls who went up and down during performances with the latest kind of antiseptic scent-spray, an ice-cream fountain, Accositcon-aids for the deaf, Synchro-Harmonic Reproduction, and deep rubber-padded chairs for refugees.

Cinema had been Nell Hall's refuge from the cares and troubles of life since first seeing Chaplin on screen. She was convinced she must have passed him and his family on the local streets years earlier. When the Trocadero was under construction, it was 'as if they was building the pyramids at the Elephant'. She waited outside on the opening night, as one of a crowd of 4,000. London was engulfed in a peasouper fog, which seemed to concentrate on the poorer, densely populated areas of the metropolis, where it was thickened by the slate-grey smoke shooting from closely stacked chimneys, and, at the Elephant & Castle, the smog and soot from the railway. The streetlights appeared to hover in mid-air, their stems erased by the density of the fog. Before the cinema opened its doors, some of the 300 staff soaked blankets in ammonia and shoved them against air vents to prevent fog seeping into the venue. Outside the crowd queued, freezing, purblind, as police stood guard.

The success of this, the first and the biggest cine-variety theatre, set a precedent for supercinemas that emerged elsewhere throughout the decade; the Odeons, Granadas and Regals that at their peak brought in close to 20 million customers each week. In *A Corner of England*, John Martin writes of the impact of cinema on working men and women of Southwark: 'it has been a new gateway of knowledge to the world around them . . . they have derived from the pictures a vast fund of information, and, what is far more important, a considerable stimulus for reflection and inquiry'.[86] With the arrival of cinema an 'ever-widening area of human experience is forced upon their attention, even though it be in a crude and melodramatic form – a spy-glass held out to them through which they can peer at the remotest corners of the world'. This new form of mass entertainment was followed by broadcasting, which would move closer to the masses as the wireless became widely affordable throughout the decade (and available on weekly instalments with hire purchase). It was reported in the *New Survey of London Life and Labour* that 'the wireless has now become a very general adjunct to the amenities of working class life in London, nor is it limited to the homes of the better paid artisans. It looks as if the wireless, though an entirely post-war development, had already become in London working class life not less important than that of cinema'.[87]

The new medium of broadcasting had begun in 1922. The BBC's founding Director General, and the 'father' of the corporation – as he would later describe himself – John Reith, filled the BBC with graduates from Oxford and Cambridge. Reith's high ideals, his bid to educate, inform and entertain, in that order, were the voice of the patrician class nannying the nation:

> Our thoughts turn to the poor, that vast majority whose children look on the streets as their playground and attend when they can the performances of the nearest Picture House. The possibilities of 'the pictures' were enormous, and at the

outset it was firmly believed that here was to be found the means of educating the masses. The ethical and educational value of the cinematograph was allowed to be superseded by sensationalism . . .[88]

Reith's attitude to cinema was a familiar one, but in Southwark John Martin believed that the working class were 'as qualified to winnow the wheat from the chaff in the films which they see as are their middle-class brothers and sisters in the plays and the books, American, French, and indeed of all nations which they so freely visit or buy'.[89] John Reith's vision of a wireless in every home was reminiscent of the missionary priests at the end of the nineteenth century, opening a settlement house in every working-class neighbourhood, to educate the locals by example. A Scottish Presbyterian, Reith was a cultural missionary, and his message spread beyond the folk at home to the foreigners in the far reaches of the Dominions.

By December 1932, the block where the Halls lived also housed Nell's sister, her husband and in-laws, the widowed Kate Larter and her youngest son. It was Christmas Day, a week after the inauguration of the BBC's Empire service, and all were gathered in the bar of The Albion nearby to hear King George V become the first monarch to use the wireless to address his subjects throughout the globe, from a small office at Sandringham. Appropriately the script was penned by the Empire's laureate, Rudyard Kipling, and addressed those 'so cut off by the snows, the desert or the sea, that only voices out of the air can reach them'.

At home, another section of the Empire was equally cut off. The unemployed numbered 3 million by January 1933. Almost a hundred years before, Disraeli had coined the phrase 'two nations' to describe the split between the rich and the poor.

Now J. B. Priestley wrote how the nation could be divided four ways, after an expedition throughout the country via bus, train and tram. He discovered the official historical England of the tour guides, the industrial England of the nineteenth century, the modern, postwar England of giant cinemas and Woolworths, and the England of the unemployed. London was perceived as the wealthy capital, with its high-wage centre, and the new light industries beginning to thrive on its outskirts. Southwark and Bermondsey may have been perfectly placed, but like the sooty little towns of the north they were depressed areas in which unemployment was concentrated. Those arriving in the capital from the north on hunger marches were surprised to find not simply support and supplies en route to London, but many people in similar circumstances. Unemployment reached 19 per cent in the early years of the decade in Bermondsey, when the London average was 12 per cent; and the rate in Southwark towards the end of the decade remained at 4 per cent higher than the London average. This paled beside the figure of 68 per cent to be found in Jarrow, but Southwark, as a borough close to the centre of a rich city, was an example of 'poverty amidst plenty'.

While Priestley was on his English journey, George Orwell was collecting material for his first book, *Down and Out in Paris and London* (1933). During his travels he spent time on the streets of Southwark and Bermondsey, where he slept in a local 'doss-house' and wrote in a local library. Like Chaplin, he had dressed down and dirtied up to create a particular persona. By putting himself in the right clothes, and with little alteration to his upper-middle-class accent, he could pass himself off as a vagrant. Once again, middle-class authors who took the working class as their subject were writing of the exceptional rather than the typical.

The cinema newsreel, and the documentary film – which

came into its own in the Thirties rather as photography did in the 1890s, along with slum fiction – offered a more general view of the working class. Orwell's preoccupation with the vagrant was rather like Morrison's attachment to the working-class criminal. He stayed in lodging houses for the homeless at this time, and later wrote how staying with ordinary working-class families 'always has a dangerous resemblance to "slum-ming"'.[90] Had someone like Orwell smartened himself up, and wandered further inland beyond the lodging house and the library, he would have returned with a more general picture of the working class of Southwark and Bermondsey. But what if he had lodged with a local family at this time? The Halls, perhaps. They could certainly have done with the money. Nell Hall said: 'You weren't allowed to sub-let.' But just suppose that someone like Orwell . . .

The first sound in the mornings was that of a 'knocker-up' who walked the streets tapping a huge pole against the bedrooms of certain homes, for men and women who needed a wake-up call. There were generally six of us in the small flat. Mr and Mrs Hall had three young children, and other relatives who lived elsewhere in the block were forever dropping by. Mr Hall was a balding, portly man, who was in and out of employment due to illness, and a lack of available local work for a man approaching forty who had only ever worked with horses at a time when the horse was becoming redundant in this urban community.

Horsedrawn trams, cabs and wagons have slowly disappeared since the beginning of this century, when electric tramlines arrived in Walworth. This decade has witnessed the invention of the pedestrian crossing, and the City of London has passed by-laws forbidding access to horsedrawn vehicles. Mr Hall told me that local harness-makers had all but disappeared, along with many other businesses that used to sit on the corner of every other street: curriers, dyers, cigar-makers. The horses now traipsing the local streets pulled the carts of rag-and-bone men, tally men, knife-grinders, totters. Rag-and-bone men collected bones to make glue; tally men sold clothes and household items, usually second-hand, on hire purchase. Each week the tally man halted his horse and cart on the forecourt of the buildings where the Halls lived. The furniture the neighbours bought from him was old, rapidly falling apart, with springs erupting from armchairs like bones breaking through skin. It was passed on to the rag-and-bone man before the instalments had been completed.

In a bid to improve his prospects of obtaining work, Mr Hall had bought a bicycle on hire purchase, but had been unable to meet a number of the repayments. Of course, as I was indoors a good deal I heard all about the Halls' woes, and how when her husband was ill Mrs Hall had to take his place in court. 'It's the first time anyone in this family has had trouble with the law since my father was a boy', she told me. Mrs Hall relayed the outcome of the day in court, a day of lost pay, as she spent it immersed in a lengthy queue of 'criminals' responsible for similar misdemeanours. 'When the judge sat down,' she began, 'I saw him pull a face and hold his back. I thought – lumbago. So when I'm in front of him, and he's looking down on me, and asking me why we can't pay, I says: "My husband suffers terrible with lumbago." So he does this, taps his nose, then he nods, and lets me pay what I can afford each week.'

There was no local park or green on which the Halls' two daughters could play. They were often on the forecourt or climbing on the costers' sheds with the other children, marching at the helm of a miniature army with a cache of homemade catapults and peashooters, with split-peas and maize for ammunition. One local boy let the others use his wooden leg as a 'rounders' bat, in exchange for sweets. The weekly appearance of the rag-and-bone man had them charging along landings, knocking on doors for any junk they could hand him in exchange for a goldfish. The youngest of the Hall children, a boy, caused a commotion within the neighbourhood when he returned home from school limping as though crippled. Mrs Hall had been unable to afford new shoes for her son, and had sent him to school in wellington boots. As punishment, a teacher had placed pieces of hard chalk inside the bottom of the boots and made him walk on these throughout the day. Mrs Hall, sleeves rolled, and apron billowing, marched to the school, with several local women in pursuit to witness the spectacle.

Whenever a depression was at its most severe, or republicanism at its most potent, a slight revival of fortunes and a royal event would kick in at the right moment and turn the nation's head. The king's silver jubilee fell in 1935. Unemployment began to drop, dipping below 2 million by that summer, which lifted the national mood. As with the celebrations of 1897, the locals of Southwark gathered on the streets. A crowd of 50,000 waited six hours for the king and queen's procession to make its way through the borough from Blackfriars Bridge. In Bermondsey, whose political administration had an increasingly radical reputation, the mayor refused to take part in the proceedings, and 2,000 residents burned an effigy of him outside the town hall.

But within the upper classes, in this decade, there emerged a generation that positively embraced the idea of the proletariat. 'Fathers in clubs complained that their sons had become Communists at Oxford and well brought up daughters suddenly announced, sometimes in the presence of servants, that they proposed henceforth to devote themselves wholly to the class war.'[91] Following Orwell, many embarked on expeditions to discover the working class for themselves. Not since the end of the nineteenth century had the pursuit of the authentic working-class experience been so fashionable. The modern-day equivalents of George R. Sims were not immaculately presented flâneurs returning from their expeditions with stories of that dangerous 'mighty mob', intended to alarm the middle classes. The message and the mission was now one of solidarity with the masses. Some wished to rally them to revolt. Malcolm Muggeridge explained the trend:

> From the London School of Economics and other places went annually many earnest persons, male and female, to plant their tents in depressed areas, housing-estates, malnutrition belts. Juvenile crime claimed their attention, prostitution was not neglected by them, birth-control clinics and after-care committees and vocational centres all were within their range. Members of Parliament disguised themselves as tramps in order to inform themselves of the circumstances in which other forms of Public Assistance than their own £600 a year, were administered; journalists settled temporarily in slums.[92]

In his essay 'Inside the Whale', Orwell writes that certain English authors embraced their new faith like boy scouts with bare knees embarking on a community sing-along, every one 'an eager-minded schoolboy with a leaning towards Communism'.[93] Rebellious upper-class offspring may have found their political faith, but it wasn't one that was shared by the majority of the urban working class, according to Orwell. 'The typical Socialist is not, as tremulous old ladies imagine, a ferocious-looking working man with greasy overalls and a raucous voice'.[94] He was likely to be 'a youthful snob-Bolshevik who in five years' time will quite probably have made a wealthy marriage and been converted to Roman Catholicism'.[95] The opinions Orwell expressed in the second half of *The Road to Wigan Pier* were like a brick through the collective windows of the upper class party faithful, who stood apart from the common culture of the proletariat with whom they claimed solidarity, in their political views, habits, interests, and the fact that they married within their class. Socialists themselves were pushing the English working classes towards fascism, argued Orwell, while communism was a creed 'never found in its pure form in a genuine proletarian'. The genuine working man 'is seldom or never a Socialist in the complete, logically consistent sense . . . I have yet to meet a *working* miner, steel-worker, cotton-weaver, docker, navvy, or whatnot who was "ideologically" sound.'[96] Orwell's observation was similar to that of Alexander Paterson some years earlier, when he recalled how the working man of Southwark rarely stopped to listen to socialist orators on street corners: 'He slides off home, with little thought of revolution in his heart.'[97]

In keeping with the tradition of Mayhew, Greenwood and Sims, those now writing about the working class were describing a race apart. 'A tribe as unknown to us as the Trobriand Islands',[98] noted the historian Hugh Massingham of his East End experiences in *I Took Off My Tie*. His jaunt was reminiscent of that of Richard Whiteing's fictional narrator in *No. 5 John Street*, who 'cannot discard his gentlemanly habits and asks for a washerwoman to wash his clothes'.[99] Massingham recalls his thoughts before beginning his trip: 'If I were to succeed there must be no half measures and I must live in the same conditions as the poor and share their privations and fears.'[100] And so the author smoked Woodbines instead of Players, and allowed himself few creature comforts for his sojourn to the east: a shaving set, pyjamas, underpants, and a choice of reading: Stendhal and Balzac. There is an element of mockery within

Massingham's musings. One incident has him standing beneath windows listening to mothers yell for their children: 'Joo-o-oey'. The author gets 'some quiet amusement from thinking what an excellent burlesque this would make of the balcony scene in Romeo and Juliet'.[101] Eventually he warms to his neighbours but writes that Chaplin's *Easy Street* reveals more about the working class than any social survey by outsiders:

> All our efforts to bring about a reconciliation between the classes are useless and a waste of time. I dare say the only way to get to know them is to give up everything and be subject to the same necessities and fears as they are. Well, I haven't got the pluck to do that, and I don't mean to try.[102]

Someone else who took Massingham's approach to understanding the working class was Celia Fremlin, who came down from Oxford in the 1930s and took a job as a charwoman and a kitchen-hand, which she embarked on 'in that spirit of armchair socialism which is so prevalent among my class and generation'.[103] Her observations were published as *The Seven Chars of Chelsea*, and the conclusions reached were similar to those of Massingham, and even G. K. Chesterton when he was commenting on social and artistic slumming. 'By working and living for a time among a class other than one's own one may learn a lot', she writes. 'But one will not become a member of that class. Between oneself and them there will remain a barrier, thin and clear as glass, but impenetrable. However one may will the contrary, one will remain essentially an outsider; everything one says or writes about one's experiences will, in the last analysis, be from the point of view of an outsider.'

In Rotherhithe, Jessica Mitford, daughter of Lord Redesdale, claimed to be going for the full conversion. She was the epitome of one of those well-brought-up daughters who devoted themselves wholly to the class war. And like the 'snob-Bolshevik', she had married well, and within her class: to Esmond Romilly, her second cousin, and a nephew of Winston Churchill. Both literally and metaphorically, the couple distanced themselves from family members, old friends, and the set that once surrounded them, by moving across the water to live in a working-class neighbourhood. Home in Rotherhithe was a house overlooking the river, owned by a friend and consisting of seven rooms over four storeys. Rent was £2 per month including the use of the grand piano. The locals were 'a shorter and paler race of people than the inhabitants of London's West End. In appearance, dress, speech they form so radical a contrast as to give the impression of a different ethnic group'.[104] The newly-weds gave 'bottle parties', which brought journalists, writers, and night-club singers across the water; they ate fish and chips, and attended meetings of the Bermondsey Labour Party, because Romilly believed the Communist Party membership consisted of too many young upper-class intellectuals like himself.

Me and My Girl was the most popular show in the West End at the time. The musical tells the story of a banana-selling, winkle-eating cockney named Bill Snibson who inherits an earldom and becomes Lord Hareford of Hareford Hall. But he simply cannot forget his cockney ways. He breaks into the Lambeth Walk at a society dinner party, and suddenly all the dukes and duchesses relinquish the shackles of their class and relish the vibrancy of the cockney. *Everything free and easy . . . Do as you darn well pleasy*. Mitford's reversal of the Bill Snibson role was a piece of prole-playing that reprised the games she participated in with her sisters as children, at their very own Hareford Hall, Swinbrook House.

Whilst living in Rotherhithe, Mitford took a job that, like her new postcode, was outside of her class, in the fresh new field of market research, but she harboured an ambition 'to prove myself as an efficient working-class wife, keeping everything bright, clean and attractive . . .'[105] She was to fall at the first hurdle, having failed to understand the logic in house cleaning: stairs had to be swept from the top to the bottom, and not the reverse.

Meanwhile, in nearby Walworth, Nell Hall, an efficient working-class housewife, worked at home when her children were babies, making paper bags, or toffee apples from glucose and colouring, before returning to full-time work at Hartley's jam factory when they were old enough to be left with her mother and other relatives. In the flat next door, the wife took in washing, and chopped up eels to earn a living. Nell Hall said: 'She'd been born with one hand missing, and every time she cut an eel she'd pin it down with the stump at her wrist, and it would wind itself all the way up her arm.'

Shortly after moving to Rotherhithe, Jessica Mitford gave birth to her first child, a daughter.

'We planned her future, growing up among the rough children of Rotherhithe Street, born to freedom and May Day parades . . .' – *everything free and easy . . . do as you darn well pleasy* – '. . . without the irksome restraints of nanny, governess, daily walks and dull dances; or perhaps we'd take her to Paris to live, a little gamine trudging to a Lycée with books in a satchel . . .'[106]

Within months of her daughter's birth Mitford endured an experience that was common for those working-class women she played at being: an event that would not have happened had she remained within her class. An epidemic of measles broke out in the neighbourhood, and her daughter caught measles, then pneumonia, and died. Here the advantages of Mitford's actual class became apparent, and made her different from local mothers. The grieving couple took off to Corsica for three months.

During the period in which they remained at Rotherhithe

Street on their return, they were hassled by a man employed by the gas company. Mitford recalled later that no one had ever explained she needed to pay for utilities, and so 'lights, electric heaters, stoves blazed away day and night'.[107] As bills reached colossal proportions, the couple began to don various disguises to avoid the gas inspector, with Romilly often concealed beneath a worker's cap and a false moustache. Again, it was just like the games and pranks at Swinbrook House. 'It was unthinkable that we should pay',[108] Mitford wrote in her autobiography. And so they didn't. Concealed beneath their fancy dress, they moved their belongings over the water, and settled in Marble Arch.

Meanwhile Nell Hall experienced her lowest point since losing her first son. Even though she and Bill were in work, their incomes could barely help them sustain a decent standard of living. The bills piled up, and she seriously considered suicide.

'It was a silly thing when you think about it, but it was because I couldn't pay the milk bill. Every day it got closer to the milkie coming on the Saturday, I got to planning it. I thought it out, how to do it and what time, knowing where everyone was. I thought to myself: "I'll put the pillow in the oven and that" – I even knew what pillow, because I didn't want the kids or Bill to have to sleep on it afterwards. And I mean, it strikes me at the time that's the best way. I didn't want Bill to have to find me hanging behind the door. That's what happened to a woman along the landing – she hung herself. Her sister used to skin rabbits and hang 'em on the railings top of The Lane. But, I dunno, somehow we muddled through it. Something happened. Somehow something always happened to help you through.'

11

THE F WORD

Fascism had arrived in Walworth early in the decade, without fanfare and without a substantial local following. Nell Hall was introduced to the new creed by a disturbance at 122 Walworth Road that spilled onto the street. A reported 300 communists armed with iron bars raided the headquarters of the British Union of Fascists, based in rooms above a shop. Word had spread through the market, as locals raked the content of the stalls, prodding veg and placing thumbprints in fatty cuts of meat. Ironically, the day before, the talk of Walworth Road had been a big wedding at the synagogue, at which the groom was the brother of the bandleader from the celebrated Trocadero orchestra.

Fascism, like communism, was largely identified with the offspring of the upper classes. Just as Jessica Mitford had jettisoned coming-out balls in favour of playing at being an efficient working-class wife, so her sister Unity hotfooted it to Germany to stalk Hitler. Her efforts at proving herself a loyal fascist back in England were as affected as her sister's bid to be a socialist. With a signed copy of *Mein Kampf* clutched to her heart, she

performed the Nazi salute and bellowed 'Heil Hitler!' at everyone she met near the family home, including the local
postmistress. At a May Day march in which 'Blackshirts were
overwhelmed by the sheer numbers of Bermondsey men',[109]
Jessica Mitford caught sight of her sisters Unity and Diana
waving swastika flags: 'I shook my fist at them in the Red Front
salute.' It was just as it was when they were girls, when Unity
clawed swastikas on her bedroom window with a diamond ring,
and Decca scratched a hammer and sickle.

The British Union of Fascists was led by the Mitfords'
brother-in-law, Oswald Mosley,* who introduced the 'black-
shirt' motif, and about whom there was a touch of Flash
Gordon: the turtle neck, the belt joined by a large silver square.
The movement's symbol, two lightning flashes, was more in
keeping with the double crosses soon to be worn by the followers of Chaplin's Führer in *The Great Dictator* than with the
Nazi swastika. Mosley was, according to Nell Hall, 'too full of
himself'. He was described by Malcolm Muggeridge in *The
Thirties* as 'a Lilliputian Führer'. 'The revolutionary voice was
more curious than impressive; the Blackshirts made but a poor
showing, notable rather for their capacity to stir up opposition
than their own numbers or prowess. One existed by virtue of the
other. They were complementary, and in some cases, interchangeable.'[110] Orwell believed that if there ever was to be such
a thing as English fascism it would be sedate and subtle and, initially, unlikely to be referred to by the f-word. 'It is doubtful', he
wrote, 'whether a Gilbert & Sullivan heavy dragoon of Mosley's
stamp would ever be much more than a joke to the majority of
English people.'[111]

---

*Diana Mitford married Oswald Mosley in 1936. Her sister Nancy parodied the politics of
Unity, Diana and Mosley in the novel *Wigs on the Green*. The book barely conceals the
British Union of Fascists behind 'The Union Jack Movement'.

Mosley's anti-semitism, like the policies relating to unemployment, was marketed at working-class men like Bill Hall,
whose promised land fit for heroes had not materialised. In the
Forties, Orwell would write that the severity of the circumstances in England, despite the extreme unemployment and the
poor living standards of many within work, had not proved
great enough for fascism to flourish. However, Mosley saw
urban working-class strongholds like Walworth and
Bermondsey as recruiting posts, and fertile soil for his anti-
Jewish propaganda. In *I Took Off My Tie*, Hugh Massingham
writes that anti-semitism in the East End, responsible for an
increase in support for Mosley, was not exclusively attributable
to blind prejudice:

> Some people have Jewish landlords and complain that they
> have been treated harshly and inhumanly. Others – especially
> women – have worked in one of those East End trades which
> are so small that the workers cannot protect themselves from
> exploitation through a trade union. Some of these trades are
> in the hands of Jews, and low wages and bad conditions have
> fanned a vague prejudice into living hatred.[112]

Mosley's proposals for greater public spending to assist the
creation of more jobs had been carried over from his time as a
minister in the Labour government. When these were not taken
on board he resigned and set about creating the New Party, to
propagate his own policies, and provide him with the leadership
role that he felt his life had been preparing him for. Had he not
met Mussolini, or been struck down with a bout of influenza,
making it impossible for him to campaign and mobilise his party
members to win seats, he might not have made his bid to
rebrand fascism, to stay in the political frame. But dressing up
and taking to the streets made him no more a likely political

leader than his sister-in-law's time of slumming it in Rotherhithe made her working-class. Just as Mosley believed his class and upbringing meant that he was born to rule, Mitford couldn't quite shake the sense of superiority that made her a snob-Bolshevik. Orwell had said that no matter what their views the upper classes all believed the working classes smell.

Among those championing the dictatorship of the proletariat, the prejudice was often more subtle. They liked the idea of the proletariat but not the proletariat themselves. Writing of his time as a communist in the Thirties from the vantage point of the 1970s, Stephen Spender remembered hoping for revolution, yet being concerned that the workers would have him scrubbing floors instead of polishing stanzas. In 1960 Jessica Mitford recalled her colleagues from her market research days in the prewar era as having brutal voices, and talking too much about sex and men:

> I was repelled yet fascinated, at the same time rather hoping these were not the workers of the world destined to lead the revolution. There didn't seem to be much danger, as none of them were remotely interested in politics; their newspaper reading seemed confined to crime news and the ever-popular antics of dear little Princess Lilibet and Margaret Rose.[113]

When Mosley's 'blackshirts' marched to the Elephant & Castle and into Bermondsey in 1937 singing 'the Horst Wessel Lied' and the hymn of Mussolini's fascist party, they were confronted by communists singing 'The Red Flag'. But all these voices were drowned by the collective renditions of 'Rule Britannia' and 'Land of Hope and Glory' from the majority of those living nearby who had turned out on the streets, or witnessed the event from windows and balconies. The march was diverted because the inhabitants had barricaded the streets with barrows and a water tank from a nearby factory. Eggs, door knobs, shoes, stones and oranges were tossed over the barricades at Oswald's army. 'Today a bridge has been built between north and south Londoners', declared an apparatchik of the Communist Party at a meeting in the Trocette, following the Bermondsey confrontation. 'One hundred per cent of cockney Bermondsey has given the same answer to Mosley as the Jewish lads and girls in Stepney just twelve months ago.'[114]

The champions of communism and fascism appeared to be oblivious to the 'Englishness' of the English working class. 'The insularity of the English is more obvious than in any other class in England', wrote Hugh Massingham in *I Took Off My Tie*. 'The slightest taint excites prejudice, for not only are the Jews, Frenchmen, Germans, and Americans regarded as "foreigners" but even the Welshmen, Scotsmen, and Irishmen.'[115] The left was forever looking to Russia for its cue, and as Orwell noted of Mosley: 'Even the elementary fact that Fascism must not offend national sentiment had escaped him. His entire movement was imitated slavishly from abroad, the uniform and the party programme from Italy and the salute from Germany.'[116] In *A Corner of England* John Martin wrote that he had seen more covert hostility towards a 'toff' than towards any foreigner. Much of the crowd in Bermondsey that turned out to see off the blackshirts would have consisted of insular 'cockneys' predominantly opposed to Mosley not because of his anti-semitism but because he was an English aristocrat who favoured the politics of Mussolini and the theatrics of Hitler, and who fronted a movement that called for an end to democracy a decade after all working-class men and women had been granted the vote.

Within a year or two of the barricades being dismantled and door knobs returned to front doors, Oswald's army had gone to ground. The leader was interned as war broke out. When war was announced, his sister-in-law Unity attempted suicide. And a fair number of those who had championed the dictatorship of the proletariat, railed against capitalism and warned of the threat of fascism throughout the decade – including Jessica Mitford, W. H. Auden and Christopher Isherwood – migrated to . . . America. Meanwhile those women who were 'not remotely interested in politics' had no choice but to stay put and watch as sandbags appeared on the street corners of Southwark and Bermondsey. They evacuated their children, waved off husbands, boyfriends and brothers, and kept their ear to the wireless and their eye on the sky. In their moments of respite, they continued to read 'crime news and the ever-popular antics of dear little Princess Lilibet and Margaret Rose', and, like Nell Hall, they drifted between the half-darkness of the cinema and that of the air-raid shelter.

At the Trocadero ('half-price Mondays and Thursdays'), throughout the Thirties, the newsreels had been peppered with men and moustaches: the late King George – a grey-brown walrus-like moustache attached to a silver beard the shape of a sporran; Mosley – straight as a freshly trimmed privet hedge, almost obscuring the top lip. Chamberlain returning from Munich had a moustache more spliced with grey. From the lips beneath these whiskers emerged the words: 'I believe it is peace for our time.' One year later, the big moustache of Stalin and the little moustache of Hitler came together for the Soviet–German pact. And finally the neat and clipped moustache above Rhett Butler's lip, like the teeth on the comb the school nurse dragged through the heads of working-class kids to purge them of nits.

During the 'phoney war', when the evacuees temporarily returned home, Nell Hall and her daughter Eileen sat in the stalls of a packed Trocadero staring up at *Gone With the Wind*. Had Charlie Chaplin's wife Paulette Goddard landed the part played by Vivien Leigh, he said he would never have made *The Great Dictator* (1940), which became his biggest-grossing film to that point. It was the part in which the little tramp's moustache – tiny, square, black and mottled, the hairs gathered like the tobacco collected from the dog ends found in the gutters of Walworth, and sold on the pavement of East Street by the very poor – came into its own. The film starred Chaplin as the poor, bemused Jewish barber mistaken for the dictator Adenoid Hynkel. It was the film that the British establishment didn't want the country to see, fearing its impact on Anglo-German relations, and the film Hitler didn't want the world to see. Nell Hall said she wanted to see it, to hear Chaplin speak for the first time. In the final speech he says:

> Let us fight for a new world, a decent world that will give men a chance to work, that will give you the future and old age and security. By the promise of these things, brutes have risen to power, but they lie. They do not fulfil their promise, they never will. Dictators free themselves but they enslave the people. Now let us fight to fulfil that promise. Let us fight to free the world, to do away with national barriers, do away with greed, with hate and intolerance. Let us fight for a world of reason, a world where science and progress will lead to all men's happiness. Soldiers – in the name of democracy, let us all unite!

By the late Thirties there had been a slight upturn in the fortunes of the Halls and many of their class. 'It is quite likely', George Orwell wrote in *The Road to Wigan Pier*, 'that fish-and-chips, art-silk stockings, tinned salmon, cut-price chocolate, the movies, the radio, strong tea, and the football pools have between them averted revolution.'[117] A form of 'affluence' had touched the lives of the working class with the emergence of more affordable consumer goods towards the end of the Thirties. Families like the Halls were fodder for Dr Gallup's market research techniques, which were adopted in the Britain of the Thirties, so that advertising could sketch a detailed picture of the British consumer. The masses were under the microscope, with surveys and statistics more in vogue than throughout the nineteenth century. And the techniques used to understand them as consumers were also used to understand them as citizens, by way of Mass-Observation.

Social anthropology had come a long way since Henry Mayhew wrote about the skull shapes of costermongers. The Mass-Observation organisation, founded in 1937 with its base in south-east London, dispatched more than 1,500 canvassers in the late Thirties to report on the everyday behaviour of the working classes. Unlike previous social investigations, the data was not defined by religion, housing and work. Among the subjects explored were the obsession with astrology and all-in wrestling, 'the cult of the aspidistra', the psychology of the dirty joke and the saucy postcard, funerals, undertakers, and the football pools. Both the term 'Mass-Observation' and the concept were the brainchild of a surrealist poet, Charles Madge, but the name with which it became synonymous was Tom Harrisson. Each had emerged from a wealthy upper-class family; each had abandoned Cambridge before graduating. As a student, Harrisson had been famous for, amongst other things, wandering through the university grounds barefoot with painted toenails. He joined forces with Madge in the mid-Thirties after returning from the New Hebrides, where he had studied the cannibalistic tribe of the Malekula. He was completing work on the book *Savage Civilisation* as Orwell was undertaking his expedition to Yorkshire.

Harrisson would soon plant himself among the working classes of Bolton, with jobs in a factory, as a lorry driver and an ice cream man, so as to apply his methods to 'the cannibals of Lancashire'. It was not unlike James Greenwood shifting his

gaze from the haircuts of the Bushukulompo to the mating rituals of the costermonger. Harrisson also dispatched spies to
camouflage themselves in urban jungles, on public transport, in
pubs, cinemas, dance halls and fish and chip shops, chronicling
the rituals, customs, habits of the native tribe. The selected areas
were kept anonymous within the published research. Worktown
was the name used for the northern outpost, and the 'sample'
working-class borough in London was referred to as Metrop.
'What a change this is from the usual subtle study of national
character by a cultivated foreign observer, who thinks England
is one big middle-class and generalises accordingly', opined *The
Times*. 'With these anthropological spies among us one wonders
how statesmen and journalists will ever again dare to speak and
write on behalf of "the people".'

Harrisson's surveys relied on 'indirect' interviews, and quotes
recorded from conversations in pubs – he described them as
'overheards'. For his lack of academic expertise and unconven-
tional methods, he was pilloried by the purveyors of the
burgeoning science of sociology. His writing style in the books
and pamphlets he published was similar to Orwell's, in its plain-
ness and accessibility. No specific qualifications were required to
be either an observer or a contributor. The author Bill
Naughton, later famous for *Alfie*, was a lorry driver who sought
out Mass-Observation so that he could write. Harrisson positively encouraged input from working-class writers. *Britain*
(1939), a book that sold 100,000 copies within weeks of publication, allots several pages to the monologue of an engineering
worker, depicting a random day from his week:

Upstairs, strip my vest off and have a dam [*sic*] good scrub,
change into clean gear, stick some Brylcreem on my nut,
shave, put my best suit on, downstairs, 'My word, what quick
work!' Have my dinner, pork chop, french beans and potatoes

and black-cherry tart and custard, tea and a smoke, feel good
once more, a new guy, getting twilighty, sit quiet, smoke and
rest my back, eyes still smart a bit, but R.I.P. for 1/4 hour.
Look at my watch, right we're off. 'Give her my love!'
'Night' – 'Night' – out.

Harrisson and his colleagues were in pursuit of an authentic
working-class experience like so many of their class and generation, but with an approach more radical and representative
than their contemporaries. No judgement or political agenda
was imposed on the data published, and their method of eaves-
dropping, recording and reporting was in keeping with the
documentary form adopted by filmmakers like Humphrey
Jennings (along with Harrisson and Madge one of the founders
of Mass-Observation). Its print equivalent was the *Picture Post*.
'Progress and reaction are ceasing to have anything to do with
party labels', wrote George Orwell in *The Lion and the
Unicorn*. 'If one wishes to name a particular moment, one can
say that the old distinction between Right and Left broke down
when *Picture Post* was first published. What are the politics of
Picture Post?'[118] Presumably he meant that the magazine, rather
like Mass-Observation, was in the business of reporting what it
witnessed without imposing its own agenda.

During the Blitz, when the London sky, where planes previously scrawled letters promoting Oxo and Bile Beans, became a
page for something more sinister, Mass-Observation came into
its own. The Ministry of Information enlisted its services to
gauge the morale of the masses, now that aerial bombardment
of built-up urban areas was inevitable. In the late Thirties a
large number of young German sociology students had carried
out their own research on the attitudes and experience of the
English working class, to ascertain how they might react to war,
gathering colossal amounts of data to send home. 'The Third

Reich must have been in possession of more factual details of slum clearance than the most efficient welfare organizations. But they could not understand the English temperament, the traditions, the cockney spirit.'[119] In *London Belongs to Me*, the German student Dr Otto Hapfel walks the streets observing the inhabitants of south-east London:

> He spent nearly the whole week, when he was not at lectures, going to the theatre, the football matches, to restaurants, to religious services, to public meetings, painstakingly observing the strange British race and making notes on its behaviour. It was his fervent hope, his prayer, that somehow or other he might hit on some single aspect of English life that had never been scientifically isolated before, something that might provide the essential key to the national character.[120]

One discovery that emerged during his numerous sociological expeditions was a ubiquitous song emanating from cinema screens between films, the wireless, fairgrounds, and the whistling lips of milkmen and butcher boys: *Everything free and easy . . . Do as you darn well pleasy*. 'The Lambeth Walk' had made the transition from the West End stage to the nation's dance halls. The craze spread to Prague, Paris, New York, and the pages of *Time*. Mass-Observation reported that a young brunette had been sent to teach Mussolini the dance, and Nazis had been inquiring about the 'pedigree' of the song's creator, Noel Gay*. With 'The Lambeth Walk', the image of the cockney, the urban working-class character so many had investigated, championed, lampooned and aped, had become a

---

*Noel Gay wrote the music for 'The Lambeth Walk'. The lyrics are by Arthur Rose and Douglas Furber.

recognisable brand, rather like Oxo. It was an image that would become identified with the 'spirit' of the London Blitz. 'German statesmen have said that they chose 1914 for the other war because they reckoned on the Irish revolt to help them. In 1940 it was the Cockney rising they believed in.'[121] The enemy assumed that heavy bombing of London's slum areas would bring about social disorder and rioting, which would further a German objective to annihilate the docks and the food industry.

From the close of the 1930s, Bill Hall drove the horses at funerals arranged by the Co-op. The job had its perks. It meant the family moved into the flat above the premises on Walworth Road. One of the few photographs of him that remains was taken by the company itself, at the head of a funeral in the Forties; it was framed and hung in the window of the shop. He looks older than his years – he had just turned fifty – with his eyes sunken above dark maps on sallow skin, and his corpulent frame sinking owl-like into the seat at the head of the wagon. He became a regular sight at the head of the funerals of a number of local casualties.

Despite the losses incurred during the previous war, and the impact of sporadic bombing on the local area, it was widely believed that wars were fought at a distance, with armies dispatched to foreign countries. Throughout this new war, those sent to fight feared for the lives of those at home as much as their own, concerned that they would have no families to return to. Some would later send home epitaphs for funerals they could not attend. In the final count the losses in Bermondsey would be 702; the figure was 925 in Southwark and 1,014 in Camberwell.

During the bombing campaign Southwark, Bermondsey and Rotherhithe suffered colossal damage. At one point, half a mile of dockland was ablaze. The Elephant & Castle was hit, destroying the building that once housed Tarn's but leaving the pubs and the Trocadero standing. The locals who failed to descend into the packed underground subways lodged temporarily in a disused tunnel from the original City and South London railway. The entrance was at the side of 'Little Dorrit's' church, on the site of Kent Street, and was known as 'The Deep'. The research carried out by Mass-Observation, in order to gauge morale, revealed that it was not the time spent in air-raid shelters and going underground that was having the greatest impact, but the introduction of the blackout, which made all that was familiar appear alien to a class so attached to their homes, streets and neighbourhoods.

There was one particular day, one particular blackout that Nell Hall recalled:

I'd been to see Eileen, where she was evacuated. Directly I gets off the train, I walk to where she's been put up, but I don't let on to the family. Have to be a bit cute, like. Don't want them to know I can't afford the bus fare. So I'm on the train back. Pitch black. What with it being late and the blackout and that. Barely a soul about. But this figure, tall fella, gets on. Turns out he's in the navy. Starts talking about himself, telling me all about his family, and him growing up. As it happens, he's from Walworth, so course he loves me, 'cos I know all the places he's talking about. As luck would have it, he's going to the Elephant. So – he thinks I'm getting on a bit – he says he'll walk with me, 'cos you can't see where you're going. We turn into Walworth Road. Further down it's pandemonium. Shop's been bombed. I hear someone say 'Co-op's been hit', so naturally I panic, thinking about my Bill. Well, it was unbelievable, 'cos the shops are being looted. You can see these shapes – people running down the street with the dummies from the shop windows, with the clothes on 'em. Woman comes running up to me, she's got her apron open and she's cradling bundles of cutlery in it like it's a baby. She comes up right close: 'Go on, mother, get yourself some crockery.' So I realise it's the Royal Arsenal Co-op with all the furniture and that. Not us – not the funeral Co-op. We're further down, past where Mosley's lot had their set-up. But when we gets to the street where the sailor's going, we can't believe it. Don't recognise it. There's women running with pails of water; men holding the hoses with the firemen. Everyone mucking in, well they did then, mind you there was some bleeders about, not just them looting, I mean a few of them ARP wardens were out for what they could get. Turns out the houses where he was going, this fella – all bombed. Nothing standing. He lost all his family. And that's when I got a good look at him, 'cos the street's in flames. All lit up. I don't think he could have been more than nineteen.

When the urban working class emerged from the subways, tunnels and rubble of the war, and into the light, once again it was the moment for the promise of something utopian. Morale and national unity required a vision of life in peacetime, and the coalition government enlisted the services of a former director of the London School of Economics to formulate a welfare plan for the reconstruction of postwar Britain. Many of the proposals in William Beveridge's famous report,* published in 1942, were taken up by the new Labour government of 1945, as the foundations were laid for the welfare state. The Family Allowance Act and the National Insurance Act were the first in a sequence of legislation that provided insurance 'for all classes for all purposes from the cradle to the grave', as Winston Churchill described it. The National Health Service Act introduced 'free'

---

*According to a Gallup poll conducted at the time of its publication, nineteen in every twenty adults were aware of the 'Beveridge plan', and 95 per cent of those canvassed had some knowledge of its content.

medical care and hospital treatment for all. The introduction of National Assistance saw the abolition of the old poor law. 'Freedom from want cannot be forced on a democracy or given to a democracy', wrote Beveridge at the close of his plan, 'it must be won by them.'

In 1941, on screen, Chaplin had closed his speech at the end of *The Great Dictator*:

> We are coming out of the darkness into the light! We are coming into a new world – a kindlier world, where men will rise above their greed, their hate and their brutality. Look up, Hannah!
> The soul of man has been given wings and at last he is beginning to fly. He is flying into the rainbow – into the light of hope. Look up, Hannah! Look up!

But it wasn't simply novelists, politicians and film directors who were becoming visionaries. Architects and town planners also had an eager eye on the bigger picture. The *County of London Plan* was published the year after the Beveridge report. 'Sir William Beveridge has talked of giants in the path of social security', wrote Lord Latham, leader of the London County Council. 'There are giants too in the path of city planning. There are conflicting interests, private rights, an outworn and different scale of values, and lack of vision. But just as we can move mountains when our liberties are threatened and we have to fight for our lives, so can we when the future of our London is at stake.'[122]

For London, ironically, the war had put visionaries in the most advantageous position since the plague and the Great Fire, for reconstructing the heart of the capital. The plan was prepared by the architect J. H. Forshaw and Patrick Abercrombie, Professor of Town Planning at University College – although it was for ever referred to as 'the Abercrombie Plan' – in response to a request to the London County Council by Lord Reith. The father of the BBC was now Minister of Works and Building, and he had picked up a title en route. Previously, the rebuilding and regeneration of London had been uncoordinated and sporadic, adding to the problems of congestion and density rather than curing them. Under the old ways, open spaces and parks were not evenly distributed, and residential units and industrial premises were lumped together arbitrarily. And nowhere was this more true than of industrial working-class areas like Southwark and Bermondsey. These were among the key areas listed as in need of urgent reconstruction. These boroughs were to have 'their dwellings grouped about their social and shopping centres, interspersed with open spaces, their schools spaced according to the new population requirements, and their industries collected into more compact areas'.[123]

When the historian Harry Williams crossed over the bridge and walked through south London in 1948, he wrote that 'the very water seems to creep past as though it were ashamed'.[124] It was widely believed that this was about to change. One of the ambitions of the Abercrombie plan was to extend the capital's civic, cultural and commercial centre across the water to the southern shore. 'For centuries the settlement on the south bank was not known as London, and even today the appearance of homogeneity is superficial', wrote Harry Williams. 'The southerners are "foreigners", still, and the threadbare town is almost unknown to the vast majority of visitors to London'. The *South London Press* had always described this part of south London as the Cinderella of the capital. This too would finally change if the plan was implemented, as its authors stipulated:

On Thames-side similar facilities for quick passage between opposite banks are of paramount importance in any comprehensive scheme in which the South Bank would be expected to develop as an extension echoing in character the area of Whitehall; and the Strand, and thereby establishing itself as an integral part of the centre of the Capital. The development of the South Bank is the opportunity for the greatest spectacular effect of the new London . . .[125]

Among the proposals mooted for the South Bank were a large assembly hall, a theatre and a concert hall. There would be land for offices, shops, a hotel or two, cafés and restaurants. Perhaps the most important news for the Hall family was that the South Bank project would 'include the complete redevelopment of the area around the Elephant and Castle, and, while this area does not immediately adjoin the riverside development, it would be necessary for the two sections to be correlated'. When at the beginning of 1949 the *Picture Post* made the 'cockney life' of the Elephant & Castle the subject of its cover story it was as though it was documenting a portrait of an area and its inhabitants that would soon be consigned to the past: 'Its voice has the rasp of trams, trains, trucks. Its eyes have the blaze of street-stalls, eel-stands, pin-table arcades and chestnut cans. Its anatomy is decked with sooty bricks, cast-iron spines, and the marble pillars of pubs. Its heart is that of its people – kind as a housewife, rough as a worker, busy as a tradesman, wide as a wide boy.'[126]

One of its people, Bill Hall, was battling with tuberculosis the following year. Two days after he was given the all-clear, he returned home from work mid-afternoon, went to bed and never woke up. His wife blamed the rabbit. Nell Hall said: 'I'd left some rabbit stew in the pot on the stove from the day before, and he heated it up when he got in. I'm convinced that's what did it. Not the TB . . .'

THE F WORD

William Emmanuel Hall
1891–1950
Abide with me. Fast falls the eventide.

'. . . he was buried by the firm. He had five carriages. All those horses – he would 'ave loved that.'

Orwell died the same year. The world that Bill Hall's children, and their children, were about to inherit was expected to be a better one than that which he had known. The older urban working-class culture that had prevailed for so long would soon be altered by the 'mass culture' of the Fifties, which would make inroads in the daily life of the masses more fundamental than the bout of fleeting 'affluence' in the late Thirties.

In 1951 Kate Larter, who had been born into an England in which universal suffrage, education acts, pensions, cinema and broadcasting did not exist, died weeks before the launch of the Festival of Britain. To kickstart the southern shore's bid to rival the frontage of the north, Labour minister Herbert Morrison had chosen the South Bank site to stage a glimpse of the future. The festival exhibits – the Dome of Discovery, the Skylon, the Shot Tower – were designed by some of the architects expected to mastermind the urban housing estates and tower blocks of tomorrow. The future was looking up from the gutter and the kerb; it was heading skyward. 'With the united efforts of all,' Lord Latham wrote of the proposed plan for London, 'we can build the new England which has been the inspiration, and must be the reward, of the citizen-soldier who "knows what he fights for and loves what he knows".'[127] The sword would not sleep in the hand. The New Jerusalem was to be built, and in part on land that was neither pleasant nor green, but decked with sooty bricks and cast-iron spines; a corner of England that was for ever grey. Look up! Look up!

PART TWO

AN EVOCATION

12

THE LAST OUTPOST

In 1961, the year I was born, the Berlin Wall went up and Yuri Gagarin became the first man in space on his street. Closer to home, an 80 foot wide silver cube appeared on the roundabout at the Elephant & Castle interchange. It's made up of 728 stainless-steel panels, and rises 20 feet above pavement level. The natives never knew why it was there, merely what it became: an eyesore on a patch of land destined to be lumbered with more doomed monoliths than any postcode in London. To its architect, Rodney Gordon, it was a clue to the urban future we might inherit, the more modern and moonstruck we became. His original concept was an even grander design. The cube was to be the first building in the capital built entirely of glass, and surrounded by a moat, but the authorities feared that local youths would smash every panel. This spot had been the scene of a riot in 1956 by a reputed 3,000 Teddy boys – an invention of south London working-class youth – after a screening of *The Blackboard Jungle* at the Trocadero. The last reported incident of window-smashing, as Gordon discovered when he canvassed local proprietors, had been on the site of the men's outfitters,

Burton's, in 1910. Nevertheless, the authorities opted for 728 panels of stainless steel.

There were many rumours as to what 'the box' was, and those of us in our infancy throughout its first decade offered suggestions that were particularly fantastic. It was a time machine. It was, when we were really thinking on our feet, the place where our dead pets and lost footballs had disappeared. For our older, smarter brothers, who were beyond *Dr Who* and Will Robinson, it became a 'space oddity'. The cube was actually an electrical generator for the Elephant & Castle underground. Its arrival was almost simultaneous with that of Southwark's other new monument, completed in 1963 – the Bankside power station extension. The valedictory work of Sir Giles Gilbert Scott,* who had introduced the red telephone booth to the capital, had proved the more controversial of the two, with its single campanile rising 300 feet facing St Paul's. The building had faced opposition from within the House of Lords, one peer dismissing it as 'introducing an alligator into a lily pond'. But its fiercest critic was Lord Latham, who believed that its presence thwarted any aspiration to create a better South Bank for the capital, as proposed in the original County of London plan. The scheme to develop a 31-acre site around the Elephant & Castle had come into being on the back of that plan, and was first mooted in 1955. The roundabout and its silver cube marked the first stage in a plan to make it one of the traffic spectacles of the world. It was expected to put even Trafalgar Square in the shade.

For me, the silver cube became a Checkpoint Charlie beyond which the West (End) beckoned via the roads stretching from the Elephant & Castle to London's main bridges and, in the

*Giles Gilbert Scott died in 1960.

words of my nearest and dearest, 'over the water'. Our elders had been content to see Southwark as a self-contained country in the centre of the most famous city in the world; as though living out the plot of an Ealing comedy. It was ignored, but at least if it was ignored, it wasn't imposed upon by the modern or the foreign. They would have welcomed a large injection of cash, a win on the football pools, an E.R.N.I.E bond coming up, or failing that, a wage that made the monotony of long hard days worthwhile; but essentially they wanted to stay put – a decision born of both desire and limited options. That network of streets of houses, local pubs and the market was still central to their lives. There was a mutual understanding, an implicit code of conduct, and for the most part a mutual respect. More significantly, unity had developed because of the absence of any prospect of mobility. The percentage that moved away was small. It was therefore not aspiration and ambition that formed part of the shared experience but the very business of keeping their heads above water.

Most of the houses were cold, sometimes damp, always cramped, never owned, and never likely to be. Still, this was home, and there was no place like it. No place so dilapidated, slate-grey, bombed out, dug up – at least not over the water. Or so we, the very young of the species, presumed. We were akin to Doris Josser in *London Belongs to Me*: 'as she walked along, she began once again going over the whole complicated business of being born in the wrong place. And on the wrong side of the river. As she saw it, she'd missed her chance by a mere couple of miles or so.'[128] We collected news of anyone raised in these meanish streets who had got out, made it over the water, through pop (Tommy Steele, Max Bygraves), film (Michael Caine), comedy or crime (the Charlies Chaplin, Drake and Richardson). We scanned television programmes and song lyrics for a mention of the place we lived, as if to find confirmation that it, and therefore we, existed in the minds of anyone out there. Evidence was scarce, even in the Sixties: two BBC *Panoramas*, one *This Week* for ITV, and the news that Twiggy's first love was a boy named Colin from the Elephant & Castle.

13

'AFFLUENCE'

If the journey from suburbs to city is, as the author Michael Bracewell has written, 'from innocence to experience',[129] that from Walworth to the West End was from exile to inclusion. A short bus ride separated the capital's two busiest roundabouts – Piccadilly Circus, and 'the gateway to the south', the Elephant & Castle – but culturally, and in terms of social class, the journey could be measured by light years. Southwark was still the city's Cinderella, natives still the 'foreigners' that Harry Williams wrote of. In many aspects the culture of the urban working class was similar to that of Nell Hall's generation, despite mutterings from various writers and historians that it had given up the ghost by the 1950s. What the *Daily Express* referred to in 1962 as the 'rollicking revolution of merry England'[130] had started in the previous decade, when the postwar austerity began to be eased out by a comparative affluence, particularly among the young working class. Those durable consumer goods that Orwell had said staved off a revolution increased a hundredfold. Consumerism, along with welfare provisions and full employment, had been responsible for a drop in trade union membership, cinema audiences and the crowds at football matches. In some quarters it was believed that the working class were forsaking a sense of community for a culture of material-ism, individualism and competition. From the world of sociology sprang the term embourgeoisement to describe those who chose a spin dryer over a mangle, and dreamed of a fridge and a television; or who entertained the fantasy that sport, show business or pop music might be a better by-road to the good life than education.

Casting an eye over these developments was the kind of middle-class Marxist[131] whom Richard Hoggart describes in *The Uses of Literacy* as someone who 'admires the remnants of the noble savage, and has a nostalgia for those "best of all" kinds of art, rural folk-art or genuinely popular urban art, and a special enthusiasm for such scraps of them as he thinks he can detect today. Usually, he succeeds in part-pitying and part-patronizing working-class people beyond any semblance of reality.'[132] These young intellectuals who believed that 'working-class culture' was in decline during the 1950s idealised it, but according to Eric Hobsbawm 'their elegies did not revive it'.[133]

It was idealised to some extent in art, by what the critic David Sylvester termed the 'kitchen sink school', of which John Bratby, Edward Middleditch, Barry Greaves and Jack Smith were the forerunners. After experiencing London-born Bratby's first solo show in 1954, one swooning critic claimed that he could make a Kellogg's cornflakes packet look like the *Rokeby Venus*. The new English social realism had arrived, but unlike the slum fic-tion movement of the 1890s it now began with art and worked its way through theatre, literature and film. Once again, its audience was predominantly middle-class. 'In the club and other local centres',[134] wrote Dennis Potter, returning to the turf of his birth, the Forest of Dean, after graduating from Oxford, 'there is little or no talk of Wesker or Osborne or Joan Littlewood (there might be about Noel Coward) and the external culture comes from the telly, and mostly from commercial television.'

In many ways the artists were as diverse as the group that made up the 'angry young men' of theatre and letters, but essentially they had a common interest: capturing the banality or beauty of the domestic environment of the working class, on canvas. The scriptwriter Ted Willis, who had a hand in creating some of the most notable filmscripts of the decade, and television series in the Sixties, later recalled that he himself was dealing exclusively with the ordinary and the untheatrical. 'The main characters are typical rather than exceptional: the situations are easily identifiable by the audience; and the relationships are as common as people', he said of the film *Woman in a Dressing Gown*. 'I am just now becoming aware of this area, this marvellous world of the ordinary.'[135] The title of the film – the point where the new wave meets an old master – could equally have been that of a Bratby painting, from that first solo exhibition. His tableaux of domestic life, depicted in encrusted, vibrant oils, from what became known as his 'tabletop' period had titles such as *Still Life with Chipfryer*, *Still Life with Wardrobe*.

When the kitchen sink theme found its way into literature the genre was dominated by writers from working-class backgrounds, born too early for the legislation that followed the 1944 Education Act, which extended the school leaving age. Each of them had left school in his early teens, experienced life during wartime, and had a stint of factory work: Alan Sillitoe (Nottingham), Stan Barstow (Yorkshire), John Braine (Bradford). There was a vast difference between the male protagonists in these novels and the working-class characters found in slum fiction. The hedonistic Arthur Seaton in Sillitoe's *Saturday Night and Sunday Morning* made his debut in a decade in which for the first time young working-class men dressed up for effect, rather than dressing down in the uniform of utility (an approach at its most evident and extreme in Teddy boys). Joe Lampton in Braine's *Room at the Top* is the scrupulous opportunist pursuing embourgoisement by marrying out of his class and into money. Vic Brown in Barstow's *A Kind of Loving* is ultimately trapped by his circumstances when his girlfriend falls pregnant, but is out to puncture the pretentiousness of anyone who fancies themselves as his cultural superior, such as Ken Rawlinson, his colleague at the engineering firm Dawson Whittaker & Sons:

He fills his glass up and says, 'I saw a very good French film last night.'

'Oh, yes?'

'"*Gervaise*"' Rawly says. 'Based on a novel by Zola.' He pokes about on his plate as if he expects to uncover something nasty. 'Do you know his novels at all?'

''Fraid not.' Zola sounds like a game, like bingo or ludo or canasta.

'An excellent writer. Surprisingly modern to say he wrote sixty or seventy years ago.'

'Oh?'

'Very outspoken for his time. They banned his books in this country. Wouldn't wear them.'

'Sexy, eh?' This is more like it.

'Shall we say "direct"?' Rawly says and I think he can call it any name he likes as far as I'm concerned. I decide to take the mickey a bit.

'Was this picture hot stuff?'

'Oh, X certificate and all that,' he says. 'Nothing pornographic about it, though. An adult film.'

'Be in French, I suppose?'

'Oh yes. Subtitled, of course, for those who don't know the language.'[136]

Almost all the novels within the canon were set in the working-class north. There were non-fiction works by social investigators who, in a bid to offer a contemporary take on work carried out by Mayhew and the social investigators of the nineteenth century, scoured the East End to examine 'kin and kinship', and fed new words into the lexicon of class – 'meritocracy' followed on the heels of 'embourgeoisement'. In the 1970s the historian Stuart Hall recalled that London's East End became 'a sort of living social laboratory for the social investigator: a place where, by patient study, some little light might be thrown on the clear gap there is between what people think is happening to ordinary people, and what is actually going on: the gap between the image, or "myths" of affluence and contradictory reality'.[137] But ultimately, he believed such investigations to be a 'thankless task':

The real processes – new kinds of industry, rehousing, property speculation, the rise in consumption, urban planning and legislation, the inexorable forces of the market – continue to make on this landscape, and on the culture it sustains, an indelible imprint.[138]

Only one London-based novel became identified with the school of the 'kitchen sink'. Ironically it was written by an heiress, born of titled parents, who, like Jessica Mitford, moved across the bridge into a south London neighbourhood and took a job in a factory. It was 1959. She was the recently married Nell Dunn, aged twenty-three, and a journalist. Her husband Jeremy Sandford, later the writer of the documentary *Cathy Come Home*, had an Eton and Oxford pedigree. The pair had been part of the Chelsea set that circled the likes of Lord Bath – who gave them pet names – before they moved to Battersea to experience the rumoured vibrancy of working-class south London.

Everything free and easy . . . do as you darn well pleasy. It was fitting that Sandford and Dunn should have been the subject of a John Bratby portrait. Like the 'kitchen sink' artists, Dunn believed that she had found a beauty in the banality of a working-class environment. The home she bought was 'the most beautiful place I had ever been to, a grapevine grew wild over the outdoor lavatory . . . At the end of the street there were four chimneys'.[139] She chronicled her observations, superbly, in the vignettes that became *Up the Junction*, published in 1963. Like much of the slum fiction of the 1890s, the portraits were purely observational, written from inside, and reliant on contemporary working-class speech. And even though much of what is witnessed focuses on bike boys who crash and burn, backstreet abortions, knocking-shops and tally men, it is essentially a study of those characters that had appealed to Ted Willis: the typical rather than the exceptional; the ordinary and untheatrical.

Shortly before Dunn began writing about her descent into another class, two other writers – one a university graduate and the other a tutor – were returning to their roots to take the pulse of the working class at a time of radical social and cultural change.

Famously, Richard Hoggart, a tutor in the adult education department of Hull University, used his birthplace of Leeds to examine the beliefs, opinions and folklore of working-class culture in *The Uses of Literacy* (1957). It was the most accurate, detailed audit of working-class culture written in the twentieth century, and could only have come from the hand of a writer who hailed from that class. Hoggart argued that the mass media had corrupted working-class culture, even though much of its oral tradition and 'habit, aphorism and ritual' still survived.

Dennis Potter used the term 'admass' to describe the process whereby advertising attempted to work its voodoo over the masses. But he still found the 'true and valuable' elements of working-class culture 'reflected in the slicker, cheapened "pop" culture, however obliquely, however much like a ray of light sliding through a filthy window'.[140] Potter took a more localised approach than Hoggart, simply documenting the changes he witnessed on trips back to the Forest of Dean. In *The Changing Forest* he writes:

> each time I return, I feel a number of subtle changes – a few pretentious wrought-iron gates, a thick platform of brothel-creeper to walk on, another juke-box, emptier clubs, a miner at a wedding in a top hat. These are small things, but each time, also, I feel a shift of values, the unrest of the anxiety behind the change . . . in the streets of a working-class town or village, in the minds of the miner and the mother, the past does not seem so quaint and manageable, less a thing for the gentle sigh and the lowered eye of sentimental scrapbook-style recognition. Instead it is there as a physical thing, eaten away in places by the hollowed caverns of chain stores and pop-record shelves, boxed around by rows of new houses with pastel-coloured curtains over their clear, flat windows, and cloaked by the dress, style and conversations of people in the streets. But it still reaches out and threatens.[141]

The working class, now considered to be more 'affluent' than previous generations because of their increased consumption, with televisions, fridges and cars, did not become middle-class and continued to have little contact with those from other classes. Essentially, life continued to be lived around those staples of working-class culture, the pub and the street market. Their outfits might have changed, but their essential outlook had not. They still expected to go into the same jobs as those of the previous generation, marry someone local, and, in the poorer London areas like Southwark, live with parents or in-laws because of the perennial housing problem. And certainly the younger generation of Southwark held fast to many of those 'older' values, living by habit, aphorism and ritual, adhering to an oral tradition, with the past still very much a physical thing that reached out and threatened, by way of the environment, until the 1960s brought change.

This was the experience of young couples like my mum and dad, Eileen and Bill, in the Southwark of the 1950s. They married in 1952, and produced their first child, John, the following year. Nell Hall's youngest daughter began dating her future groom on the day of her father's funeral. The couple knew each other from the pubs, cinemas and milk bars that peppered the area. They were both regulars at the dance hall above Burton's at the Elephant & Castle, its alabaster vanilla pillars an effort to introduce something like glamour in the early postwar years. The impact of the war was still visible in the abundant bombsites within the area. The bombing campaign had taken out the roof of the Elephant & Castle pub, as well as that of the Tabernacle. All the same there was enough left standing for this patch of the district to remain the centre of social life in the evenings, as the market on East Street was during the day. Bill had returned to the area after two years of National Service in a converted holiday camp in a foreign land: Llandudno. The young conscripts were alien to the locals because of their nationality, and to officers because of their class. For the duration they were treated with disdain by both.

He bumped into Eileen outside the Albion, where her dad's wake was taking place. She was smart, in full black, a three-quarter-length coat with leg-of-mutton sleeves, strawberry blonde hair moulded around a half-moon cap. He was sporting the 'demobbed' look: trousers beginning just below the nipple, jacket stopping short of the knee, moustache as thin as the seam pencilled on a woman's leg in wartime.

'What you doing done up, out here in the cold?' he asked.

'We've just buried me dad.'

Weeks after they began dating he took Eileen to meet his parents. Sitting in the saloon bar of another local pub, and settled with a drink, her face was suddenly ashen.

'What's the matter, Ei?' he said. 'You look like you've seen a ghost.'

'Who's the old bloke in the corner?'

'That's my Uncle George.'

'He's got death on his face.'

'What you talking about? Don't lark about.'

'I'm telling you he's got death on his face.'

Little more than a week later, they were all gathered in the pub for the wake for Uncle George.

Bill's family had been in the area for generations, as long as the Larters, possibly. And in that time they had lived in the streets that made up the 'coster colony', and established themselves on the market stalls, selling fruit and veg. Bill's dad now had a tiny greengrocer's on East Street, and would become a local publican before the end of the decade. His grandfather had been known locally as 'Punch', for his ability as a street fighter in his youth. The market remained the draw that it had always been, and in the early postwar years it was home to the 'spiv', who could get his hands on rationed goods for the right price. In the Fifties there were the 'cosh boys' reputed to hover in the midnight hour, preying on lone strangers at coffee stalls. At the Elephant & Castle, the cosh in question was often a passenger strap that had been snapped from the carriage ceilings of Bakerloo Line trains.

The term 'cosh boy' was a contrivance of the press, and the news stories exceeded, by far, the actual extent of the crimes.

The tone of the reports resembled that used to promote the hooliganism campaign of the 1890s, and as with the case of Patrick Hooligan, the powder keg of moral panic would be ignited by a notorious crime. In this instance it was the murder of a policeman on the roof of a south London warehouse in 1952, with which Derek Bentley and Christopher Craig were charged. Both of them, on the night they set out to commit the felony, were wearing drape jackets and crepe-soled shoes.

For a number of younger men, the drape jacket was the garment of choice – a hybrid between the zootish demob suit and the Edwardian dandy look that upper-class youth were being measured for in Savile Row. It was a look they quickly jettisoned when they realised how much it had become the wardrobe of the urban working-class youth, and particularly the 'cosh boys'.

Apart from the 'cosh boys' there were the burgeoning gangs of which all the locals appeared to be aware, that dealt in petty theft and robbery, and were known in pubs and spotted at boxing bouts. In 1959 a government report entitled *Penal Practice in a Changing Society* acknowledged that 'in the years since the war, rising standards in material prosperity, education, and social welfare have brought no decrease in the high rate of crime during the war: on the contrary, crime has increased and is still increasing.'[142]

The past persisted within the landscape, and, like the memories, stories and superstitions of its human relics, it was fragmented and incomplete. It existed between bombsites left untouched since the last war; cavities between terraced streets that survived. In the Sixties, shops, tenements, houses and streets would be removed crudely and rapidly, in the willy-nilly manner in which the older generation had teeth extracted. When the Elephant & Castle was laid waste, the first casualty was the landmark pub itself. The major transformation of the district began in the wake of the erection of the silver cube. The Rockingham Arms and the Alfred's Head went. The Trocadero closed its doors after its final leading man, Laurence Harvey, disappeared beneath the credits of *Running Man*. The dance hall, with its semicircular exterior and Grecian pillars, came tumbling down, along with the island on which the old Elephant & Castle pub stood, and the remaining shops and restaurants and cafés that congregated around the main junction.

Finally, the shell of the South London Palace disappeared. For years it had fallen into disrepair, dismantled by kids and occupied by tramps. The lower part of its skeletal façade had been fenced in by hoardings prepared with advertisements informing me and my family as we stood at its bus stop, 'You can't help falling for a Walls', and playbills promoting Palladium shows (*Stars in Your Eyes* with Russ Conway, Cliff Richard, David Kossoff . . .) that would once have had their equivalents on this very spot, twice nightly. It was as though the venue had been left to deteriorate for years because it *was* haunted by nuns, and no one would deal the fatal blow. Skeletons from its previous incarnation as a burial chapel were discovered when it was finally reduced to dust. When all at the centre of the Elephant & Castle was demolished and replaced, initially, with the silver cube, the area may have kept its heart – 'that of its people' as the *Picture Post* once described it – but it had stopped beating.

14

CITY OF TRANSFORMATIONS

Nell Hall's ground-floor flat was so dark it could have been below ground level, rather like the basements of the tenements that surrounded her as a child, in which the gaslight burned all day and wooden banisters were used for firewood. She had whitewashed the oblong yard outside her living-room window, believing it brought more light. The door to the yard was never open; it was blocked by buckets, and an iron bath, which she still used when she wasn't making the trip to the washrooms at the swimming baths.

I was sitting with my brother in her living room, stuffing bits of newspaper and scraps of fabric into old stockings, making 'snakes' to put at the bottom of the doors to keep out the draught. The pattern was repeated each November, when she helped me make the legs and arms for a guy. It was a day in January 1965, and almost dark enough to be evening. The room was lit by the two long orange fingers in the electric fire, perched in a fireplace that was never used. A stabbing breeze found its way down the chimney behind and into the room. The tiny black and white television screen, drowning in its own cabinet, like a face poking from a balaclava, shed further light. It was intermittently silent, a nasal whistle from the chimney the only noise. On screen was a blurred image that meant nothing to me, but was significant enough for Nell Hall to remain transfixed, and hush me when I broke the silence with a question. The sporadic commentary dominated the room: *How slowly they seem to creep away upstream towards the bridges of London.* The image was reminiscent of what she had witnessed first-hand, aged barely twenty, when on the say-so of Winston Churchill a destroyer had ferried the bodies of the boy scouts up the Thames. *There behind lay London on this day of mourning.* Now the body was Churchill's own, and as on that day the Thames was as still as when it was frozen. *The only movement on this bustling, thriving waterway of ours, this small flotilla . . .*

The cranes were dipped, the wharves and factories silent; as silent as they would become when the working lives of many of these buildings came to a close the following decade.

Churchill had died a few months after Nell Hall's working life finally ended. At seventy-two, she left the company where she had been employed as a cleaner for twenty years with a golden handshake of thirty pounds. Her working life ended as my education began, at the very school she had wanted to attend: 'My mother sent me to clean the house next door to St John's', she said. The school and its church had changed little since she was a girl. A peppery scent from a small factory nearby filled the playground. The part of the road in which she had lived had been demolished, along with its pubs and its foundry, leaving a small street of houses further along known as 'Little' Larcom Street. On one side of the street was a line of garages protected by tall grey gates, topped by spiked railings, on the other were ten small, two-storey Victorian houses. This was where I was born, and where we lived until the mid-Sixties.

We occupied the two rooms on the first floor. There was no bathroom. There were a kitchen and a toilet along the landing. The family downstairs had the yard and the outside lav. They were a married couple with a daughter who had been named after Judy Garland. There was no partition separating these houses into flats, and so the strangers living in them for years became like one extended family. The father downstairs loved routine and lined his shoes up at the bottom of the stairs every Sunday morning without fail, ready for polishing. The mother often sat in our narrow kitchen, at the yellow formica table with its pattern of gold hair-like threads, cracking one-liners ('A bloke asked me how I got into this dress. "I was poured into it", I told him') or airing her concerns ('My sister, my Bet, has became a Christadelphian'). In the evenings, she was a barmaid at the Albion on the corner.

Sometimes Bill sat on the other side of the bar.

'You've always got a glass in your hand, Win.'

'That's right, Bill. An' it's always empty.'

My dad's cousin and his family had the upstairs of the house next door; on the other side lived a woman known as 'Pissy Kate', with her two brothers. She was a permanent fixture in the pub, and always dressed in black. The kids in the street were terrified when she approached, stooped like an eagle in astrakhan, promising a sweet and almost toppling from the kerb in an effort to retrieve her keys from the bottom of her handbag. One of the other neighbours was a driver on a number 12 bus. His wife was full of superstitions and old wives' tales. She'd pause midway through scrubbing the paving outside her home to reveal how the 'old workhouse' was haunted: footsteps could be heard at night on the stairs of the empty block, and the shade of a dead child could be seen wandering the corridors. The morning after a particularly bad storm, she had found her mother dead in her downstairs bedroom. She sat in our kitchen and revealed that throughout that previous stormy night a black cat had been moaning and knocking itself against her front door. It was an omen.

One day, two men turned up in the front room in which the four of us slept, and positioned themselves at the window, returning to this spot for several hours over each of the following few days. They said little; drank a lot of tea, smoked a lot of fags. They were plain-clothes policemen who had been tipped off that there was a 'drugs racket' in operation in the Greek café that could be seen from the bedroom window above the garages opposite. Bill felt obliged to let them use the room as a stakeout. The day of the 'bust', everyone was on the street watching the habitués of the café escaping out the back, climbing drainpipes and darting across the roofs of the garages.

At the time Eileen was close to a story of sex, scandal and the establishment that was making the national newspapers. From when I was six weeks old she had left home in the early hours to do office cleaning in various buildings 'over the water', before returning home and taking up the role of mother, while Bill went to work. In 1963 she was cleaning offices in the West End, close to the osteopathy practice of Stephen Ward, at the time when he emerged as a key figure in the intrigue of the Profumo affair. This infamous annus mirabilis in which, according to Philip Larkin, sexual intercourse began just as the Sixties were about to swing, initially had little impact locally. But there was one piece of legislation introduced as the Sixties began, that revolutionised the lives of the inhabitants of Southwark: the Gaming Act of 1961, which legalised betting shops and bingo. Bill got a day job in one of the former, and became adept at the art of Turf Accountancy, and Nell Hall was unleashed on the bingo halls. But the clearest indication that the times were changing continued to be the regeneration of the landscape.

Throughout its history the Elephant & Castle had never been improved by an overall plan. Like other developments within the borough during this and the previous century, reconstruction had been piecemeal, and schemes had been thwarted by the depression of the Thirties, and the last war. Now architects got to play Kubla Khan, or at least Fritz Lang, in creating a veritable Metropolis at the gateway to the south. There were tenders, competitions, and visions. The money was in place, and now after five years utopia was beginning to be realised. By the end of the 1960s the heart of the old Elephant & Castle would be almost entirely eradicated. Along with the 80 foot silver cube, there would be a shopping centre, surrounded by a forecourt at lower-ground level, with an office block sprouting from the complex itself. Its height competed with the 170 foot glass and aluminium tower of the London College of Printing, and the modernist block, Alexander Fleming House – described by someone in the trade as 'Stalin's buildings as they should have been'. The latter was the work of the architect Erno Goldfinger, who also designed the cinema next door, which took a mere portion of the land once dominated by the Trocadero. (Ironically, it was the ABC opposite that screened *Goldfinger* the following year.) Where the dance hall had stood, an expansive council block emerged. Finally, a tubular high-rise, lauded as the tallest residential block of flats in London at the time, looked askance at Spurgeon's Tabernacle, its Corinthian columns making it a gatecrasher in this spanking new scene.

When flagstones were laid for the Elephant & Castle shopping centre it was to be (like the Bull Ring in Birmingham, built simultaneously) the biggest shopping complex in the city. An advert declared it was 'setting the standards for the 60s that will revolutionise shopping concepts throughout Britain'. The initial reaction to the shopping centre was tentative. It was almost as big a curiosity as the space oddity on the island. Those who entered returned rarely, preferring East Street market, and the still abundant shops in the dilapidated streets behind south London's aspiring Xanadu. Nevertheless, the revolution had arrived in the shape of a vast, largely empty shopping hangar that housed the Golden Egg restaurant, a Green Shield stamps centre, 'June's Bingo', a passport-approved photo kiosk, moving staircases, and the Charlie Chaplin pub. Like its sister project in Birmingham, the whole endeavour was dismissed as 'ill-fated' before they'd even got the roof on.

Meanwhile, the press canvassed the locals to discover the reason for their absence from consumerism's brave new world. 'I've walked the length and breadth of it and can't find a bread shop' was the response of one elderly female shopper. Both the Walworth and the Birmingham projects were described in Oliver Merriot's *The Property Boom* as 'two major and uncomfortably visible blunders, born of overconfidence'.[143] But the biggest misjudgement was the way the shopping centre was made accessible from the new tower blocks, via an intricate web of underpasses. There were two miles of tunnel. The architectural historian Nicholas Pevsner went underground here and emerged 'deafened by traffic and crushed by the ruthless scale of the surrounding towers, confusingly similar at first sight'. The subways became the ideal location for the perfect crime. Those who could navigate their way overground by jaywalking did so. What started as one of the biggest inner-city redevelopments ever implemented materialised into one of the worst planning failures of the Sixties.

But the apparent failure of the venture did not dampen the ardour of the council, the planners and the architects. The future of the urban working class was in their hands. It was as though they were making up for the centuries of neglect that had shrouded the area and its natives. A scheme was conceived which, in its embryonic stage, involved the construction of a huge housing estate in Peckham – part of which now fell under the aegis of the London Borough of Southwark – along with two similar ventures in Walworth and Camberwell. This ambitious triptych would be linked by walkways and ramps, ensuring that pedestrians would never have to touch the ground until they reached the Elephant & Castle, at which point they could disappear into the subways: 'a massive complex of deck-access, multi-rise housing sprawling from Elephant & Castle to Peckham. The pedestrianised, high-density estate would have stretched for two miles'.[144] Ultimately the vision stopped short of this last utopian detail, but the creation of the three megalithic estates went ahead. The last of these would cover the land behind the new shopping centre, Lock's Fields, where lepers once roamed with bells to warn others of their presence. Now the noise was the death rattle of bulldozers.

Stories and rumours circulated about these planned changes within the landscape. It was said that planners decided which streets would be erased, on the acres required for the regeneration, in the back of a taxi, as they were driven around the neighbourhood. One of their digits, the finger of God, swept across our home. It was just a matter of time. We moved.

15

THE MIDWIVES OF NEW ENGLAND

Our new home was footsteps away from the one we left, just out of reach of the regeneration area, and therefore escaping demolition. It was a long blind alley of a road, with a pub on its corner, and plugged at the other end by the rear wall of a boys' school. By then The Street, as it was always known, was almost the last of its kind, serving as a reminder that the area was once crammed with similar streets, that married couples moved to and stayed until the hearse carried each of them away; where children remained, and grew into their parents. The summer we moved in, Geoff Hurst's hat-trick took the national team to World Cup victory. The big news was that locally-born villain Charlie Richardson and his gang had been arrested. They were soon sent down and the trial was reported in the press as though it heralded the end of south London's rising tide of gangland crime, notorious since the Fifties. The Richardsons and the Krays had almost come to blows as part of planned gang warfare at the Elephant & Castle itself. But the newspaper reports revealing the tactics and the torture employed by both gangs when dealing with their enemies did not draw total condemnation from the locals. 'They only hurt their own' became a mantra whenever the subject was raised.

The bulldozers moved in. The new world they brought would be a grey world, but not the grey of age, soot and grime that it promised to replace. In the meantime we waited. We watched. If there had been any indication that the planners might sweep a finger over The Street, doubtless a riot would have ensued, the kind of insurrection not witnessed in these parts since mobs gathered on St George's Fields, or at least the kind in which Peggy Mount and an army of charladies took on the authorities in British films. Over the years, rumours would circulate that these houses were next in line for a demolition job, and immediately the women, for it was mostly the women, would be tanked up on something like Dunkirk spirit, ready to batten down the hatches, pile up the sandbags, evacuate the kids and prepare for invasion. More than only bricks and mortar, they were protecting their past, as well as their present and their future. Some were keen to protect their territory from newcomers – even if they'd simply arrived from a neighbouring street. The day we moved in a woman poked her head through the front-room window. She was typecast, and wouldn't have been out of place alongside Peggy Mount: a dishevelled nest of hair badly underpinned by kirby grips, and an apron worn like armour. She announced to my mum: 'I'm telling you now, before you start, if any of your kids lay a finger on mine, I'll be over here. Mark my words.'

Welcome.

She had seven kids. The older daughters would often be found embroiled in a fight, in the middle of the road, each trying to drag the other one's head towards the manhole cover. The younger son was often found crawling up a drainpipe in his underpants. Years later they moved, and my dad's relatives occupied the house. Inside, all the rooms were darkened by red paint, as though it were bought as part of a job lot. My uncle's wife stood, surveyed her new domain, pulled on a cigarette, nodded, and announced: 'I reckon their old man must have worked in a fucking fire station.' One of the other brothers in this family would one day be best man at my brother's wedding. But during the Sixties, as teenagers, the pair caught the tail-end of the Mod boom, before shifting from mohair to long hair, and growing sideburns so thick, so long, they could stuff a chair. They were in a gang of four mates. Born in the early 1950s, they were the first urban working-class generation to sustain an uninterrupted formal education, undented by child labour or evacuation. It was this generation that the developers were targeting with their schemes, as they would be the ones likely to move onto the new estates after they married – or rather, after they married and were expecting their first or second child, as only this would guarantee them enough points to move far enough up the council list. My brother and his mates fantasised about being millionaires by the time they were thirty, yet couldn't see their career prospects as anything other than that of finding a trade, 'a job for life' in the print or the Post Office.

Meanwhile, somewhere out there, there was talk of revolution, one that went beyond that trailblazed by the *Daily Express* – a social revolution. It was all so – and here was a word that became shorthand for that very spirit – classless. It was the season's accessory, something to be worn in the streets of Chelsea, possibly Notting Hill, Kensington, where a privileged few were creating the folklore of the Sixties. And oddly, it was heralded by the Conservative prime minister Harold Macmillan, who declared after his victory in 1959 that the class war was obsolete.

By the mid-Sixties, Harold Wilson's Labour Party was in government, the Beatles were in the charts, and David Bailey's costly *Box of Pin-Ups*, featuring portraits of the key players of the new classlessness – the Krays, Michael Caine – was on the shelves. This was the wonderful, wonderful world that the children of the revolution were born into, and of which our elder brothers and sisters were rumoured to be the main beneficiaries. And not only had the revolution arrived, it was about to be televised.

The BBC had sold itself as harbinger of the new order of classlessness, revolution and change since the arrival of Hugh Carlton-Greene as director general in 1960. It was a radical departure from its original patrician approach. The shift was partly because of the success of commercial television from 1955, with its wider appeal for the working class, and partly because graduates, the middle and upper classes, had tapped into the dominant popular culture of the working class. A minority were creating their own opposing elitism. Dennis Potter described it as the popular culture of the working classes on one side and 'the Sunday critics, Monitor, hush, hush, hush, hushed on the other, chinking light refracted through brandy glasses'.[145]

The BBC was in the business of educating and entertaining the masses, but it never got around to employing them. Despite the talk of revolution that emanated from its upper echelons throughout this decade, it continued to operate a form of institutionalised classism. The Oxbridge graduates favoured by Reith continued to dominate, and the general traineeship scheme introduced by the corporation in the 1950s continued to draw from these sources. Almost all of those who enlisted for these schemes to become producers, directors and managers were culled from the confines of Oxford and Cambridge.

Throughout this revolution emphasis was placed on the few working-class dissenters who had found their way to university or into the glare of the spotlight via their photography, acting ability, musicianship or football skills. As the journalist Christopher Booker wrote in his summing-up of the decade in *The Neophiliacs* in 1969:

> little attention was paid to the origins of those New Aristocrats who were upper or upper middle class. The fact that Lord Snowdon (Eton), Mark Boxer (Berkhamsted), David Hicks (Charterhouse), not to say Mary Quant's husband, Alexander Plunket-Green, had all gone to public schools was somehow not in accord with the 'classless' image.[146]

In the Sixties, those who had chosen careers in the relatively new field of communications rather than, say, politics became what Booker called 'the midwives of New England'. Those working in the field of television and journalism in particular had their hands on the controls and sold the idea of a social revolution by way of some selective reporting throughout the media. Classlessness was the new faith, and it was being spread as though, with the advent of the Sixties, the working class at large were benefiting from some new inclusiveness, when this was only applicable to a small minority:

> Just to what extent there had been a real 'class revolution' in these years is open to argument. Perhaps, in the long run, it had amounted to little more than a continuation of the same revolution which had been taking place for forty years or more, coupled with a general relaxation of social attitudes and barriers and, of course, the new prominence of that glamorous little 'classless' minority publicised through television and the mass media – which together gave a somewhat misleading impression of the extent to which class barriers had broken down through the nation as a whole.[147]

The majority of the working-class youth did not go into further education, and were employed in the same industries as the previous generation.

The 1960s revolution was ultimately not about the breaking down of the barriers between the classes, but about erecting an even bigger one between the old and the young. Our older siblings were more attuned to the rumoured revolution than anyone else, and often returned with dispatches from its front line: Carnaby Street. They were more like tourists returning from day trips to a foreign country than a young generation of Londoners at the fore of a cultural revolution that was apparently on their doorstep. The artefacts they returned with were embraced, hoarded and given pride of place, rather like the bullfighting posters brought back from Spain in the early Seventies, when a neighbour became one of the first to go on holiday abroad, via Pontinental. And so the official Sixties arrived and stayed in my room by way of a Smiley sticker, and a mocked-up newspaper with the headline: 'Michael buys out the whole of Carnaby Street'. My brother's bedroom, like that of his mates, was the point where the reported spirit of the age made an appearance. Wires sprouted from an old portable record player, the Caramac beige of our local doctor's surgery. It was connected to a makeshift speaker in a bid to bring *Disraeli Gears* in stereo to a home that had been given a second-hand 'radiogram' from a neighbour, on which the LP *A Pub, A Pint and A Song* livened up the preparation of Sunday roasts, Christmas dinner, and old year's night.

My brother's attempt at state-of-the-art technology was perched on the cabinet that previously housed the television on which we'd witnessed Churchill's funeral. The cabinet was now a shell with the screen removed. Next to it was a bedside cabinet that entered the family in the Fifties, when Nell Hall put down a deposit and bought it on the never-never as part of a suite from the Royal Arsenal Co-op. My brother painted it white, in a tribute to *The White Album*, and pinned the four individual portrait photographs of the Beatles which came with the LP to the wall above it. Another wall was peppered with pictures of England's triumphant 1966 team, and the Manchester United line-up. Above the bed headboard, and plastered across the chimney breast was a massive poster of Elvis from the '68 NBC special, the King in leathers.

In these bedrooms, with their pop artefacts and reconditioned props, there was a hint of the present, whilst downstairs seemed closer to the Fifties or even the Forties. But there were signs: our budgie was christened Twinkle in salute to a Sixties singer. The cat, Justin, was bought from the manageress of the one boutique in the market, Downtown. His sister, Twiggy, was passed on to a relative.

The elderly, and especially those old enough to remember when they were without a vote, a basic education or a National Health service, witnessed these changes, and saw elements from their past taken out of their original context to become the objets d'art of modern popular culture. The last time Nell Hall had seen the face of Lord Kitchener was on the walls of Walworth when he was recruiting the young for the First World War. Now a generation of a similar age were putting his face and his finger on their bedroom walls, and wearing old military jackets. During a week's holiday in an uncle's caravan at Reculver, my brother bought a second-hand undertaker's tailed coat for five shillings. It was never worn beyond that day, but hung for years behind the curtain in a recess in the bedroom, along with the waterproof Post Office mac the company provided for him to wear when working outdoors in bad weather, but which he was too vain, too modern, to be seen in. The undertaker's coat seemed to hang there defiantly as a symbol of Sixties youth. When my mum cut part of the tail off and used it to patch up the elbow of my school uniform, he was incensed. It was 1972. He was nineteen, and Mott the Hoople were singing: *My brother's back at home with his Beatles and his Stones/Guess he never got it off on that revolution stuff.*

The houses in The Street were old. Over the years tenants installed inside toilets, sometimes bathrooms, and a kitchen where the scullery had been. For decades, a man turned up regularly, dressed in black, like Shadrach from *Billy Liar*. He looked like he might be collecting bodies, but he collected the rent from every household. A man walked the street offering to sharpen knives; another sometimes called out for 'rag 'n' bone'. These characters were more suited to another era, but like the tipsters, quacks and sarsaparilla sellers on the market they remained until the 1970s. They were the bottom note to a weekly routine that had persisted since Nell Hall was young. There were Sunday roasts, and Sunday tea, always with prawns, winkles, cockles. There was the equivalent of the 'Steve' from the end of the nineteenth century, with the 'radiogram' replacing the piano and the collective singing of that era. A hairdresser living in The Street did the sets, perms and colours of other women; another neighbour, a dressmaker, was always in and out of houses doing alterations. Kids went swimming at the municipal baths or watched relatives box there as part of a family night out. The pattern was sometimes shattered by mothers almost coming to blows defending their children, or the rare occasion when a man left his wife for a woman further along the street, leading to the very public bust-up of a marriage.

Like most of the neighbours, we lived in a home where no one bothered with books. The television had more of an impact on cultural lives than the paperback. I was named after the actor Michael Landon, who portrayed Little Joe in the TV Western *Bonanza*. From her hospital bed, a day after the birth, my mum wrote a note to my brother, informing him of the fact and asking 'did Brownie in *Emergency Ward 10* get better?' The note survives stored in a battered suitcase along with photos, postcards, wedding invitations, memorial cards ('Abide with me. Fast falls the eventide'), and irrelevant relics that have found their way there, and to which time has awarded a strange significance: an old beermat on which the measurements for – something, were scribbled decades ago . . . a Nat West diary from 1974, with few entries: Weight Watchers on a Monday in April, and the date the Christmas Club pays out.

Back in 1950 the *Daily Mirror* had issued a warning that 'If you let a television set through your door, life can never be the same again.' By the following year television licences in this country had reached the million mark. The working class were early adopters, thanks to hire purchase and TV rentals. A majority of those sets were in the homes of low-income families. Seventy per cent of those with TV licences had not been educated beyond the age of fifteen. Broadcasting would finally become the educator that John Reith hoped in the days of wireless – but not quite in the way he had anticipated. By the mid-Fifties the BBC monopoly had been broken, with the arrival of commercial television. The campaign for it had been organised by a former BBC insider, who was also the author of the novel *London Belongs to Me*, Norman Collins. Information from the global village flooded into family homes.

In the Sixties television championed the ciné-vérité style of the documentary in drama as well as current affairs, in the by now traditional pursuit of authenticity. The masses may still have favoured melodrama, as G. K. Chesterton had said, but equally the gritty realism found in the weekly visits to Weatherfield's *Coronation Street* was to have a lasting appeal. By creating the series Tony Warren said he wished to explore 'The driving force behind life in a working-class street in the north of England'. The programme focused on the traditional staples of the working-class neighbourhood – The Street, The Pub, The Corner Shop – that were fast disappearing in the urban areas of the city, and even more so in London; replaced by the growth of high-rise housing estates. Like Andy Capp, who had emerged as a cartoon strip in 1957, *Coronation Street*, transmitted three years later, was largely peddling nostalgia for a way of life that appeared to be dying out. Even the habits of the families on *Coronation Street* owed more to the previous generation. It's ironic that in a series depicting the working class, whether it was the Ogdens in Weatherfield in the 1960s and 1970s, or the Fowlers in the Walford of *Eastenders* in the 1980s and 1990s, one crucial point was overlooked: the effect of television in the home. In these programmes, the television was almost never on, and on the occasions when it was, or is in the Coronation Street or the Albert Square of the twenty-first century, it only ever screens Westerns.

When the screen was silenced in homes in The Street in Southwark, the oral history of the neighbourhood and its inhabitants was relayed in monologues in which all of the hardships, trials and tribulations were transposed into comic stories. These were told by neighbours and relatives, like stand-up routines – performed on a mat in front of the coal fire, burnt bald in parts by the hot coal chippings it spat, and covered in cat hairs. Our fathers and uncles stood in these rooms, rattling loose change in their pockets, rocking on the balls of their feet, the way they did at weddings, funerals and anniversary parties. Each of them in serge or two-tone suits (custom-made; Levy & Sons) with slicked-back hair (Eau de Portugal). The Blakeys on their shoes tapped a rhythm on the pavement, announcing their return to The Street after work. The look of their younger selves had been maintained. One said: 'I know I'm getting on a bit; but I like to think I can still look the part of Jack-the-lad.'

It was also the look of the smooth criminal, whom many of them knew by a few degrees of separation; some had drunk in the clubs run by the Richardsons. Many had links with the local boxing fraternity, and crime and sport came together in certain local pubs, notably the Thomas A Becket on the Old Kent Road, with its gym and ring above. It was here in the late Sixties that film director Donald Cammell sent James Fox to mingle with south London wide boys to create the persona of Chas for *Performance*. Here he discovered a local, Johnny Shannon, and cast him as the Kray-like gangster Harry Flowers.

Friendly disagreements occurred outside the houses in summer, as neighbours sat and put the world to rights. The couple opposite fancied themselves as communists, and threatened to put a red flag in their window on election day. 'They're not communists', someone once said, 'They're just tight.' There was one issue that united all the neighbours: they loathed two kids in The Street – twins, who made the transition from spitting and swearing at anyone who passed when they were infants, to threatening them with fists and crowbars by the time they were in their adolescence, and who fancied themselves as miniature Kray brothers, having earned the names Flash Al and Nutty Ray.

The Street began to represent both a haven and a time capsule harbouring the rituals, the routines, the culture that had been the lifeblood of the neighbourhood and the area at large for so long. As the walls came tumbling down all around, as rubble settled and dust rose, it was as though the time capsule itself was being buried underground. But the future would have to wait, whether it was housing estates as wide as their accompanying tower blocks were tall, or the influx of interlopers. Homes, heritage, homogeneity, the holy trinity of the neighbourhood and the wider community, were the territory that was now being protected, defended even.

16

PALIMPSEST

The redevelopment of the neighbourhood brought more open spaces than the war. The bombsites that remained, on which relics of former homes hovered, exposed broken fireplaces and floral or barley corn wallpaper that had witnessed births, deaths, Christmases, parties, tears, arguments, laughter and sex. In the rubble beneath, broken furniture and souvenirs – the hood of a bassinet, a lidless ottoman, things that us younger brothers and sisters, in our infancy, collected, and from which we built lairs on the waste ground that were stoned and destroyed hours later by older boys in bigger gangs.

So quickly was the past being buried, it was sometimes hard to tell which buildings still clung dearly to life. One day we climbed over a wall into the yard of a house remaining in Little Larcom Street. We armed ourselves with the bits of debris that were left undisturbed: a flower pot covered in shells, a wooden crate on which the words 'Worthington E' resembled the washed-out tattoos of the man who sharpened our mothers' knives. The following day we returned, bigger in number, intent on raiding the vacated house for whatever contents remained.

Except we discovered the house still had an occupant – the last to leave, with nowhere yet to go. The kitchen door was unlocked and the house appeared to be furnished. From another room, stickleback-thin, with not even a shadow adding weight to her frame, a figure materialised in the passage, let out a frightened roar and put the fear of Christ into the lot of us. We retaliated with a chorus of 'It's Pissy Kate', and one of the boys literally shat himself.

There were scarier figures. We came across one or two when they sheltered on the bombsite, within the remains of Guinness Buildings – now derelict – where Nell Hall had lived. We knew that Hayley Mills had discovered the bearded, dishevelled murderer Alan Bates in a barn, and mistaken him for Christ, but the figures we found were as red as burns victims, with eyes that seemed to be those of murderers rather than 'methers'. These figures could barely stumble to their feet to aim a bottle in our direction. An older boy sent several stones flying in the direction of one of these tramps, and cut his forehead. We saw him fall, and spent the night believing that he was dead. When we returned the next day he had gone; he had probably joined forces with the gangs of similar men huddled and drinking outside the few remaining missions, the dosshouses that once provided George Orwell with a bed, or even the former workhouse, now The Lodge.

The workhouse had been a hostel for years, and very soon the subject of several articles in the press because of the conditions inside. The BBC and ITV had turned up and made programmes about it for *Panorama* and *This Week*. In 1965 it was used as a setting for scenes in *Cathy Come Home*. This, along with the TV adaptation of *Up the Junction*, spearheaded the trend for provocative television plays for which the urban working class were the subject, and authenticity the aim. The latter was televised the night Edward Bond's *Saved* was staged at the Royal

Court. Its abortion scene, and the stoning of a baby in Bond's south London drama, were a modern take on the themes of the slum novelists of the nineteenth century.

The old workhouse was eventually demolished because the land it stood on was required for the second of the megalithic estates planned for Walworth. The day it went I was part of the crowd that turned up to watch. Nell Hall and her sister had hurried me from a jumble sale in Camberwell that was to be opened by Katie Boyle. The name meant about as much to me as that of Winston Churchill. We found a place in the small crowd that had gathered to watch the first brick of the old workhouse being removed by the mayoress of Southwark for the cameras.

'Is she Katie Boyle?' I asked, bored by the prospect that I might have to wait while an official-looking woman in a two-piece and a feathered hat dismantled the neighbourhood's remaining link with the nineteenth-century Poor Law brick by brick. Nell Hall and my aunt silenced me, as though it was Churchill's funeral all over again.

The silence of the crowd during the short ceremony was broken by an old man behind us, who seemed close to death, but was hanging on for this moment, simply so that he could see the building crumble, and spit: 'Good job an' all.'

Whatever else those present had to fear about the future of their neighbourhood, they now had one less reason to fear the past, although they continued to jokingly taunt the young with threats of the 'bunhouse' and the 'workhouse' that had haunted their formative years. The building's demise finally laid to rest the stories of ghost children's calls and footfalls. But other, more contemporary tales were spread in which the truth became blurred.

It was November, so the kids in The Street kept off the building sites and went 'guying', with our guy made from the stuffed stockings that could double as draught-excluders. The pitch was the same spot every year; on top of the hatch where the barrels were delivered outside the pub. It was where kids stood and waited in summer if the elderly in The Street went on a beano. The coach waited while from the windows the daytrippers lobbed pre-decimal pennies, each of which seemed the size and weight of a discus. The same patch was used by a boy from a neighbouring street who played the mouth organ outside the pub on Sunday lunchtimes to get loose change from the regulars, taking our trade, and consequently reducing our firework money. Bizarrely, he was the only person at the time, apart from Sandie Shaw, who performed his act without shoes.

'You wanna be careful sitting here asking for money.' It was the bus-driver's wife and two mates returning from their cleaning jobs. She seemed to be addressing the guy. 'Didn't you hear about the boy kidnapped outside the butchers'?'

The story was that a boy had been dressed up as a guy by his mate, and a man had whisked him away. Where to? We toyed with the idea that maybe he had gone the way of all flesh, dead pets, and lost footballs – The Silver Cube. There was never any further news of either the boy or the guy, and it seemed as though the tale was apocryphal. However, the rumour put the locals on edge and on their guard. One day a man working in a depot behind The Street downed tools and came running towards me. He'd seen a man pull up in a car and talk to me before driving away. 'Did you know that man, son? What did he say to ya?'

'He's my dad. He said: "Go home."'

Two minutes later one of my uncles spotted me.

'Who was that bloke, boy? What did he say to ya?'

'He asked me who the man was in the car, and what he said to me.'

'What did you tell him?'

'He's my dad. He said: "Go home."'

The Street was a dead end that enclosed its inhabitants like a glove, and at this point the neighbours did the same in an effort to protect their young because of the aftershocks of the Moors Murders a couple of years before. There was one line forever on their lips: Don't talk to strangers. Don't take sweets from strange men.

'What about Mr Peach?' one of our number asked his dad.

'That's different.'

His name was a clue to his nature: a name like Tom Larter, Harriet Hackett, that wouldn't have been out of place in the pages of Dickens. Mr Peach lived down The Street in a house that held all the promise of a grotto, because of the wealth of gifts that he produced from it, and passed on to the children of neighbours. Yellowing veils hung like mosquito nets at his windows. Girls were given miniature bottles of dusty perfume; boys, bags of sweets – 'lucky bags' – that he had cobbled together: peppermints, Dairy Maids, Parma violets, fluff. He did this regularly, and for years, until one day he simply disappeared indoors. Mr Peach was not just old, but ancient. He was tiny, hunched, his frame curling like a Swiss roll unfolding, and bringing him closer to the size of the children that he called to his doorway. He was forever with a cane, and dwarfed by a mandatory Homburg. He was 'a widower', a term implying that he was once young and had a life, unlike those described as a 'bachelor', which hinted that life had never made it to their door.

Another man lived alone, in a house said to be 'like something out of Dickens'. Reports of what lay beyond the front door were swapped among neighbours over the years: 'He's very clean in himself but I bet he's not got so much as a scrap of lino in there' . . . 'He can't be short of a few bob; he must get a good pension from Sainsbury's.' To local kids, his thin, towering figure cast a giant shadow. We fell silent as he passed, and steered clear of his doorway. His house was always in darkness, as though he existed in a single room somewhere to the rear. When he died, it emerged that most of the developments of the twentieth century had not actually touched his austere, Amish-like existence. There was no television. No bathroom. No sofa. But quite a lot of cash concealed in the 'coal cellar' under the stairs.

These were the characters from another era who were grad-ually vanishing like local shops and houses, many of them with one or two decades left on the clock. They were ill-equipped for the present, having come of age in an era when to reach adult-hood was a blessing, to meet middle age a bonus, and to live beyond retirement a veritable miracle. Those living alone appeared to be most at odds with the modern world. They dreaded the rumble of the distant bulldozer that began to make its way into the neighbourhood, almost as much as they once feared the doodlebugs and bombs. Louder and closer it got, and one day, with the merest of warnings, and no say in where they might end up, their home could be a target.

They hated noise, unless it was the hustle and bustle of the market. And it was the noise of the young they hated most. The repetitive slash of a skipping rope, the bounce of our brothers' football, the banging of a tin can – three times – when one kid has spotted another behind a car in a game of hide and seek. Every so often, a stray ball would bounce on the front-room window during a game of rounders. That's when they would be roused, immediately at their front door and shouting at the kids responsible. The same phrases throughout the years: *Go and play up your own end . . . I know where you live . . . Wait till I tell your mother.* They were part of a wider collection of stock phrases relating to prices, high-rises, foreigners, and again and again, the younger generation: *Hanging's too good for 'em . . . Bring back the birch . . . Bring back The Cat . . . Bring back National Service.*

Maybe it wasn't simply the noise but the games themselves, many of which were variations on those they recognised from their younger days, made-up games born of hard times on hard streets. Those of us on whom the gift of youth was wasted glimpsed the past they had known, when their doors were ajar in summer, or above the half-nets of their front rooms if we dared walk on the short walls beneath their window sill. Here they kept the aspidistra flying. Antimacassars kept the chair-backs clean, rent money was kept in the teapot, and insurance policies hidden on top of pelmets in the spare room, a room that housed amongst other things 78s, draughts, Christmas decorations, and perhaps a collection of buttons in an old Empire biscuit tin. Fuzzy sepia prints captured the memories of distant holidays. Somewhere there was a horseshoe. Beyond the front door a dark, heavy curtain was sometimes suspended midway along the passage, and stairtreads held down a strip of linoleum so used, so old, so polished, its pattern had faded into the blur of a bruise. The banisters might have been painted a chocolate brown. The walls were mushroom and cushions were mustard. Elsewhere curtains, eiderdown, candlewick bedspread were the jaded red of salt-beef. The front room, the parlour, remained silent, even on Sundays.

In the summer the old women would be stationed like a sentry at a window – first floor front – arms nesting beneath them, the net curtains swept behind their heads like a bridal veil. Their ample frames were parcelled in pinafores, or housecoats, and some of them wore bottle-thick spectacles in which their tiny eyes appeared like sediment. On summer afternoons, if the sun cast their side of the street in the shadow, they'd be perched on the wall outside, on an old cushion as flat as spam, cradling a cup and saucer, having executed all the rituals of cleaning, ironing, washing and scrubbing that they had carried out religiously, like their mother before them. And like their mothers before them, they were part of that group of women which played many roles within the neighbourhood. Now, they were attendants in its museum, ensuring that everything remained as it should, as far as it could, for as long as it could. They harboured a knowledge of the history of its paving stones, bricks and windows that was encyclopedic. They remembered the accidents, fights, funerals and marriage break-ups that were played out before these walls, doorways, windows, kerbs and drains. It was a secret history, an oral history of the London that almost nobody knows.

And as with the major sights on the capital's map, this London also had its landmarks, even though many had disappeared with the passing years. On the wall above the shop on the corner, there was once a wrought-iron sign on which was carved the word 'telephone'; the low walls outside the houses had railings that were removed during the last war: *Harry wassname's mum jumped from that top window – her husband died a fortnight later of a broken heart.* The young, milky-white slab of paving, at odds with the rest, was where a solitary tree once stood, before it was removed because it attracted too many flies.

These women, and the men who had lasted to a similar age, were survivors from the previous century. They had stories to tell, and these stories were revealed piecemeal, with parts missing, to anyone who would listen, particularly the young. Those of us born in this decade, in between incessantly bouncing balls outside their homes, or knocking at their doors and running away and laughing as they passed, would sometimes, and very fleetingly, listen, deigning to give the very thing the young could give the old because we had so much of it – our time.

17

JUMBLE'S ISLAND

Towards the end of the decade, one phrase in particular began to fall from the lips of locals: *Enoch was right*. Those of us too young to understand when that speech, guided missile that it was, catapulted from Birmingham to the television news on 20 April 1968, and onto the cover of all the Sunday papers the following day, didn't know exactly what he was right about. We knew he looked like the kind of stranger we shouldn't take sweets from. We knew that here was someone else in this decade famous enough to have only one name: Pele, Lulu, Twinkle, Twiggy, Cliff, Elvis . . . Enoch. The name came up as men stood on mats covered in cat hairs, rattling loose change in their pockets, pointing an accusatory finger at an invisible enemy; as women gathered in a neighbour's doorway on dark summer nights, lit by an amber streetlight; as relatives debated over bars in pubs, whilst ash built and stooped like a leaning tower on the tip of an Embassy nestled in an ashtray, as nods of agreement arrived and the full stop descended: *Enoch was right*.

There had been previous speeches from Enoch Powell on the issue of immigration. His constituency in Wolverhampton had been transformed by neighbourhoods of 'coloured' immigrants, he said, in the way that some had been transformed by the bulldozer. Fear and frustration had taken hold of the indigenous population and yet, much to his amazement, there had been little sign of antipathy. Major unrest in response to 'coloured' immigration had been rare – compared to what it might have been. The most infamous was that ignited by 400 white men, mostly Teddy boys, who, armed with knives, bars and razors, descended on Notting Hill on August Bank Holiday 1958 for a bout of 'nigger hunting'.*

Two years prior to this, the author Colin Macinnes – a relative of Rudyard Kipling and Stanley Baldwin – attempted to create a better understanding of black men by white English men, with an essay entitled 'A Short Guide For Jumbles (to the Life of their Coloured Brethren in England)'. The Jumble of the title was a corruption of 'John Bull', used by West Africans to describe Englishmen 'in a spirit of tolerant disdain'. In his bid to enlighten the Jumble, Macinnes seemed to be inadvertently confirming certain fallacies, as well as stereotyping both whites and blacks to a risible degree:

> The reasons for this critical distinction between us is probably that African and West Indian children are brought up much more strictly in respect to manners than our kids – who, though of course delightful, are utterly uncouth. This courtesy – digni-

---

*The events of that weekend were reported as a clash between white and 'coloured' hooligans. But in August 2002 the Public Record Office released internal police reports written at the time that had remained confidential, protected by the 75-year rule. No reason was offered as to why these should be made public early, and at this time. And what was taken up by certain newspapers as a revelation had for a long time been regarded by numerous academics and journalists as axiomatic: the disturbance was not merely a battle between troublesome youths, but one triggered by the racially motivated violent intent of a white gang, with a counterattack by black men armed with similar weapons. There were 104 arrests, 72 of which were white men; four of whom were sentenced to four years' imprisonment.

fied and quite unservile – is one of the most attractive qualities of coloured people. Though they can be casual, quarrelsome and even treacherous, it is extremely rare to find them rude.

What most differentiates an African from an Englishman is that our chief ambition is to put our lives into a savings bank, while he firmly believes that every day is there to be enjoyed . . . Of course, this wonderful instinct for the pursuit and capture of joy goes with a certain fecklessness. They aren't responsible in the way so many Englishmen are; but then, so many Englishmen are little else.[148]

The 'vitality' that previously appealed so much to certain younger members of Macinnes's class, and which was believed to be synonymous with the white working class, was now the signature of the black immigrant, with his bank-free, carefree ways. *Everything free and easy . . . do as you darn well pleasy.* Meanwhile the white working class were now bundled in with the more general white Englishman, with his lack of spontaneity, uncouth children, and silly little concerns about something as inconsequential as solvency. What was also coming to the fore even more was his bigotry and prejudice – neither of which was the patent of whites, English, working-class or otherwise. Writing of this period in *Working Class Cultures in Britain (1890–1960)*, published in 1994, Joanna Bourke argues:

Racist and anti-racist activity was carried out on the humdrum level of day-to-day interaction. 'White' working-class rejection of the 'foreigner' did not seek justification within a rhetoric stressing biological inferiority, but the opposite: 'foreigners' were proving themselves superior in the fight for scarce resources. In particular, the fight centred around three sites: the body, the home, and the marketplace. Although no one 'racial' group was regarded as threatening one of these three sites exclusively, racialist rhetoric tended to link Irish 'dirtiness' and vulgar fecundity with fears relating to the body, West Indians and Africans with the menace to housing, and Jews with the challenge to 'British' standards of employment.[149]

In Walworth and Bermondsey the population had altered since the 1920s when the bishop of Southwark wrote how the borough had not been 'invaded' by Jews or Chinese.[150] But in the 1960s Walworth was still only peppered with a 'foreign' minority, none of which was concentrated in particular streets or neighbourhoods. Meanwhile nearby Peckham, and Brixton in the neighbouring borough of Lambeth, were increasingly regarded by locals as 'black' areas. The change had begun in earnest in the postwar period. The country was rebuilding itself, the labour market was overstretched, and so the call went out to Europe, and eventually the Commonwealth, for unskilled manpower. Until then, as the economist Bob Rowthorn wrote in *Prospect* in 2003:

> There had been no sustained immigration into Britain, other than from Ireland, since the Norman invasion. About 100,000 Huguenots arrived from France in the 17th century. A similar number of Jews arrived in the late nineteenth century and around 70,000 refugees from Nazi Germany were admitted in the 1930s. Sustained immigration dates back only to the 1950s, when migrants from the Caribbean and south Asia began to arrive in Britain.[151]

By the time Enoch Powell stood up in Birmingham in 1968 and shared his apocalyptic vision, the black and Asian population within England and Wales was quadruple the figure at the beginning of the 1950s (the level of Irish immigrants was double this for the same period), but still constituted only 2 per cent of the national demographic. In the capital it was 3.2 per cent.

Powell predicted that by the year 2000, there would be a non-white population to equal that of greater London.

And so, in Walworth, somewhere between the bombs stopping, the bulldozers starting, and kids being warned about strangers, 'the coloureds' had become a talking point. The inhabitants had witnessed changes within their communities without consultation – streets, cinemas, shops and pubs had been eradicated; cubes and doomed shopping centres erected. They now felt powerless in the face of further change. Their prejudices may have been based on bigotry, but their fears were not totally unfounded. In the Sixties in these areas employment was once again becoming an issue. The workforce was predominantly unskilled, and many still worked locally. When the manufacturing jobs in certain industries were relocated to the new towns beyond the capital's green belt, a number of skilled workers opted for the chance of resettlement.

If the argument by elements of the white working class that 'foreigners' were taking their jobs and houses was widely exaggerated over the years, so was the response from certain media pundits, who argued that since the beginning of the 1950s blacks did the jobs that whites didn't want to do. In that post-war period of labour shortages the urban white working class was largely unskilled. They didn't suddenly get contracts at the BBC, as that reported social revolution got under way. And they didn't stop working for London Transport or the National Health service, where a large percentage of immigrants from the New Commonwealth found employment. They were essentially doing the kind of work they had always done.

Enoch Powell delivered his speech shortly before the Race Relations Act was debated in parliament. Between the classical allusions ('Like the Roman, I seem to see "the River Tiber foaming with much blood"'), the fire-and-brimstone histrionics ('It is like watching a nation busily engaged in heaping up its own funeral pyre'), and the racial caricaturing ('charming, wide-grinning piccaninnies'), Powell capitalised on the alienation of a group he believed were beginning to be disenfranchised:

> The discrimination and the deprivation, the sense of alarm and of resentment, lies not with the immigrant population but with those among whom they have come and are still coming . . . The sense of being a persecuted minority which is growing among ordinary English people in the areas of the country which are affected is something that those without direct experience can hardly imagine. Now we are seeing the growth of positive forces acting against integration,* of vested interests in the preservation and sharpening of racial and religious differences, with a view to the exercise of actual domination, first over fellow immigrants and then over the rest of the population. The cloud no bigger than a man's hand, that can so rapidly overcast the sky, has been visible recently in Wolverhampton and has shown signs of spreading quickly.

Fearing that cloud might descend sooner rather than later on inner London, 4,000 dockers downed tools and 800 marched to Westminster in protest against the sacking of Powell by Conservative Party leader Edward Heath in the wake of his speech. The marchers were supported by Smithfield porters; and in Wolverhampton factory workers, and an official from the Transport & General Workers, armed with a petition of support from local members, backed Powell. The opinion polls swayed heavily in his favour, and mountains of letters supporting his views arrived at Powell's house, on the desks of MPs, and at the

---

*Ironically, the point Powell seems to miss was that the legislation was intended to prevent discrimination in housing and jobs, thereby preventing the creation of ghettoised immigrant communities, and creating greater integration.

offices of local and national newspapers. The wave of support was not entirely attributable to a support for Powell's opinions, or the manner in which he expressed them, but for his right to air them. Unfortunately the inflammatory nature and the hysterical tone of his speech made it impossible for a rational discussion to take place within the media on the issues of immigration and race. It was as if the issue was only being addressed from the hysterical Powellite position, or the other extreme, whereby white working-class concerns on immigration and race were dismissed as entirely racist and unfounded. Certainly, rumour and falsehood, not to mention the press, may have played a major part in generating these concerns, but they were not entirely attributable to white racism and xenophobia. Nationally, the levels of those emigrating from the UK often outweighed new arrivals, but this was not the case of the urban areas in which they settled. These densely populated areas swelled, particularly as during this decade, as Peter Clarke writes in *Hope and Glory: Britain 1900–1990*, 'immigrants (not least the Irish) were having bigger families than natives – their average family size was about the same as that of English families half a century previously'.[152]

In the wake of the Powell episode, race was a topic many were eager to avoid; 'community' also seemed to become a dirty word, to those champions of the proletariat who previously believed the word was inextricably linked to the British working class. The collectivism and the shared experience of working-class communities were now viewed in a different light. In certain white northern towns it was possible to maintain the notion of a working class dominated by the local industries – a community and culture identified entirely in terms of its labour. But many of the urban white working class saw themselves more as part of an ethnic group united by colour and culture, than as a class united by their work. Those on the left, who argued that working-class culture had been threatened with extinction by American-style consumerism, were confronted with the fact that the white working class themselves believed the greatest threat was the arrival, en masse, of black immigrants. Suddenly the issue of fridges in the home paled beside that of foreigners in the street.

18

THE RISING GENERATION

In 1974, the first of the two general elections ignited the imagination of a teacher at my secondary school. Pupils were selected to represent political parties and deliver a manifesto to the class, and votes were cast at the end of the lesson. From the mouths of babes came the clichés and platitudes they had picked up from parents. Coming out for the blue corner, the Conservative candidate was a girl everyone said looked and behaved like someone's aunt, even at this tender age. She was accused of trying to speak posh. The word pencil she pronounced *pen-seel*. Her dad was in the police force, which made her even more unpopular, and less likely to muster votes. By the last year of school, and looking even more like someone's aunt, she would achieve notoriety by being the first girl in the year to declare she was having regular sex with her boyfriend. In a housecraft lesson, she summoned classmates to help her remove a stain from her school skirt.

'What is it?' asked Sandra ——.

'It's what boys do', she said.

The girl who took up the Labour candidacy, Linda ——,

would never make it to housecraft lessons, and her hands-on experience of boys came not long after her appearance in the general election. She disappeared from school a year later; occasionally showing up at the school gates with a smoker's cough, her baby in tow, looking sallow, haggard, and more like someone's aunt than the Conservative candidate. In her bid to win votes, she informed the electorate that the Tories were for 'the posh' and Labour were for 'us'. Her Conservative opponent promised to make 'us' rich. The boy who offered himself for the Liberals was distinguished by being the best white fighter in the year, living in a prefab, and revealing in the showers on Wednesday morning at games that he had developed a veritable topiary of pubic hair. He promised to lower the voting age to fourteen, and create 'more discos'.

The critical moment in the brief campaign arrived when the final speaker was given a platform representing the National Front. The selection for the candidate stirred up some laughter when the tallest black girl in the class, with the highest afro in the year, possibly the school, jokingly raised her hand. Her best mate was the tiniest, skinniest white girl in the class. The job of representing the National Front fell to her. Like her fellow candidates, Tiny addressed the class with slogans that had been relayed ad infinitum back at home. Essential to her address, in between giggles, was the slogan that 'Enoch was right'. Using an overhead projector as a rostrum she could barely reach, she declared: 'Well, we are gonna send back the blacks, right. 'Cos, like they come over here, and they take our council flats—' At which point she cut off, looked across to her best mate, and said with a giggle. 'Not you, Sue.' She continued in the vein of a politician touting for votes, and in the absence of a baby to hold, introduced the personal touch. 'I mean on my estate, like, old girls are always getting mugged.'

The mugging issue had gone national in the summer of 1972,

when the *Daily Mirror* reported a new name – it had crossed from the USA – for what was essentially an age-old crime: street robbery with threats or violence. The country was reputedly in the throes of a crime wave. On paper there was little to distinguish this brand of crime from that practised by the 'cosh boys' of the 1950s, and even some of the more insistent pickpockets who carried out their trade in the 1890s and who provided the model for *The Hooligan Nights*. Those critical of the term have, over the years, pointed out that 'mugging' is not a statutory crime, and therefore since the word came into common usage no one has ever been charged with it. The website 'Blaqfair', which was established to 'record the social, political, cultural and economic experience of Black people', currently carries an essay referring to the days when 'mugging' first became a talking point:

> The Police manufactured the mugger label in the 1970s. Their purpose in doing so was to re-brand robbery. They aimed to make the label mugger a code word meaning black criminal and mugging a black crime.

Statistics revealed that street crime in which a robbery was carried out on an individual and involved violence or the threat of violence was almost exclusively committed by young black males on white victims, who were largely female and frequently elderly. This was the case in key urban areas that were increasingly multiracial, and where the proportion of this crime was high compared with the percentage of young black males resident in these neighbourhoods. Even allowing for some creative rigging of statistics by prejudicial police, and the scaremongering and racial stereotyping of certain newspapers, this was an issue. And what made it a relatively new phenomenon to the urban white working class – whether they were victims of the crime, relatives of victims, or possessed by a not altogether unfounded fear that they might be a victim – was race. Theft may have been the primary reason for the crime, but because of the apparent absence of cases in which both assailant and victim were black – had this been the case the term black-on-black crime would have worked its way into common parlance a lot sooner than the twenty-first century – urban working-class whites believed they were being targeted because of their colour. The details of these black-on-white attacks, whether stated as fact, personal experience, or rumour, always seemed to be reported as being particularly savage. As with the previous issue of immigration, the official reporting of the issue of 'mugging' and race was split between two extremes: those implying that street crime committed by young black men made all black males potential 'muggers', and those who, when confronted with what was seen by many as essentially a black-on-white crime, were as creative with the statistics as they believed the Metropolitan Police to be. They argued that if these crimes did occur, it was because of the impoverished circumstances of the assailant (even though in these urban areas, the white victims were largely in the same economic boat as the black minority). And those same middle-class commentators, in the press and elsewhere, would dismiss any suggestion that a racial element played a part, arguing that the white victim merely *perceived* there to be a racial element because the assailant was black.

My school was notably multiracial. Most of the white pupils had grown up in predominantly white neighbourhoods and gone to primary schools that were a street or two from their homes. As part of the overhaul of the borough, two comprehensives had been amalgamated, and resettled into one new building in Camberwell, integrating pupils from Walworth, Peckham and Brixton. Its Caucasian contingent was the first to attend schools in which non-whites constituted a substantial minority. The friendships were largely divided along race lines, although not from any racist motivation. There was little sign that the fights and arguments that occurred were ever brought about by colour. And when it came to fisticuffs, the white kids saw the black kids as either contenders or aggressors, and never as the defenceless victim at the mercy of racism from other pupils.

There was little to distinguish the school itself. It had been used as the setting for the Jack Wild film *S.W.A.L.K.* By the mid-Seventies, had it needed to boast, it could list among its pupils the child of a Great Train Robber, and the daughter of the actor who played Harry Flowers in *Performance*. In the staff room, an art teacher was rumoured to be the sister of Stephen Spender, which meant nothing to most of us; the headmaster, an uncle of Brian Eno, which meant everything.

Older boys pinned younger ones against the cold walls in stairwells, and punched their circular scars fresh from TB injections. Others threatened to 'wind them' unless the captive recited a nursery rhyme. Cornered, and overwhelmed, they could do nothing but eke out a verse, whilst focusing on the stone floors that, on sunny afternoons, shimmered like the glitter on Marc Bolan's cheeks. Pop and television continued to provide us with reference points; book reading remained anathema, unless it was related to these topics. Pop was our native language and the cue to other tongues. When Bryan Ferry sang 'tous ces moments/perdus dans l'enchantement', French lessons temporarily appealed. It was worth showing up to get a translation. When Sparks put 'potentate' in a lyric, we reached for a dictionary. One teacher got wise to the idea that smuggling in a stereo, and bookending lessons with *Ziggy Stardust* and *Natty Dread*, might wake white kids from their slumber and encourage black boys to arrive on time for more than just games.

There were the strict teachers who knew everything about education but nothing about the young. They could get the attention of a class, but not the interest. It was as if they believed that boys who wore their heels high and their hair long should be flogged or hanged, depending on the height of the shoe and the length of the hair. Those of us heading into adolescence in the mid-Seventies were the tryout generation; the guinea pigs for the radical philosophies that teachers were keen to put into practice, including the belief that creativity should play a greater part in education, and that pupils should be introduced to content relevant to their lives. And so before those final years in which we were expected to concern ourselves with exams relating to Shakespeare, the lifecycle of the spirogyra and the logarithm, we were introduced to the football hooliganism of *Zigger Zagger*, the gang brutality of *Saved*, and, absurdly, the drug addiction of *Gail Is Dead* (we could barely navigate our way to the tuck shop, let alone a heroin dealer).

In week one, a drama teacher arrived, introduced himself, and told the class to form the circumference of a circle with him at the centre. 'I want you all to take your shoes off', he said, kicking away his sandals, and revealing ill-matched socks. Education thus far had meant short trousers, no Christian name, and kids pissing themselves rather than raise a hand to be excused, fearing the wrath of Miss Tracey. Now, it was standing in circles, shoes off and . . . 'I've got this football', he said, 'and what I'd like you to do is to catch it. Whoever I throw it at – catch it. But I want you to imagine that it's been dropped in shit.'

Another teacher later informed us he believed his home had been burgled and trashed by the National Front because his posters of the black US activist Angela Davis had been slashed. He later brought in a soldier who had seen combat in Northern Ireland to give a speech on why we shouldn't join the

professionals. The fact that the pupils had about as much interest in pursuing a career in the British Army as they had in the
existence of Angela Davis seemed to pass him by. More impor-
tantly, the class always knew when they were being had, when a
member of staff was trying just a bit too hard to prove that they
were down with the kids. And those that did try too hard were
greeted with the apathetic response given to the strict, bald,
bespectacled old men who rattled on for double periods on
damp afternoons about kings, queens, commerce and 'con-
tainerisation'.

'Exams mean nothing', a teacher declared one day. Like pop,
it was music to our ears.

'Exams mean nothing', we told the teacher in the class that
followed.

'Who says so?' she asked, eyes widening.

Smugly, everyone chorused: 'Mr —— in the last lesson.'

The anger visibly welling up inside her, she picked up the
chalk and proceeded to cover two blackboards with all the letters said teacher had after his name.

'That's how much they meant to him', she said.

Others, younger teachers, drifted into the abyss of a dark
and deep humiliation each week, finding themselves at the
mercy of unruly teenagers who would shower them with paper
pellets, elastic bands, matches, spit. In one instance, a teacher
had brought in two goldfish in a bid to arouse some interest and
enthusiasm, and was reduced to tears when a group of boys
attempted to staple the fish together. It was the one moment in
the lesson when the rest of the class were captivated, their
silence broken only by the teacher screaming, picking up the
goldfish bowl and, before making a quick exit, shouting: 'I'm
fucking pissed off with the lot of you. I am a good teacher. I am
a good teacher.'

*

The fleeting silence that descended when there were confrontations, fights, or the tears of a teacher, paled beside that which fell on the classroom the day Pam's baby was stoned to death. She left it with Fred and his mates. Pete pulled the baby's hair. Barry said: 'Gob its crutch.' He bent into the pram and spat. The baby messed itself. Pete smeared it over its face. Barry did the same. Mike dropped burning matches into the pram, and all of them – Mike, Barry, Colin, Pete – started aiming stones at the child, with Barry making the final lethal throw.

'I gotta get it once more!' he said.

He takes a stone from the pram and throws it at point-blank range. Hits.[153]

An English teacher arrived in class with Edward Bond's *Saved* weeks after The Tallest Black Girl in the Class had an epileptic fit. Alexander Paterson had written of that genius of watching among Londoners: *A funeral appeals to all. A fire engine. Unrest in a street. An epileptic fit.* One minute everyone was sitting there in the new chairs, with the flaps that pulled down over the lap, making desks redundant, and the next they were being ushered into the playground, listening for the ambulance. If we were mature enough to witness this, we should be able to cope with the reading aloud of a play set on a south London housing estate, in which a baby is stoned to death by a gang of men barely out of their teens. Nothing throughout school could quite capture the attention of the class to that extent, apart from the news, weeks later, of the death of The Tallest Black Girl in the Class. She was fourteen years old, and it was this – her age – that shocked our parents. It was the arrival of death into our young worlds that shocked the rest of us. The silence shifted from the gym, where we were gathered together and told the news, to the playground during the afternoon break. Black boys and white boys tapped a ball to each other as though in slow motion.

Some had made the transition from George Tremlett pop biographies to books in which the pages were earmarked to signpost passages that could shock. The most popular book in the school library, forever on loan, was *Up the Junction*: the 1966 Pan paperback. A decade on, and the abortion page, signposted by a frame of biro from a childlike hand, had caught the imagination of a group of teenagers that rarely read books – if at all. *Finally the ambulance arrived. They took Rube away, but they left behind the baby, which had now grown cold. Later Sylvie took him, wrapped in the* Daily Mirror, *and threw him down the toilet.*[154] Aborted babies, babies stoned to death, managed to touch the parts that logarithms and amoebas couldn't reach. Bond's set-piece of social realism was presented by the teachers as though the pupils might be plummeting to these depths in adulthood or sooner, on these sprawling estates that had erupted on the local landscape. As though there were a thin line between throwing matches and spitting at a teacher and doing the same to a child; from stapling a goldfish to stoning a baby; a baby like that which Linda —— left with her mates outside the school gates.

In the spring of 1977 the school was the subject of an ITV documentary that set out to illustrate the inner workings of a typical, underachieving, urban, multiracial comprehensive whose first language was that of social engineering. It was timed to coincide with a wider debate concerning the performance of comprehensives, and the standards of the larger inner-city examples. As a teacher pointed out in the programme, a high percentage of the pupils possessed reading abilities several years below their age. Nationally, only 60 per cent of school leavers had succeeded in gaining some form of exam pass.

The school's careers officer suggested the bank life for the girls, and the print, Post Office or police force for the boys.

THE RISING GENERATION

Among those who remained pupils beyond the call of duty, a couple would enter a polytechnic. In a monologue within the documentary, a student reveals all she hopes to get from the world – and she was thinking big, as big as a dreamer and a visionary: racehorses, swimming pools of champagne, a castle – but 'I don't think I'll get any of these things and will probably end up working in Woolworths.'

19

JEERUSALEM'S DEAD

The Estate was finally completed in 1974. It housed a number of families who had previously lived on the land it occupied, but most had been dispatched to newly completed estates elsewhere in the borough, or further afield. To some it was a bad hangover from the neo-brutalism that urban architects embarked on in the Sixties. One of its inhabitants put it more succinctly when BBC's *Nationwide* canvassed her opinion outside the off-licence. 'It's a concrete jungle', she bellowed.

In the summer of its completion our hopes were as high as our heels – those of us hitting adolescence. It was the year of *Diamond Dogs*. *The Great Gatsby* was on at the Elephant ABC. The Sound of Philadelphia had reached SE17, with 'When Will I See You Again' oozing from every pub and car radio. After dark, in the stairwells of these modern blocks, as moths flapped and died in the lights above our heads, we became fuzzy figures behind frosted glass. Here we 'bum-sucked' Consulate; sometimes St Moritz. 'Bryan Ferry smokes them', someone said. It was a moment of glamour: a chalk-like tube, with its bridal whiteness broken by a ring as golden as a wedding band where the filter began; perched between fingers dotted with biro marks, wrists manacled by elastic bands.

To paraphrase a song lyric: *There was concrete all around but not in our heads*. Defiantly we blew smoke rings to the sky, and gave the finger to the past, as epitomised by The Street below, where I lived. It was stuck at the entrance to the spanking new estate, with its cavalry-grey thoroughfares and flats the white that Daz promised, with their floor tiles, fitted bathrooms and kitchen cabinets. As soon as the first blocks were completed, a group of us spent hours dismantling the lock of one of its maisonettes, before finally breaking in as darkness descended and, guided by a succession of Swan Vestas, feeling our way around the formica, as though discovering an alien planet. Like the Silver Cube, The Estate seemed to bring the future closer to home.

No one ventured too far from these thoroughfares. An older girl, with a bob the colour of beetroot, made it to Kensington for shoplifting trips to Biba. On the estate, in the clubroom disco, dancing to 'Judy Teen', she looked like Gatsby's love, Daisy Buchanan, in white gloves and a wide-brimmed hat that hid her face like a surprise, and was more suited to the cocktail hour in another time, another place. Another class.

Streatham sometimes beckoned, with its Silver Blades Ice Rink. On the train home, the boys – boys who smelled of Juicy Fruit and nicotine – twisted the lightbulbs from the carriage, and aimed them at the wall as the train headed towards the tunnel. As the tunnel enveloped the carriage in noise and blackness, there was a muffled yell. Immediately the train sped into the sunlight everyone present saw the blood splattered over the fawn V-neck with its map of brown diamonds, beige flares spliced with cream pinstripe. (It was the best the market could offer, in transforming a local boy into Jay Gatsby.) Everyone on their knees searching for his three missing fingertips, and abandoning the hunt as the train rattled into the Elephant & Castle station. Slotting a St Moritz between two fingers would never look as swish again. Later his mates sat on his bed at Guy's, aiming grapes at the gaping mouth of an ancient, comatose man in the next bed. He looked like Mr Peach without his Homburg and his teeth.

'He can't feel nothing', one of them said, aiming another grape.

Mike said the same thing about the baby, before they stoned it.

At the heart of The Estate, at the end of its first summer, we sat on a bench, five teenagers, our heads tilted to take in the surrounding high-rise blocks. From this angle, the upside-down estate looked like a mighty concrete claw, into which the sun was stubbornly wedged. We kept the pose, the five of us spotting and following a drifting stretch of cloud as it dispersed. First it resembled vertebrae, then it grew thin, and smoky, and split further into vaporous trails that passed over London like letters. One of us said: 'This could be an LP cover.' Soon some of these boys would discover unprotected sex, Old Kent Road pubs, and concept albums. It was as if we were marking this spot in time, recording this moment that summer, in case we might one day need to call it up as a keepsake.

There was concrete all around. It covered much of what was once Lock's Fields. The Estate was built over land where previously there were streets of houses, tenements, a stretch of shops, a small tabernacle and a synagogue. It was the last of those three megalithic estates that would alter the make-up of the borough, each of which was completed in the 1970s. These had not become joined as part of that original plan of 'south London link-ups'. Nevertheless, Southwark was one of the boroughs used as a testing ground for the revolutionary deck-system. This was an attempt to create a 'street in mid-air' – 'a safe pathway' free of the noise, dirt and fumes on the ground. The Deck was built into housing estates at the second-floor level. The front doors of the second-floor flats opened onto it. In some instances there was a pub, a clubroom, a laundry and shops on The Deck to recreate a sense of community. This was the layout for the North Peckham estate, which covered 1.4 miles and was her-alded by a local newspaper with the line: 'a new type of home and environment will be ready for five and a half thousand lucky people'. The second estate crossed the Walworth and Camberwell borders, on the site where the workhouse, R. Whites and numerous factories once stood. It also took out much of the old 'coster colony', creating 2,000 homes with 43,000 cubic yards of concrete, and was famous at the time of its completion for having the 'largest frontage of municipal houses in Europe'.

The Estate on the former Lock's Fields was made up of stretches of high-rise flats, and two-storey blocks of maisonettes, planted between blankets of grass that rose to a hump. The occasional tree sprouted between beds of concrete. Weaving through its centre, and connecting small arterial walkways, an intestinal deck began at the top of The Street, several feet above ground level, and came to an end at the Elephant & Castle station something like fifteen minutes later. For the young of the neighbourhood, the walkways, stairwells and landings were a maze in which to play, and an improve-ment on Gaol Park, which had previously provided them with an outlet. This site, where a gibbet once stood, where Dickens and maybe a Larter or two witnessed the hanging of the Mannings, was now a stretch of tarmac, edged by an island of balding grass which had become a stopover for the 'methers' chucked out of the car park behind the Elephant & Castle, where they started fires, fell asleep in the sunshine, drank, argued, fought, pissed themselves and sometimes flashed at passing schoolgirls.

To adults The Estate was as crude and spartan as the past from which they had emerged, but no one fresh to their teens believed it at the time. Even the previous decade was a foreign country to us. At family get-togethers, family photos came out. In the still-life scenes from the Sixties, the subjects were caught unprepared at Christmas, not quite presentable, in rooms dishevelled at the end of a day. So much was old: home knits handed down from brothers, nylon pyjamas we had outgrown, carpets threadbare and balding in places, like the pates of our fathers; sofas that dipped and ever so slightly protruded from missing springs beneath, like the bellies beginning to show on our fathers; copies of the *Mirror* and the *Sketch* spread out beneath cups and saucers with tea the colour of our mothers' stockings; cigarette smoke and a horseshoe reflected in a wall mirror. Flowerless vases that were dumping grounds for Green Shield stamps and Esso coins.

Nell Hall is there. She wears a hat indoors, and her boots are unzipped, with fur trim rolled back, making allowances for swollen feet. There is a thick crepe bandage around her leg. She had been changing a lightbulb in the hall of her flat, where it was as 'dark as the docks.' She fell off the stool, and as she fell her leg scraped a trail of tacks jutting out from the wall. The skin peeled open from the knee to the shin ('It was like a zip coming down'). She wrapped a towel around it and hobbled to the doctors. In the afternoon she put a bet on. In the evening she was sat in our living room.

My brother said: 'Nan, I'm gonna take your picture.'

'Does it hurt, mum?' our dad asked.

'I'll be all right', she told us all. 'Healing skin, you see.' She tapped the leg as the camera clicked. 'My mother always told me that. She always said that to you Eileen, didn't she? Always said: "All the women in this family have got healing skin."'

People were getting more things now – filling out their homes with new carpets or new sofas. An older generation had seen kids marry and move out, and others pay their way within the home. Charles Booth's survey had noted that there was a brashness about the clothes that costermongers chose. By the Seventies, much of the brashness was concentrated into one particular home. He'd been in the market all his life, and now his kids were working there. He and his wife had the cash; they had the parties – they had transformed their house on The Street: dimmer switches, knotty-pine wallpaper, a bar in the corner, an L-shaped Campari red leatherette sofa, and in one wall a sheet of glass the length of a door coated in the pearlised silhouette of a horse, raised on its hind legs, and lit by a tubular light behind. He is standing in front of it. He has his arm on the bar. There is an identity bracelet on his wrist, an anniversary gift from his wife. He'd bought her a gate bracelet. When he handed her the gift he serenaded her with 'My Old Dutch'. The gang of four behind the bar are dressed in shirts from Take 6. My dad stands in front: that slicked back hair, two-tone suit. Minutes earlier he'd been saying: 'They say that him out of Peters & Lee was blinded in a fight down the Old Kent Road.' Bill worked nights, in the print. Eileen is seated, her hands raised, she's laughing, and the gang of four jokingly restrain him. They are all urging him to forget work and stay at the party. *Dad, don't go. Bill, stay*. There's a flash. A snapshot – a still life from the Seventies: pink eyes and glasses half as full as the smiles.

Three years after the Peckham estate was completed, so the story goes, its American architect returned to the site, and, after witnessing what had become of her vision, committed suicide. There was also a story that a tenant in the estate on the old Lock's Fields had jumped to her death, frustrated by the noise from the lift shaft beyond the living-room wall.

Throughout these estates The Deck system did not create mid-air communities and safe walkways but, like the network of subways beneath the heart of the Elephant & Castle, notorious paths that would become synonymous with 'mugging' and vandalism. Someone came up with the idea of community murals created by local students in an endeavour to beautify these thoroughfares. The crimes continued, but at least the victims got to bear witness to painted images of smiling multiracial faces for the duration of the attack. In Peckham, by the 1980s, the milkman that dared to venture into the estate arrived in something similar to a Securicor van. Giro cheques were stolen from letterboxes. And those living beneath these pedestrian decks, where the staples of the community, the shops, laundry and pub, were battened down with plywood and masked by mesh, if they stayed in business, were forever complaining about the noise from above.

The neighbours on these estates who had attempted to recreate the community of old threw in the towel, retreated inside and eventually protected themselves with bolts, grilles and gates. Increasingly, the prospect of living in these quarters became less appealing to a younger generation of newly-weds doing their time on the council waiting list. With the arrival of the 1980s, many took the opportunity to live on credit, as mortgages became more readily available to those who were employed and skilled in some way. With a number of long-term council tenants taking up the option of buying their council houses the percentage of owner-occupiers, nationally, rose to 67 per cent by the end of the decade. 'At the outset finance was guaranteed by local councils; but the building societies soon saw their

opportunity in advancing the vast majority of mortgage loans',
writes Peter Clarke. 'On council estates, a freshly painted front
door and a copy of the *Sun* in the letterbox was a signal of
Thatcher's achievement in remaking the Conservative Party.'[155]

There had been little emigration from Southwark in the
1960s, beyond the few skilled workers who followed their jobs
to new towns, or those uprooted to make way for the new
estates who opted for a council home on the outskirts of the
Greater London area. In the 1980s, the younger generation of
families who had been established locally since as far back as the
1890s and beyond broke the chain to form part of a mass
exodus to the satellite suburbs of Greater London that spilled
into Kent – Bexley, Eltham, Welling, Erith, Sidcup. And when
their parents retired, if they had managed to buy a council
home, they sold up and followed on, purchasing a cheaper
property even further afield, just as their East End equivalents
made inroads into Essex. In Southwark this was the first major
exodus since that of the middle class in the nineteenth century,
when the proletarian forefathers of those now migrating began
to colonise the area. Those who moved away lived like ex-pats,
attempting to recreate aspects of the old neighbourhood within
their new environment. Still they returned to their old neighbourhoods for the things they missed – the staples that remained
in some form: the market, a particular pub.

This development in the 1980s brought about a resurgence of
those thoughts expressed when consumerism began to have an
impact on working-class culture in the 1950s; fears that the
working class were forsaking a sense of community for a culture
of materialism, individualism and competition. Instead of living
behind the same cobalt-coloured door as all their neighbours
they were choosing their own, and maybe even adding a pane of
glass with a rain-effect, and a brass doorknob. The concern
now appeared to be not that the owner-occupiers from the

working class might become bourgeois, but that they might not. They were becoming something far worse apparently – lower middle-class. First they had failed to keep to the Andy Capp image, and a life with no mod cons, by succumbing to fridges and televisions and losing 'the remnants of the noble savage', then it emerged that they were largely united on grounds of ethnicity rather than class and labour. Now, when they got the chance, they had done the unthinkable: moved to the suburbs but failed to become traditionally middle-class.

This new breed of working class made it in large numbers into the lower middle class. Many struggled to pay mortgages, working in several jobs, rather like their parents, stacking shelves of the expanding superstores and DIY stores nearby at weekends. But when they began to get enough cash to install central heating, maybe a conservatory or a lean-to, or a proper kitchen, and then start on really decorating their homes inside and out, well, these homes apparently didn't look right. They forked out for pelmets, cornices, carpets as high as pampas grass, and sofas in which the TV remote control could be lost amongst the plump cushions and the printed chintz. Television screens grew, picture frames expanded, became padded fit to burst in mock-William Morris fabric, and novelty magnets crept over fridges like ivy.

The exteriors of the homes had begun to change too. Lead strips criss-crossed windows. There were Welcome mats and plaques, and at Christmas, exteriors framed by lights with Santas and reindeer glowing on the rooftop. Had the young Tom Harrisson been around in this decade, he might have headed for these colonies on the cusp of the city and reported for Mass-Observation on padded picture frames and plump sofas. In his absence, others from the middle and upper middle-class were only too willing to do so in the spirit of mockery.

George Bernard Shaw once said that it was only possible to bring a working man onto the stage as an object of compassion.

Orwell claimed that Shavian drama failed to do even that, frequently using him as a figure of fun. Throughout the twentieth century, on stage, film and television, the working class, and specifically the cockney, were frequently bought in to be the butt of the joke. Often as the lazy beer-swilling, fag-smoking, chip-eating, wife-hating, armchair reactionary, or the autodidact whose efforts at self-improvement are blighted by uncouth relatives, malapropisms or Franglais. On screen, in the Eighties, the cap and the tea cosy moved aside for new staples of modern working-class life, and into the clearing came a figure who was brash, tasteless, uncouth, ill-mannered, upwardly mobile with a wad of new money. He was to be found in Loadsamoney, the character created by the comedian Harry Enfield, who caricatured the working-class builder as a con man with a big wallet. In sitcoms he had usually made a killing from scrap metal, and was a lethal concoction of chunky jewellery, stained singlets and towering cocktails. On the big screen he was the wealthy wide boy, living a life of excess and extremes, along the lines of the central character of Peter Greenaway's *The Cook, the Thief, his Wife and her Lover*, with his restaurant Le Hollandais as the backdrop. And ever since Beverley put the Beaujolais in the fridge in *Abigail's Party*, director Mike Leigh has mocked the working class's efforts to move into the middle-class territory of 'culture'. He has barely made a film that didn't include a dysfunctional family that had run to fat and moved to Essex in a house that was as loud as their clothes and their voices, with at least one lamp-post, and a fountain with cherubs urinating. And this, in films that would claim to be representative of the ordinary and the untheatrical.

The terms 'Essex Man' and 'Thatcher's children' were touted about as shorthand for those who had made it into the lower middle class via new money, rather than into the middle class via education. Yet there were probably as many millionaires made from the industry built around anti-Thatcherism, particularly within the media, as in the upwardly mobile white working class of the 1980s. When certain media pundits talked of the Tories being 'vulgar', or their voters being philistines, it appeared to be code for those from the working class who had helped them to power (an unprecedented number of trade union members had voted Conservative in 1979). When Hampstead-based writers rattled on about the abundance of Barratt homes clogging up the English countryside, they were essentially criticising social inferiors who inhabited them. Ironically, those who had championed regeneration and redevelopment in the working-class urban areas of the 1960s were now calling for restoration and renovation, as the new lower middle class moved closer to rural areas.

Redevelopment in Southwark continued with the conversion of warehouses in the docks that had been redundant since the Seventies. They were turned into lavish private flats for very high earners, much to the chagrin of local pressure groups who argued that available buildings and land should be used for housing 'locals'. A number of these locals were now, in the 1980s, a younger, middle-class generation, some working within the council or education. Those who had recently completed student life elsewhere arrived in London and found their way into housing association property, co-ops or squats, and were eager to bring the word 'community' back into the area. They were unmistakably middle-class, but in a decade in which a money system was rumoured to be replacing a class system they believed that being cash-poor made them working-class. Some made a hobby out of politics and 'revolution'. I recall coming across a group of middle-class men and women in Bermondsey trying to rally some local interest in Wages for Housework. For these, and many like them, 1979 had been their *annus mirabilis*, in which the election of Margaret Thatcher and the death of the teacher Blair Peach at an anti-National Front march provided them with a muse and a martyr. That's what someone told me, as he slid his tongue along a Rizla's edge and the landlord called 'Time': *Blair . . . Peach . . . was . . . a . . . martyr.*

And within this section of the local population were those who attempted to reinvent the word community by way of community art, community theatre or community politics, and who, rather like the political priests of the settlement movement, set out with good intentions. These also operated in local 'garrisons of culture', some of which were based in the old mission halls and institutes, which they referred to as 'spaces'. Some succeeded in involving the young of their areas in creative activities that might otherwise have passed them by. Others took a heavy-handed approach in introducing the white working class to a burgeoning 'multiculturalism'. There were actual sightings of some of these turning up at community centres for the elderly and attempting to evoke memories from those of a generation raised on music hall, by playing 'world music'. Even more misguided, some of those practitioners of 'performance' began bending and turning septuagenarian females who barely knew what day it was in the name of 'dance in the community'. In such cases, it was not the local working-class residents who were in need of enlightenment but the former students themselves. 'We are always ready to make a saint or prophet of the educated man who goes into cottages to give a little kindly advice to the uneducated',[156] wrote G. K. Chesterton about the slum journalists and missionaries of the 1890s. But the 'mediaeval saint or prophet was an uneducated man who walked into grand houses to give a little kindly advice to the educated'.

20

IN MEMORIAM

As workmen paused to cuff the sweat from their foreheads, temporarily silencing drills and retrieving them from Bermondsey's tarmac, the raised voice of a woman, near hysterical, could be heard. Traffic was bumper to bumper, and she was weaving between cars pounding on bonnets and half-wound windows, as drivers looked on stunned. It was a glazy, sweltering September day; lunchtime. Suddenly she was at my car, as the traffic reached gridlock.

'Can you give me a lift, mate? My little girl's had an accident.'

'Where to? I live in Rotherhithe.'

'Yeah, she's had an accident at nursery, they just called me.'

'Where is it?'

She was in the passenger seat in no time, and fiddling with a seat belt.

'Old Kent Road', she said.

'Whereabouts?'

'Opposite the big Tesco. Other side of the road to Tesco.'

'By the Thomas A Becket?'

'I dunno – um, yeah, I s'pose.'

It was 1992. I lived on Rotherhithe Street, minutes from the house that Jessica Mitford and Esmond Romilly had shared. Back then it was one of a run of similar tall narrow houses, pressed between the pubs and warehouses on the river. It now stood alone, with nothing to support it on either side, its life assured – as rumour had it – because it was the house where the liaisons between Princess Margaret and Anthony Armstrong-Jones took place before their marriage at the beginning of the 1960s. Twenty years later many of the nearby warehouses had been transformed into shell flats, bought by the young, wealthy and upwardly mobile – previously as rare a sight in Rotherhithe as royalty. Others became converted flats managed by housing associations and co-ops.

Seated and strapped in my car, the hyperactivity of the distraught mother momentarily melted into stillness. She fumbled for her cigarettes, and lit up: the worried mother steadying her nerves. Her skin seemed the colour and texture of cuttlefish. I had her down as twenty something, but she looked older, and she was thin, waiflike, her frame swamped by an oversized Club Sport tracksuit top and baggy jeans; a tissue bulging from her cuff like a trick. She puffed frantically on the cigarette, and let her hand rest and tap just as frantically on her lap. It was a skeletal hand, with veins as blue as the ink scrawled across it spelling: 'Call Baz.'

The tapping built into a state of agitation again. Understandably, she was distressed.

'It shouldn't take us too long', I said. 'What happened?'

'What?'

'What did they say about your little girl?'

'Oh, she was on a swing, she fell off the swing in the park.'

'How old is she?'

'She'll be seven. She's seven.'

'My niece, my brother's daughter's seven. I've got two nephews; one's nine, the other's nearly three.'

She was slumped at the window, oblivious. I asked: 'Have you got other kids?'

'No, mate. How long's this going to take?'

'Shouldn't be too long, once we've passed the roadworks. I'm in a hurry myself. I've just driven from Welling. I've got to get back there for two o'clock.'

She didn't respond.

'My brother died yesterday', I said. 'I've got to get back to go with his wife and my dad to the funeral directors. His body is being taken there today from Guy's.'

She looked at me, as if in disbelief, sunk down into the seat, and rested her feet on the dashboard. A taxi-driver had recently informed me that on this stretch there had been a number of incidents where a young woman had got in a cab and taken the driver to a desolate street, where he got jumped by a gang of her mates. But this was not a cab. It was daylight. The Old Kent Road would be throbbing with traffic and people. And yet there was something not quite right about the distressed mother, feet on the dashboard, holding a cigarette ahead as though it were a pencil, and blowing the ash off the tip. She turned, and for the first time showing an interest, asked: 'Did your brother die of drugs?'

I was reminded of a Saturday night early on in the 1970s, about the time when older brothers had George Best beards and lean and hungry white bodies maintained by lager top, tinned food and twenty Rothmans a day. A police car had pulled up in The Street and parked itself opposite, outside the home of The Communists. Curtains were soon parted in the darkness of other homes, and news soon spread among those curious enough to hover in their doorways, that drugs had something to do with it. It was a first. If the police visited The Street it usually had something to do with rolls of wallpaper, shoulders of lamb, clock radios, Teasmades, and other things that had fortuitously fallen from the backs of lorries – and once, a job lot of portable televisions that actually made it on screen when Shaw Taylor covered the story on *Police 5*; wrapping it up with 'keep 'em peeled.' But drugs? The son had been smoking something apparently. And some said, if any would, he would, as the signs were there – his bedroom in the top front had no nets, no lampshade, and a red lightbulb.

When the intrigue had subsided, and The Street's inhabitants. closed down for the night, the gang of four stumbled drunk into the gaze of the amber streetlight outside our house, stifling giggles, before dispersing. John was found a short time later spread-eagled on the settee, out for the count, dribbling on a cushion, tie loosened, and cradling the sleeping family cat on his chest. Bill stood over him, and Eileen was on her knees peeling back his eyelids and looking into his eyes. He jumped up, startled.

'Mother, what you doing?'

'Are you on drugs?'

'No, I'm drunk. What you doing?'

'I was looking to see if you was on drugs.'

'What d'you think you'd find in my eyeball?'

Did your brother die of drugs?

'He died of lung cancer', I said. 'He's the third member of my family to die in the last couple of years. He was thirty-eight. Him and his family moved to Welling in the Eighties.'

'Did any of them die of drugs?'

The traffic moved on from the snail-like pace, and each car broke its link with the one behind. I shifted up a gear or two, and built up speed.

'No, not exactly. My mother had a massive stroke. She was paralysed, and then a few years later she had to have her leg amputated. She never survived the operation.'

We were speeding though the backstreets of Bermondsey.

'I know all the backstreets', I said. 'My nan died nine months ago. New Year's Eve. Her flat was burgled the next day. She was ninety-nine.'

'She'd had all her insides out, but she could still play the piano in the pub at the Elephant', Nell Hall said, apropos of nothing, during her final days. In her mind, she was spooling through her life, oscillating between the past and the present. She was in the oldest block in Guy's, and was convinced the staff were taking pregnant workhouse girls downstairs at night to carry out abortions. Moments later she said: 'If I'd known I was gonna live this long, I'd have bought myself a white bedroom suite.'

We had paused behind several cars at the traffic lights. I said: 'You'll have to get out here.'

'No, look, it's only across the road. Over there.'

'I can't see a nursery. I can see a Londis. I can see the Thomas A Becket.'

Here James Fox hung out with south London villains and became 'Chas'. This spot was where Chaucer and his pilgrims paused for refreshments; their first port of call after a night at the inn off Borough High Street. Where the courtyard of the inn stood is an annexe to Guy's Hospital, its mouth as wide as a garage door, concealed by wide translucent strips. Above, in capitals, and a font that could almost be art deco, the word MORTUARY.

Everything suddenly pointed to death. This city was in the throes of another transformation, long after the vision of the planners and architects that had been on the agenda since the early postwar years had been brought to life. DIY warehouses and drive-in fast-food takeways were burying land once reserved for housing. Everything suddenly pointed to death. Roadworks everywhere, and the bulldozers moving onto the Old Kent Road, for ever the cheapest street on the Monopoly board. Soon I would move. The last one to go; the last one left. The final link in the chain that could be traced all the way back to the Larters on Kent Street. It had taken death and the diaspora to bring about this full stop.

Superstores with strange names – Lidl, Matalan – were appearing and altering the landscape, and coming up on the outside, something else was bringing another kind of change. Something previously rare to this neck of the woods was rumoured to be getting a stranglehold – drugs. In the stairwells of local estates, in odds lifts and evens lifts, in pubs, clubs, shops and solariums, and there in the passenger seat—

'You'll have to get out here', I said. We were first at the lights and the lights were red. She hadn't listened to a word I'd said. 'I've got to go. They'll be bringing my brother—'

She wouldn't get out of the car, and rolled up the sleeve on her tracksuit top, as though expecting violence. There were track marks on her forearm. Green for go.

'Just over there', she said, and we pulled up. There was a man in a doorway that most definitely didn't lead to a nursery. Baz? She waved at him, and pulled out some rolled notes from her pocket. 'Is that for him or your daughter?' I asked, but she was already out of the car and disappearing into the half-light beyond the doorway.

PART THREE

AN EXPEDITION

21

THE WHITE MAN'S BURDEN

When Richard Hoggart embarked on his study of the working class it was a time when working-class culture, urban and rural, north and south, was becoming supplanted by a mass culture, dominated by television. At the fag-end of the century, beyond the debates around language, history and national identity, came the news that a monoculture had finally been superseded by multiculturalism. Things were once again fragmenting. Even the media was diversifying with the arrival of the multichannel age – the 'digitopia' as the BBC's then Director General christened it. Furthermore, new media was creating more personalised technological pastimes. The common and shared experience was giving way to the niche experience. Within the media itself, the word multiculturalism became as key in the opening years of the new century as 'classlessness' was in the 1960s. Before that decade started to swing, Hoggart highlighted how journalists and authors self-consciously declared themselves keepers of the faith of classlessness:

we meet the popular novelists' patronizing flattered little men with their flat caps and flat vowels, their well-scrubbed wives with well-scrubbed doorsteps; fine stock – and amusing too! Even a writer as astringent and seemingly unromantic as George Orwell never quite lost the habit of seeing the working-classes through the cosy fug of an Edwardian music-hall. There is a wide range of similar attitudes running down to the folksy ballyhoo of the Sunday columnists, the journalists who always remember to quote with admiration the latest bon mot of their pub pal 'Alf'. They have to be rejected more forcefully, I think, because there is an element of truth in what they say and it is a pity to see it inflated for display.[157]

As race was embraced and class relegated to the back burner, the contemporary model of those columnists materialised, inflating their affiliation with minorities, ethnic or otherwise, for display. Many of them came across like the middle-aged teacher desperate to appear to be down with the kids. The satirist and columnist Jeremy Hardy informed us that Gay Pride had become a fun-day out for all south London families (but our survey says Thorpe Park and Alton Towers might just have the edge). 'It's an Ali G world where all the hip kids talk Brixton,'[158] was the analysis of leading political columnist Polly Toynbee. Almost half a century after Colin Macinnes supplied 'Jumbles' with a guide to understanding 'the life of their coloured brethren', the *Independent*'s in-house revolutionary Mark Steel was one of many who made a bid to point out the discrepancies between the races. For this reader the experience conjured up images of those white liberal characters lampooned in the Lenny Bruce routine 'How To Relax Your Coloured Friends At Parties': *Joe Louis is one helluva fighter. That Bojangles, boy can he dance*. Or those funky chic society girls whom Tom Wolfe once quoted; bored by hunt cups and cotillions they spent 'last weekend at the day-care centre, looking after the most beautiful black children . . . and learning from them'.[159]

At an old people's home exclusively inhabited by black pensioners, Steel excitedly pointed out how the residents were having the time of their lives in a way that old whitey never could: 'Old Jamaicans wear splendid Rasta hats, where white 70-year-olds wear cloth caps . . . throughout the day the tape blasts out reggae . . . can you imagine the uproar if someone stuck that on in a pensioners' centre full of white people?'[160] And when he'd finished on the dominoes, the dancing, the chicken and rice, the big, wide smiles, you couldn't help thinking, all that's missing is the watermelon.

And so, long after the cosy fug of the music hall came the summer haze of Notting Hill's annual Mardi Gras, through which black men and women were viewed by certain white middle-class columnists of the left, patronisingly and exclusively, as victims or exotica. It was a view as parochial, and as much the stuff of cliché, as anything the extreme right had come up with when portraying them solely as muggers or murderers, or white society in general when it was rumoured to have them down as minstrels or maids. In short, it seemed to be the contemporary take on those white working-class Londoners of the 1890s who believed in 'touching a black man for luck'.

Meanwhile, the modern-day white working class had a more varied, more honest, more intimate experience, having known non-whites as lovers, muggers, husbands, killers, wives, victims, neighbours, rapists, friends, foes, attackers, carers. For decades, the urban white working class had largely been educated in multiracial schools, worked in multiracial environments, and lived in multiracial neighbourhoods. Many may not have wanted this, and many escaped it in the form of 'white flight', but many more accepted it – or at least didn't manifest their opposition by rioting or carrying out racist attacks.

In 1997, the Prime Minister's favourite think tank, the Institute for Public Policy Research, investigated white racism in Britain, while tackling the side issue of reactions to interracial marriage. Non-white ethnic groups were polled on their views on 'marrying out'. They were not asked for their thoughts on marrying white Britons, although whites were quizzed about marriage between different races. It transpired that 32 per cent of Asians and 29 per cent of Jews claimed they would have a problem if a relative married an Afro-Caribbean, whereas only 13 per cent of white Britons expressed reservations. The statistics were similar when whites from all classes were canvassed on their opinions on marrying those from other ethnic groups. It therefore emerged that if interracial marriage is a gauge as to the extent of someone's racism, then white Britons are the least racist, followed by Afro-Caribbeans.

A further investigation into the area of interracial marriage would also have revealed the fact that historically, the melting pot of interracial relationships has been dominated by those from the tribe cast as racist, xenophobic, reactionary – the white working class. It was in white urban working-class areas that ethnic minorities settled en masse, and despite the polarisation that persisted, the postwar period brought a fair amount of miscegenation. Yet still the survey garnered little press coverage. Its coordinator was reported as saying: 'The mistake we've made is not thinking about white identity enough over the years. I feel "multicultural" wrongly meant the non-white culture. Anybody who tried to assert white culture was automatically a member of the British National Party. That was wrong. We're going to have to look at people being proud of being British and white without them necessarily being the enemy.'[161]

There was therefore something bumpkin-like about white middle-class journalists from white middle-class backgrounds, living essentially white media-class lives, taking on the mantle of the missionary and spreading the word of their new-found faith to the white working class. But the vision of a multicultural utopia needed its common enemy, and increasingly it was the tribe that played a major role in previous utopian fantasies. Julie Burchill captured the mood with accuracy in the *Guardian*:

> The white English working class is now the only group of people that the chattering classes are happy to hear mocked and attacked. Whether it's Louis de Bernières decrying the 'anti-education, anti-culture attitude of the white working class', Keith Waterhouse's tired old routine about the moronic Sharon and Tracey (but never Winston and Leroy, let alone Seamus and Paddy) or Jon Snow chiding the white working class for not being prepared to work all the hours God sends like those nice Indians/ Kosovans/Algerians, but rather wasting their time 'sporting a red cross daubed across their faces watching Sky digital'. What we now have is a new version of the deserving and undeserving poor – the noble new British working class, who are ethnic, and the thoroughly swinish old working class, who are white.
>
> If you want a full-on race-hate revival, just keep on telling people, as Robin Cook did, that there was no such thing as the British race (why is it on the Census, then?) or implying that, before immigration, this country was some sort of cultural wasteland . . .[162]

This argument about there being 'no such thing as the British race' had been the opening gambit in a debate on notions of 'Englishness' that took us through multiculturalism, ethnicity and whiteness. In the wake of the death of Princess Diana, the English themselves were put under the microscope. The phenomenal outpouring of emotion that followed news of her death was seen as emblematic of a number of developments. A psychologist in a TV debate suggested that the mood was one of relief and release: England was finally revealing its feelings, and not just for the late People's Princess; it was expressing relief at the arrival of a more liberal government, after years of Conservatism. The mass mourning, along with the growing craze for counselling in the UK, the plethora of books and broadsheet columns in which journalists wrote of romantic rejection, marital break-up, loss of loved ones, terminal illness, or their imminent demise, even British TV's attempt to create its own homegrown Oprah Winfrey, signalled that the nation was no longer characterised by what H. G. Wells described as that 'English shyness' that overcomes us when we talk of 'moving, grave or beautiful things'. England was getting in touch with its inner feelings.

A more abstract argument came from hacks and authors not riding the wave of emotion. We were mourning ourselves. This relaxing of the traditional English reserve was more than a mourning for the death of a princess – it was a veiled lament for the death of England, they argued. The blankets of blooms outside the London palaces, like the laying of flowers at the scene of accidents and murders, was seen as the expression of a need for rituals and customs, to replace traditions that had ceased to exist. Rituals that would involve us in a shared experience, make us feel part of a community. Love, culture, race and religion may often tear us apart, but death will bring us together. Indeed it does, from boy scouts and the The Tallest Black Girl in the Class to the death of a princess.

The 'sound of keening in Kensington was the sound of a nation doing death differently', wrote the author Kate Berridge. 'For 80 years after the first world war we tried to live as if death didn't exist, but when Diana died there was no place to hide.'[163] And here is where class comes into the proceedings. This entire argument was actually relevant only to the English middle and upper class, who had traditionally cornered the market on the issue of reserve. If the English had embraced a new openness around mourning, it was a development peculiar to the middle-class and the columns in national broadsheets. It was here that grief had its glasnost. And if official public mourning had died in the wake of the First World War, and only expressed itself with a black armband, a poppy and two minutes' silence every November, in the culture of the English working class funerals had stayed as significantly ritualistic as they had ever been. This had remained the one area in which this section of the public never failed to be lavish and expressive, despite their circum-stances. In fact, even more so since the Eighties, as funerals like homes, became more customised in the choice of song at the service, Whitney Houston or 'Wind Beneath My Wings', and with personalised floral tributes – creating wreaths in the strip of football teams. This way of mourning spilled onto the street, with the shrines that built up on pavements, at tower-block entrances, at the gates of parks and traffic islands, and the call for commemorative plaques where victims fell.

All of this evoked a cynicism in some commentators, not unlike those who mocked the decor of the working and new lower middle-class in the Eighties. It was an attitude epitomised by the hack Norman Miller, the narrator of Gordon Burn's novel *Fullalove*:

As soon as the tape markers are removed, women begin steer-ing children forward clutching thin, apologetic bunches of pinks and gyp and grade-two tulips in flattened cones that imitate laminated woodgrain and fake marble, beaten copper and satin-aluminium fire surrounds, duvet- and ironing board-covers, silver-frosted ceiling sconces, the technologised waffle-treads of trainers, glancing football shirt shadow-patterns, blistery thermoplastics, the foam-backed leather-like finish of wedding albums. The effect aimed for in the impromptu pavement shrines marking the site of the latest nail-bomb or child-snatch or brutal sex-death is peaceful, pastoral, consolatory – the evocation of some dappled blue-bell wood or country churchyard or Dairylea buttercup meadow, a world away from the 144-point hurts of the raw modern city.[164]

The reaction to the death of Princess Diana among the masses was not exactly a new development: it had been there in the mourning for the boy scouts in Walworth in 1912. Despite tabloid coaxing from the sidelines, the response to the death of the princess was spontaneous. It was a mood that wrong-footed the monarch in a manner not seen since the disaffection that gave Queen Victoria the jitters in the late nineteenth century. And similarly, the current monarch would only find her past popularity restored, temporarily at least, when the press and the PR machines got to work in preparation for the jubilee. The working class never looked on the monarchy in the same way again after Diana's death. It had always harboured elements that expressed anti-royal and republican sentiments, or a simple indifference, but now there was wider dissent. Even with the Queen Mother's death, rumblings of complaints could be heard, despite the purple prose and the plaudits in the right-wing press. There was talk about the debt she left behind and the news that her daughter wouldn't be paying death duties. The death of Diana was therefore more about the last of the Windsors than the last of England. It was as though the crowds that queued to view the Queen Mother's coffin, or lined the streets for the jubilee, were offering their final goodbyes to an institution that was finally on its way out. Meanwhile the spotlight fell on the issue of Englishness, which the white working class were said to be as attached to as the aristocracy. This has been my experience of the tribe, who see patriotism, even nationalism, as an extension of their attachment to a street, a neighbourhood.

Before long the soundbites, the essays, the books came thick and fast, in which the whole construct was dissected. 'Most of us look with longing to the republican countries across the Channel', said the playwright David Hare. 'We associate "Englishness" with everything that is most backward in this country.'[165] (Strangely, some of these countries at the time, unlike the United Kingdom, appeared to be taking a liking to right-wing politicians.) Former prime minister John Major talked of 'long shadows on county cricket grounds'. None of the conclusions came close to Orwell's seminal essay in 1941, 'England Your England', but Orwell was writing when the country was at war; when patriotism was the unifying thread that could overcome the conflict and discrepancies between classes, whereas the recent debate took place at a time when the very notion of a national identity was said to be in crisis – or at least in need of a rethink. What could be a pain-free Englishness that wouldn't upset the sensibilities of any of the nation's citizens in these post-imperial, multicultural, EU days?

Englishness was compared to, amongst other things, an exclusive but dilapidated club whose survivors lived in fear of the future. A number of pundits claimed that the blindly faithful were lingering in Housman's land of lost content. Others pulled out particular historical attributes as the case for the defence – tolerance, pragmatism. The historian Tristram Hunt chipped in with news that the English were also known for their militancy, radicalism and religiosity; notably during the civil wars. He added by way of a footnote that this might be preferable to the red pillar-boxes and cycling maids that George Orwell cited. Elsewhere the English were written off as unloved, and unable to love themselves. They were like the Millwall fans who used to chant: 'No one likes us/no one likes us/and we don't care'. Even the beautiful game itself, as a unifying experience, was called into question. During a spell of intense patriotism for the England squad, when there was some national exultancy over a win – nothing riotous; no mafficking – a leader column in the *Guardian* commented:

> only a minority of English people follow football and only a tiny handful play the game. We mustn't confuse the sociological observation that people have a need for common symbols and shared points of reference (the function after all, of *The Archers*) with some wild equation of national character . . . And furthermore, the England team itself (all male, all young, non-graduate) does not personify the country.[166]

It doesn't, it's true. But England's multiracial team, assembled solely on the grounds of merit rather than class and nepotism, is far more representative of the national demographic than the editorial team of a British broadsheet.

The Englishness which Orwell had identified in the past was dismissed as a starchy culture bereft of vibrancy, without any notable cultural or culinary inventions to call its own. Mushy peas, morris dancing, maypoles and football hooligans in Marseille were exhibited as evidence. When Jean Bailhache compared his native France with England in the Forties, he wrote: 'We have one church and many sauces, they have one sauce and many churches.'[167] Had culinary invention rather than nonconformism been our forte things might have been different. Had militancy and rabid religiosity been more characteristic of the nation it wouldn't have assimilated and absorbed the influences that have contributed to the change that brought about this debate.

It was a debate that swiftly moved on to the issues of identity and language, following the inner-city riots of 2001, that erupted after conflict between white working-class and Asian youths, who existed in separate enclaves. Here were parallel lives of races who inhabited separate housing estates, streets, social networks, and increasingly different schools, with some groups demanding faith-based education. This polarisation was highlighted by prominent black pundits. Bill Morris, the former general secretary of the Transport & General Workers' Union, pointed out that schools were being divided into black and white, and Lord Ouseley, in his report on the riots as head of the Commission for Racial Equality, made the same point. The voices of the white middle-class writers who made multiculturalism their specialised subject were silent, as though they were waiting for black figures to make the first move.

Ironically, what emerged simultaneously from the CRE report and the investigations of Bradford council was that, according to the council leader, 'white middle-class political correctness has impeded attempts to create racial harmony' in the area. It emerged that no one had the nerve to tackle the subject of race and culture, even if it meant dealing with problems that might prove detrimental to a child's education. When the Labour MP Anne Cryer weighed in with the view that Asians who didn't speak English at home were excluding themselves from integration, she was all but blindfolded and lined up against a wall.

Fear was the reason that white middle-class professionals failed to address these issues, as though to intervene would be the equivalent of slipping into Kipling's shoes and imposing the white English way – whatever that was – on others. (And this would apply even to practices these professionals themselves would regard as illiberal.) Yet it seemed strange that these same people, particularly writers, who argued against the idea of a 'host' culture, the concept of Englishness, the notion of a nation state, and supported a single European currency and the global village as one nation under a groove, objected to the idea that one language might be the currency that could bring about a more integrated society, particularly as the UK had one of the highest rates of illiteracy in the English-speaking world.

Ultimately, what emerged from the reports and debates on this issue was a compromise: citizenship. Michael Willis was appointed by Tony Blair in 2002 to explore national identity, and the core values of the British. He was dubbed the 'minister of patriotism'. Apparently, what was needed was a code of citizenship to which all sections of the community could be expected to adhere. How this would work and what it would entail for the country's citizens hasn't yet been formulated. But a Home Office panel, after much consultation, did propose a citizen programme for the immigrants who apply for British citizenship each year. Once again the argument levelled against such a move was that it might tend to colonise the cultural identity of the new arrivals. Anticipating detractors, the programme kept things pure and simple. First, it would inform potential citizens of the nation's values, which included tolerance and fair play; second, it would convey what those common principles might be that bind the everyday existence of a community. As 'what makes a good neighbour' was one of the themes introduced, those principles might well include mutual respect rather than antisocial behaviour. 'We all have a common experience, and Englishness resides in that sense of belonging', said the musician Billy Bragg in 2002. 'But there is no sense of belonging, because there's no identity. We don't take ourselves seriously enough to have formulated one.'[168] England had never really had to seriously check itself in the mirror and offer up a definition before. It was always left to foreigners like Jean Bailhache to conjure up an image. Orwell seemed to come closer than most: 'It is somehow bound up with solid breakfasts and gloomy Sundays, smoky towns and winding roads, green fields and red pillar-boxes. It has a flavour of its own. Moreover it is continuous, it stretches into the future and the past, there is something in it that persists, as in a living creature.'[169]

This English white working class, the only group in this age of multiculturalism and citizenship that 'the chattering classes are happy to hear mocked and attacked', was not those resident in the capital, where they themselves are becoming a minority (as the term urban becomes a synonym for 'black' or 'multicultural'). It was essentially a reference to those who made their exit as part of the diaspora to live like ex-pats in white enclaves, those who opted for council homes on 'white estates' further afield during the redevelopment of the 1960s and 1970s, and poor whites sighted elsewhere. These became the subject for journalists who, like George Sims in the nineteenth century, intended to go out into the field.

This time, however, it was not simply a case of crossing the river to the south but of crossing the boundaries between central London and the satellite suburbs and beyond. In media terms this was now the north/south divide, the contemporary take on Disraeli's two nations: the urban, edgy, multicultural city dwellers and their burden – the culturally impoverished, hickish whites everywhere else. It was once the cockney's ignorance of the country that made him the subject for middle-class mockery; now it was the fact that he didn't live in the modern inner city. And the issues here were not those of putting Beaujolais in the fridge, calling a napkin a serviette, and using the wrong knife. These days, it was the lack of modern etiquette on race that was keeping the white working class below stairs. And so, ironically, the people of the press who took up the missionary position did so in a spirit reminiscent of Kipling's class:

THE LIKES OF US

Take up the White Man's burden –
Send forth the best ye breed –
Go bind your sons to exile
To serve your captives' need;
To wait in heavy harness
On fluttered folk and wild –
Your new-caught, sullen peoples,
Half devil and half child.

22

POPULISM: A MANIFESTO

Shortly after Henry Mayhew's survey in the nineteenth century, religious revivalists took to street corners and music halls as part of their 'missions to dockers, cabmen, costermongers'. By the 1950s the London City Mission had produced a book on its efforts to convert publicans and cabbies with a chapter entitled 'Evangelising London's Taxi Drivers': 'Who are the men who drive our London taxis? They are Jews, Gentiles, Italians, Frenchmen, Scotsmen, Welshmen – indeed, they represent a wide range of nationalities . . . and will not tolerate the missionary.' Fast-forward to the twenty-first century, and a trend similar to that road-tested by revivalists intent on transforming the white working class into temperate keepers of the faith. In this instance, multiculturalism was the faith, and racism, rather than drink, the demon in need of exorcism. 'Multiculturalism is faith-based', wrote Matthew Taylor, then director of the Institute for Public Policy Research. 'Its creed assumes that human beings who are properly educated and guided can live together harmoniously, preserving their own cultures while respecting those of others.'[170] The rioting and the increase in the levels of racist violence suggested the liberal dream had failed, he argued – it had been 'translated' into the policy and practice of multiculturalism. 'As our idealism fades, so we turn increasingly to the law to enforce attitudes that we once might have hoped to have instilled.'

In short, those who once believed in the liberal tradition of educating the white working class on these issues were taking a line on crime traditionally touted by the right, but only with offences linked to racism: more laws, stronger sentences, zero tolerance. Elsewhere, some became positively evangelical about their mission, recommending their own strategies. The columnist Decca Aitkenhead wrote of how 'people who do not consider themselves racist find themselves in taxis listening to tirades about immigrants; every day, they sit in pubs and hear appalling racist opinions spat casually across the bar from publicans.' The solution was a simple one, she wrote: when faced with racist remarks from white working-class taxi-drivers or publicans – *confront* them.

Long after James Greenwood referred to cabmen as a 'ruffianly, blackguardly, bullying race', and Richard Whiteing's coster caricature Josef Sprouts put forth his opinions, the cabbie was cast as the ultimate conduit for racist remarks and 'populist' opinions. A report in 2000 revealing that the hippocampus, the part of the brain associated with spatial memory – where it keeps its maps – is larger in London taxi-drivers than in the average motorist was possibly the best news to hit the profession since one of its number took the *Mastermind* title in the late Seventies. Whatever others might believe, at least cabbies themselves had reason to assume that things had evolved since Henry Mayhew referred to the profession as 'a degraded body', with 'a greater development of the animal than of the intellectual or moral nature of man'.[171]

This staple of working-class life, a pioneer of the diaspora, had always been the first port of call when a vox pop was needed on race and immigration. The camera would seek them out in the hope of coaxing something close to the N-word from their lips. Failing that, the choice would be a pensioner, often female, propped against an expanse of white woodchip and prodded off-camera by questions desired to cut to the chase: the word immigration is the cue, as that (rather than 'multiculturalism' or 'minorities') is more likely to register and stir white folk of her class and generation. The camera scans the room for an image perfect for her voiceover; something indicative of her class, as a way of mocking her taste, a way of demeaning anything that she might have to say – a novelty ornament, or an air freshener not quite concealed within the inner skeleton of a radiator. And the soundbites come thick and fast, as expected. *Well, I mean, I'm not racialist but we're treated like second-class citizens . . . We're like foreigners now . . . We're not allowed a say . . . I mean you're frightened to open your mouth.*

These documentaries seldom went beyond the soundbites to examine what contributed to the foundation of these views, such as that insularity and attachment to place that defines the white working class, and which is born of a lack of opportunity. Or how the noble values that have traditionally brought them together as a community can set them apart from outsiders. By the twenty-first century, this kind of documentary had moved beyond the soundbites to examine the lives and experiences of those that aired them. In the 2001 documentary *I'm Not Racist But . . .*, Matthew Taylor argued that there was a danger that multiculturalism was solely being presented as the process of white people learning to tolerate difference. 'Diversity can bring new opportunity and wealth to an area, but the process of change does put strain on people. The reality of most immigration to Britain (repeated in the process of asylum-seeker dispersal) has been that those expected to cope with the most profound change have always been those with the fewest economic and educational resources.'

To those living in these areas, this argument has been axiomatic for decades, but seldom acknowledged in liberal middle-class circles. 'That the working class might have a thoroughly legitimate reason for becoming more agitated about immigration than the tolerant middle class, with their health insurance, private schools and comfy cars, is never considered by these usually oh-so-caring types',[172] wrote Julie Burchill, responding to the CRE 'witchhunt' whereby MPs had to swear not to mention immigration during the general election campaign. Taylor's documentary was part of a Channel Four series entitled *How Racist Is Britain?* This theme was also the premise of the series *White Tribes*. A variant on the traditional 'race' documentary, it cast the black man as the social anthropologist exploring white islanders at an 'interregnum'. The presenter, Darcus Howe, proffered his answer to the question posed by the series:

> I only really saw it badly in two places. I saw it in Oldham, which is now really, really poor. The white people are what they'd call in America 'white trash'. There are also lots of young Pakistanis, and most of them are making money, wheeling and dealing, wearing the suits – and the hatred from the whites, the real, bitter, twisted hatred. I'd never come across that before. It was a violent hatred. They wanted the Pakistanis physically eliminated.[173]

But it was a far cry from the day when Teddy boys went 'nigger hunting' in Notting Hill, or when Howe arrived here from Trinidad in 1961. 'Racism was much, much worse back then, when I first came across. We have come a very long way. You should understand that when something is coming to an end, such as racism, it can be much more violent than it was in the beginning – thus Stephen Lawrence.'

The savage crime of the young Patrick Hooligan in the Southwark of the 1890s led to his name becoming a brand for any boyish working-class male who committed a felony – or at least looked capable of committing one. Hooliganism created a moral panic, stoked by the press ('We rub our eyes, hoping the ugly thing is a passing nightmare'), during which journalists descended on the area to alert middle-class readers to the evil that thrived there. One hundred years later, with the failure to convict the Lawrence suspects, and following the inquiry at the Elephant & Castle, it was as though every group of white working-class boys had the potential to be racist thugs or murderers. The moral panic around racism that received extensive coverage within liberal broadsheets at the time was matched only by the tabloids' excessive coverage of paedophilia. Whilst the former dismissed the latter as alarmist and populist, the two approaches were not dissimilar. Any day you expected a name-and-shame campaign listing convicted racists, like the roll-call of paedophiles compiled by the *News of the World*.

Rather like Clarence Hook descending on the Southwark of the 1890s in search of hooligans, contemporary journalists headed to Eltham, and returned with their dispatches from the front line. In the *Guardian* Jamie Wilson and Vivek Chaudhary reported:

> During the day Eltham High Street looks like any other semi-suburban town centre. But at dusk, as the shoppers scurry home for their cars and buses, small groups of young white youths begin to descend on the town. Young boys in designer clothes compete for the attention of teenage girls, smoking, shouting and swearing at each other . . . Opposite McDonald's

stands the Greyhound pub . . . In a room at the back a group of twentysomething boys are playing pool. They are wearing sweatshirts emblazoned with Armani and other designer logos: de rigueur for urban white youth.[174]

Strange how dusk in Eltham should be so different from that time of day in any other semi-surburban town centre in the country, as though it's built on ley-lines that attract the worst of the nation's youth just as the locals are settling into their sofas and checking their lottery numbers. It's as strange as the news that taking to the street in designer logos, smoking, shouting and swearing to get the attention of girls is somehow exclusive to urban white boys. Strange because, well, you'd find black boys down the road descending on Lewisham town centre and Catford, doing exactly the same thing; in nearby Plumstead, Asian boys are equally embroiled in similar activities. If you came to this passage cold, unaware of the climate and the newspaper in which it appeared, you could mistake it for the musings of a portly upper-class old-school Tory who had stumbled with a sense of foreboding on a phenomenon called 'the teenager'. Close to Eltham, and covering a far greater stretch, from Welling High Street to the expansive car-free tarmac outside Bexleyheath shopping centre, the same scene is intensified a hundredfold every weekend, when teenagers whose first language is texting, and who form part of the 70 per cent of the nation's sonic youth more familiar with a computer screen than a book, descend on the nerve-centre of the neighbourhood. Here, they are the nucleus of a network of information, channelled from the benches at bus stops, to Bluewater shopping centre, to pubs, to McDonald's, to football terraces, to sports shops and clothes shops, to homes, via multicoloured mobile phones. All that is being decided and discussed is in preparation for the big Saturday Night Out.

Boy racers are sometimes spotted on Saturday evening, and on this patch some have ended their lives at the wheel; friends lay flowers and toys where they crashed, and every birthday since, their names are listed by their families in the personals of free papers circulated in local superstores. Here, the obligatory McDonald's, Asda, Woolworths remain, and kebab shops and those outlets that are a dry cleaner's one day, video rentals the next, and finally an everything-for-a-pound-shop before the hardboard goes up and bill posters bury them, are slowly disappearing. TK Maxx has arrived with cut-price designer gear. There's a multiplex, a massive bingo hall, Pizza Express, and increasingly, pubs and more pubs, where stocky men check for fake ID, and confide in headsets as though preparing for trouble or royalty. There are often reports of sporadic shootings, the most recent a 'Yardie' killing that occurred minutes from the shopping centre: a young black woman ambushed at the traffic lights after leaving the police station.

Whatever role racism or racist attacks play in these areas there are greater concerns; statistically, violence and crime among the young in which race doesn't feature is the more dominant issue, particularly around the new monolithic modern pubs – now as much a chain as DIY stores and bingo halls – introduced in these neighbourhoods to pull in teenagers and draw the equivalent from areas further afield (Thamesmead, Plumstead). Consequently, the gang culture based on territory has become more defined. Often, but not always, there is further conflict beyond the main stretch and the residential streets that are interchangeable with those in Welling and parts of Eltham and Charlton. On the tiny high streets within Erith and Slade Green, the occasional housing estate exists, overlooking streets of bungalows, many with half-finished walls and slabs of stacked paving, awaiting the DIY mood of the next Bank Holiday. Here, a few weeks ago, I was queu-

ing at a fish and chip shop. It was no later than 9 o'clock. At
the takeaway pizza place opposite, barely wider than a kiosk,
drivers pulled up in their cars, stocked up their insulated sad-
dlebags and shot off to dispatch their deliveries. Into this scene
a group of teenage boys and girls descended, out of the darkness, dodging the hooting cars that could have turned any of
them into a statistic, and came to a halt at the bus shelter outside the fish and chip shop. The boys bent to catch their breath
from running. They were dressed for summer: girls in crop-
tops, short skirts and trainers, boys in T-shirts longer than the
girls' skirts, and the odd baseball cap. The broken conversation,
between the panting and the catching of breaths, was a touch of
Bond, Edward Bond:

'I didn't think we was gonna lose 'em.'

'That fat one, that fat cunt, he could narf run.'

'I didn't think he had it in him – fat bastard.'

'Yeah, what a fat bastard.'

'D'you see his mate's face when we legged it?'

'He was getting well wound up.'

As if from nowhere, having taken a detour, and sprinted from
a sidestreet, the three men in pursuit were suddenly upon them.
At the head was the 'fat cunt' they'd been talking about: shaved
head, topless, his belly flopping over his tracksuit bottoms.

'Gal, Gary, steady', one of the henchmen called.

A trail of hair rose above his navel, and the drawstring from
his tracksuit dangled beneath his belly like an umbilical cord.

The teenagers were backing towards doorways, unpeeling to
reveal something at their core: one boy, skinny, almost emaci-
ated, in an Adidas top, and the target for the fat man's wrath.

One of the kids said: 'Mate, mate, he's only fourteen. Mate.'

The boy looked like a cornered seal cub, staring up and ready
to be clubbed. The topless man went directly up to him and
pushed his fist into his face with such force it produced a crack

like an axe on wood. The boy was down in a second, seemingly without bending for the drop. The fat man stood, looked at another boy and yelled: 'You want some?' He hitched up his tracksuit to conceal the crack of his arse, and seemed ready to take aim at another boy, but the two other adults pulled him away.

'All right, Gal, leave it now, leave it.'

The boys were watching, stunned. The girls shrank into one another, arms folded. The owner of the fish and chip shop came out onto the street. He recognised one of the adults, who stayed and explained, whilst the other ushered the topless man away. With the kids in earshot, Gal's mate revealed how they had been turning up at the pub throwing stones through the door. One of them took a brick from the forecourt of a nearby bungalow and put the window in. The 'fat cunt' was the publican.

'Do you want us to get your dad?'

The group of teenagers gathered round the boy. His shirt was splashed with blood; his nose and mouth were a bloody blur. His mates began to lift him up. One of them looked at the publican's mate standing with the owner of the fish shop.

'He's only fourteen', he said.

Here and now, the mood is an altogether different one.

'I'm writing a book about south London', I say, and when I say 'south London' he pats his heart, his Moschino-shirted heart. He lived in the heartlands of Bermondsey until his mid-teens, when his family made the voyage out. He's twenty. We are at an eighteenth-birthday party in a hall behind a pub, anchored in one of those suburbs where the fluttered folk of the white flight settled. His younger brother flops down to the side of us. He's thirteen, and wears a football shirt crowded with the obligatory logos and brand-names. His mobile has his attention; its skin, like his shirt, is in the team colours. He likes Dizzy Rascal and 50 Cent, and exists perhaps in an 'Ali G world where all the hip kids talk Brixton'. Those here of Moschino's age, many the children of a cab-driver or a market seller, were born and raised in these parts, and yet it is to the neighbourhoods and the culture of their parents they look with awe. Some, either searching for an identity or clinging to a past they never knew, have taken on the mantle of a caricatured cockney and lapse regularly into their very own modern interpretation of rhyming slang, in which pubic hair and Rubik's cubes are inextricably linked.

When the phone rings it plays thirty seconds of 'In Da Club' and a phrase arrives on screen. As he's about to demonstrate, a new arrival to the party catches his eye.

'Oi, Coxy, you gay life', he calls out. Before he darts off he flashes the screen in front of me. It says: *English and proud*.

They devour football, just like their fathers. When their fathers were young they took up the designer logos of the football casual in the early 1980s. Living at home with their mum and dad, and with, for the first and last time in their lives, a bit of disposable income, they bought The Car, the Bally shoes, the Pringle jumpers, the Lacoste shirts. In fact, it all got so big it was rumoured that Harrods had stopped stocking Lacoste because of the clientele it was beginning to attract. So a couple of shops sprouted locally, selling these names on the Old Kent Road between the pubs and snooker halls, where the clothes got an airing on a Saturday night. It became a bit of a problem locally because so many young men were getting stopped and robbed, for the Lacoste crocodile motif. And you could spot a fake. That's what they said at the bars in these pubs on a Saturday night, as they got the rounds in: *You can tell if it's the real thing*.

He's wearing a Moschino shirt with a print that owes a debt to op art. The girls here, at this party, want Tiffany ('anything – even a key ring'). The mothers love the scent of Versace – although not Blue Jeans ('it's a bit young') and the original

Gaultier ('I like the bottle'). It's Bluewater that's done it, the huge shopping complex down the road, in a scooped-out desert in Dartford, that brought a bit of Bond Street to this neck of the woods. Not that everyone here can afford to buy there ('only the young ones').

And so suddenly this generation got the taste for the West End, and started heading for Bond Street, and it was almost the Lacoste at Harrods thing all over again. The men on the doors of those big shops got a bit twitchy when they noticed. Even when they realised the money was as good as anyone else's, the accents erupting from the faces of those heading for the glass doors were not quite what they were used to.

Coxy joins us, blond as Beckham, and points to Moschino's shoes. He says: 'Whoa, you got your Guccis on then.'

Moschino raises his sockless foot, to reveal a shoe the colour of fudge speckled with dots like tiny liver spots.

'Gucci', he says to me. 'The real thing.'

Most of this generation are the first to come of age in these parts, the children of the diaspora. The schools were rumoured to be better, the roads were wider, and the shadows cast by tower blocks and housing estates were few and far between. Yet still only a small percentage go on to higher education via polytechnic or university. Sport dominates. A number of those in their mid-teens have taken up golf – Tiger Woods on their bedroom walls, and golf clothes in their wardrobes that make them over into mini-me versions of their fathers. The girls, and the mothers, get the football bug on the days national matches are televised: *English and proud*.

The generation that moved here as part of the diaspora, now fortysomething and rising, are concerned that the violence, drugs and crime that had begun to characterise the area they escaped are getting a stranglehold. Beyond that, what unites them is a desire to protect themselves from further disruption. In conversation, you can expect them to put their weight behind individuals imprisoned for protecting themselves from serial burglars, be opposed to convicted paedophiles living locally, or against an influx of asylum-seekers. The pundits who dismiss these concerns as part of populism's manifesto do so with knee-jerk responses as tired, well-trodden and burnt-out as those they impute to the people they are attacking.

Traditionally, the white working class would only take to the street for the end of a war or the beginning of a sale, with the exception of the death of a princess. Naturally there were other exceptional occasions: Jarrow marchers, the dockers responding to the Powell furore, and in the Eighties, in Southwark, there was rumour of revolt when the call went out for the muzzling of Staffordshire bull terriers. But more recently within the working class, still defined by Mayhew's nomenclature, there were those women taking to the streets against paedophiles. There were the taxi-drivers protesting during the petrol price debacle, and the Billingsgate porters' bid to reclaim the streets when they marched on City Hall, angry at the introduction of London's congestion charge. Those who champion democracy, direct action and single-issue pressure groups were suddenly referring to many of these protesters as 'mobs', and even suggesting that the police be sent in to form a thin blue line. Then there was the more pressing concern of a growing support for the British National Party. In Slade Green a BNP member beat the Tory candidate to second place in a by-election. It's a fact that when the issues of crime and antisocial behaviour have been addressed by the authorities in collaboration with residents, in areas such as Slade Green, support for the BNP has diminished by the next polling day. Somehow half-baked opinions about repatriation have no impact when local politics is about getting the bins emptied and more police on the beat. You wouldn't have to go far, in fact no further than the party leader's minders, to find burly bald men with a headful of bigotry under Burberry base-ball caps. But those who have voted for them more recently do not necessarily fit this bill.

Editors who have allotted unprecedented column-inches to this development argue that support comes from traditional working-class Labour voters disgruntled by the Blair adminis-tration. Which is odd, as these and similar journalists previously maintained that the extreme right was dormant during the 1980s because its support came from Tory voters. Actually, behind this 'protest' vote – as it has been described in the press – are work-ing-class whites in poor areas who believe they have been neglected and ghettoised, and others angry that any attempt to tackle the asylum issue is attacked from the sidelines and the gov-ernment backbenches as an appeasement to populism.

Finally, there is the fall-out from the Macpherson report, and the way that the implementation of anti-racist policies is begin-ning to owe a debt to McCarthyism, with working-class whites exclusively cast in the role of villain. By 2003 Phil Woolas, MP for Oldham East, the scene of previous rioting, warned that politicians from all parties were failing to openly condemn vio-lent racist attacks against whites as forcibly as those against blacks or Asians. 'We need a radical change in our race relations policy to reflect the fact that racism exists against white people,' he said, 'that this can take the form of discrimination in the workplace, in physical violence and in neighbourhood rela-tions.'[175] These attacks were predominantly recorded in local newspapers. Following the Macpherson report, they were finally accorded the status of a racial incident: 'any incident which is perceived to be racist by the victim or any other person'. In Catford, a knife assault by a gang on one man was described as 'a vicious attack which bears the hallmarks of the Stephen Lawrence murder – but in reverse'.

Traditionally, there had always been a moral abdication by certain broadsheets when it came to reporting crimes in which whites were the victims of racism. Even the Runnymede Trust overlooked the issue of anti-white racism in its recent report on the future of multi-ethnic Britain: 'Due regard must be paid to racism's different targets: anti-black racism, anti-Muslim racism, anti-Gypsy racism, anti-Irish racism, antisemitism.' The selective reporting on this and other issues concerning race resulted in black and Asian pundits themselves becoming quite perturbed. 'Our entire struggle against racism, its moral and ethical foundation, stands to be discredited because we are not paying enough attention to white victims of black and Asian hatred',[176] wrote the journalist Yasmin Alibhai-Brown. Professor Lola Young, project director at the Archives and Museum of Black Heritage, currently archiving a black presence in Britain that can be traced back 500 years, described how her work involves 'all our histories, not just those of black peoples. It's a strategy to raise awareness, and disseminate information about the rich texture of British history'.[177] It must have come as a snub to white academics who at forums on multiculturalism, in the presence of black academics, behave like those readers of the *New Yorker* who Tom Wolfe said became 'white liberal masochists' after reading a James Baldwin article: 'Flay us, flay us, James, us poor guilty, whitey burghers.'[178]

Elsewhere the historian Stuart Hall opined: 'If you're serious about a multicultural society, you would address the sense of alienation of white working-class people, who have to be won over to a new conception of themselves.' Towards the end of his stint as chairman of the CRE, Gurbux Singh announced: 'Our way of thinking has changed. Tackling the perceptions and poverty levels of poor white communities is almost as important as tackling ethnic minority deprivation.'[179] When the broadcaster Trevor Phillips took over the reins of the CRE, one of his first moves was to dispatch colleagues to the recent areas of unrest, to understand why people might be opting to vote for far-right groups. You could almost believe that taking up the missionary position and striking up a dialogue with the white working class in the twenty-first century had become the black man's burden. And the approach, at least at the outset, was as distinct from that of certain contemporary white middle-class reporters as that which, according to G. K. Chesterton, divided the two tribes who had traditionally gone down and out with the white working class, long before they could put Gucci on their feet and Moschino on their heart: 'The missionary comes to tell the poor man that he is in the same condition with all men. The journalist comes to tell other people how different the poor man is from everybody else.'

Epilogue

TOMORROW, LONDON BELONGS TO ME

London Transport recently applied a scent to the floors of tube stations; it's entitled Madeleine, as though a nod to that which inspired Marcel Proust to embark on his quest for lost time. Disembarking on the Bakerloo platform at the Elephant & Castle, it's difficult to conjure up a vision of the future as promised by planners intent on regenerating the area at the beginning of the twenty-first century, or misty watercoloured memories of the past. Here, the childhood images that spring to mind are far from Proustian: dusty crisp packets crushed behind the radiator of The Estate clubroom, chewing gum rooted to the underside of school desks and pub benches, lolly sticks sinking in liquid black as ink in the drain outside our house. The past is dead, and this is often how we remember our dead, by the things that were so commonplace they didn't register at the time.

The tube station gave in to dilapidation long ago, but has never surrendered to total destruction. At this subterranean level, it feels like a throwback to its days as an air-raid shelter, whilst up above, in the open air is – the land of lost content or the land that time forgot? A land currently in the process of being discovered, or rediscovered, as though a sunken city waking and finally learning to breathe again. Change is in the air.

The Silver Cube remains the space oddity it always was, but is now an anachronism, a crude vision of the future conjured up in the dim and distant past. Evidence of the future that failed to register in the schemes and dreams of past visionaries is present on a glass door of the shopping centre: the remains of a poster, now the vanilla of parchment, at whose centre is the face of a young boy: Damilola Taylor. His death occurred on the Peckham estate intended for the jettisoned 'south London link-ups' scheme, from that last major overhaul of the borough. The tragedy brought a final demand for its demolition.

The shopping centre, which spent much of the Nineties the pink of a seaside rock, has now softened to the red of a gash. Rumour has it that it was painted this shade for Comic Relief, which makes it even more tragic. Goldfinger's Alexander Fleming House is a testament to a certain gentrification. Its bank of offices has been converted to high-priced flats. It is now Metro Central. There's life here, but not as we knew it. A Wetherspoon's and a Nando's caters for the dominant student population from the London College of Printing, and the South Bank Polytechnic, which has expanded like a tiny empire. Another fixture, almost nudging the rear of the site that once housed the South London Music Hall, is the Ministry of Sound, which arrived in the early 1990s. The redundant cinema, where Redford once bought Gatsby to life, has been converted into a concert venue.

If a modern equivalent of Henry Mayhew embarked on an expedition to these parts, he might classify the diverse factions within the borough by race and nationality. Yet the original blueprint would still suffice, not least the dominant presence of a criminal class operating with different codes and existing within its own culture. But equally, a report carried out in 2000 revealed that 54 per cent of residents here live in financial hardship, which was the fourth highest percentage in the country. Certain groups, like Southwark Mothers Against Guns, and their equivalent in other areas, march through local streets by the scenes of shootings and stabbings. On some of the big estates locals have formed credit groups to rescue neighbours from the grip of moneylenders. This is the real modern face of urban activism, by those attempting to reclaim their neighbourhoods. It doesn't attract the numbers or the column-inches it warrants. And holds no appeal for the professional protesters who can be relied upon to take to the streets of urban areas on selective issues, or those found outside the Elephant & Castle tube station, flogging copies of *Socialist Worker* to students.

When I contact a childhood friend, Julie, after decades, and tell her I'll be returning to the area to write about it, she says: 'Just keep driving. Or you'll get mugged.'

We meet in the area – on the brink of middle age. We talk about the mates we had when growing up here. Martin has moved back after living abroad. Linda returns to visit family. Debbie lives locally. Julie comes back to see her relatives on The Estate where she lived after marrying, before becoming part of the diaspora of the 1980s.

'You know who I married don't you?' she asks. 'Charlie no-fingers.'

Marriage, divorce, parenthood, death, have become the themes in lives where once the big news was the report of how one of our number lost three fingers at Silver Blades Ice Rink, during the estate's first summer.

The two of us walk through local streets, agreeing that we have become reminiscent of the older generation that surrounded us as kids, for whom London was summed up by certain buildings, and an intimacy with their intricate detail. Another mate from our formative years has returned to live in his parents' home, since his marriage broke up. We pay him a visit.

I say: 'The last-ever conversation I had with you was when you were on a bus coming home from hospital. Guy's, I think it was.'

'When?'

'We were about eighteen. You'd been stabbed.'

'Where?'

'A pub on the Old Kent Road.'

'No, I mean, what bit of the body?'

Turns out he had been stabbed twice, at different times, on different parts of the body and in different pubs, but on that same stretch of road. Each incident the result of a drunken fight. It's been so long that time has all but healed the scars. There have been more significant wounds: he recently lost a parent. And more significant triumphs: the proud father of two teenage boys.

He looks me up and down, as though checking to see just how much I've changed. I've kept my figure; he's kept his hair. He's checking for battle scars.

'I bet you ain't got a mark on you', he says.

He likes being back because it's local, but hates what it has become. I mention the imminent plans to improve the place. This section of south London is being described by planners and estate agents as 'the lost quarter' of the capital. Someone has taken a look at London and realised that if you stand at Victoria you are the same distance from the West End as if you stood at the Elephant & Castle. Yet the reputation of this locale doesn't compare; doesn't match up to having a neighbouring Kensington, Chelsea, or Belgravia. Now London is opening up, expanding across the Thames, further south, this area is being recognised as a prime location.

'People around here have heard it all before', he says. 'And, anyway, it's too late. No matter what they do to this place now, it won't change anything. It's because of the people that are here now – a lot of them anyway.'

'That's the trouble', Julie says. 'It's some of the dregs you've got here now. I was walking through the estate a little while ago, with my little one, and someone threw something out of a top-floor window. It just missed us.'

Picture Post once referred to the anatomy of this area with its 'sooty bricks, cast-iron spines, and the marble pillars of pubs', and its heart which 'is that of its people'. Historically, it was never healthy, and the sporadic attempts to correct its ailments frequently brought further afflictions.

The three of us sift through the names of demolished streets and attach names to faces long forgotten. We agree on the sequence of certain memories potent enough to become a talking point in the present, and leave the flaws, the fears, the fights in the shadow of the past. We recall that ubiquitous eye of the neighbours that helped cocoon us as kids, translated into nosiness and interference when we were adolescents, and how it seemed to be checking for a code to which we were expected to conform, and which appeared to threaten any ambitions beyond the familiar and the well-trodden, when we were heading for adulthood.

Unlike those who once stood on mats the colour of old mustard in front of open fires, and recast hard times as one part idyllic and two parts comic, we are too cynical for our memories to be rose-tinted or misty watercoloured. We arrived after the bombs brought people together and before the bulldozers pushed them apart. And for us it is merely the backdrop to the beginning of our biographies, not the beginning, middle and end. We couldn't find the words, couldn't articulate exactly what the heart is or was – but before I leave I get an inkling of the spirit of sociability, and trust, that was traditionally at the core of working-class communities. That which Alexander Paterson identified as the generosity that 'touches a point reached nowhere else, and does so by the prompting of instinct, rather than as the result of exhortation and conscious virtue'.

'I've got to go', says Julie. 'I've got to pick up little one.'

He looks at me and says: 'I've got to go out – what are you gonna do?'

'I've kind of got to hang around', I say. 'I'm meeting someone on the estate in their flat, in about an hour. I'll have a wander.'

'Stay here, if you want', he says.

'What, on my own?'

'Yeah. You can watch a DVD if you want. I've got *Shrek*. Just make sure you shut the door when you go.'

'But what if your dad comes back?' I say, sounding twelve again.

'He'll be all right. Tell him who you are. He won't recognise you. But he'll remember you.'

Outside, The Street on this sunny morning in autumn is a thing of beauty compared to the haggard estate: trees are more prominent than the gates protecting its houses (but only just). In recent years, as though in preparation for the forthcoming wave of change, it has partly become something it never had the potential to be: middle-class. Even the previous property boom passed it by, and headed to the docks. The house where Mr Peach once lived – owned and made over by a couple in PR – has been the subject of *Relocation Relocation*. The two residents traded it in for a bijou pad in London and a house in the country. There are doctors. There are students. 'Mad' Frankie Fraser has moved back to the neighbourhood – the stamping ground of his youth. There are even members of the media class. An actor from *Notting Hill* has bought a house in The Street, and doors and decades on from where I once discovered pop, and my balls dropped, the late Ruth Picardie wrote of her final months for the *Observer*. Now the pubs that pepper the streets on the periphery of the estate are being refurbished in anticipation of the developer's new dawn. Only the Prince Regent remains untouched. It is dark, dilapidated, as though a memorial to the past, whilst the flowers and messages on its steps are a stark reminder of the present. They mark the spot where a teenage boy was stabbed.

I meet Doreen. She moved onto The Estate in its early stages, when the paint was barely dry. She and her late mother had been shipped out of their house in a nearby street, which was soon demolished. She recalls that most of the neighbours wanted to stay put, as their homes were not as wrecked as some were. But the guts were ripped out of the neighbourhood, when they should have simply removed the slums. Meanwhile I, Julie, Martin, Debbie and the rising generation welcomed every breeze block that brought change.

Like many flats on the estate, her home is manacled by a gate and window grille. Elsewhere, the surgery is defended by a halo of barbed wire, and the clubroom caged. Almost anything that resembles a walkway is fenced in. Signs and faded posters make points about the perennial problems of dogshit, drugs and syringes.

Doreen's home is bright, immaculate. The only indication of the world that lies outside the neat, peaceful flat, apart from the shadow cast in her kitchen by the bars of a grid, are two scars on the wall. Her flat was flooded twice by a former neighbour above. 'The problems on the estate have stemmed from drugs, crime and antisocial families', she says. 'The council don't do what they should do to keep it in a decent state. And they move in a lot of antisocial tenants. It's about lifestyles. I've seen flats that are filthy and have cockroaches at the window. It makes people want to get out of here as quick as possible. It's gone down in the last three years as much as it has in the last twenty.'

The turnover of residents on the estate is rapid. A number of tenants are subletting their homes while the council seemingly turns a blind eye. Another resident, Maggie, believes that the students in the area add to the itinerant nature of the population: 'They don't have a stake in the neighbourhood. And they don't need to care about it because they don't stay here.'

Both Doreen and Maggie have been actively involved in the Tenants' Association for years. Its efforts have been largely responsible for the attempts to curb crime. During my short time in Doreen's flat, a window shatters several doors along, and two joyriders skid a car onto the forecourt below, crashing it into an oncoming car. The other driver, dazed and confused, attempts to give chase. These are now rare occurrences, apparently.

For several years these women have given much of their free time to working as part of a group set up to liaise with the planners and the council on the issue of future development. After a history of being disenfranchised, the denizens of this estate are trying to find a voice. Maggie got involved in local housing issues the day someone told her there was asbestos in her flat. 'I stay involved because of my grandchildren. I want these changes to the place so that they will have the chance of a better future.' Her children live nearby, in the high-rise built in the Sixties and championed as the tallest block of flats in London.

'I've been a bit of a nomad', Maggie says. 'I've lived in different parts of London. But I've settled here, and it's because of some of the people.'

'I've lived here all my life', says Doreen. 'I like this area. I want to see everyone here that deserves a decent home get one. But I worry that the only people that might be able to one day live in the area are those that are well off, or those that have everything paid for by benefits. And people in the middle, like me, will be forced out.'

The Estate is to be demolished and replaced with new homes. The shopping centre is to be transformed into a new city centre with low-rise terraces, garden squares, and a tower block at its hub. These at least are the developments rumoured to be on the agenda as once again the council, visionaries, planners, architects warm up in the wings. The Elephant & Castle is about to become the canvas for one of the biggest urban regeneration schemes ever to occur in Europe, and to the tune of a cool £600 million. The future is making its way here for the first time since that particular planet was symbolised by silver cubes. But the current vision of the future actually owes a great debt to the past. It seems the infrastructure that was demolished to make way for brutalist estates and a passport-approved photo kiosk in the late twentieth century might be about to enjoy a renaissance, to get rid of what the Southwark plan describes as:

A fragmented and disconnected urban form, a confused, disjointed and inhospitable network of streets and space that actually discourage and prevent pedestrians . . . single districts and neighbourhoods which are inward looking and operate independently of each other.[180]

Long after the Greater London Council was dismantled, the Greater London Assembly came into being with the arrival of the twenty-first century, and at its helm a mayor who was expected to coordinate a strategy for the restructuring of London. The fruits are to be revealed in 2004 with the publication of the official London Plan, which is expected to bring change on a scale not seen since the implementation of the

County of London Plan in the postwar years. The fundamental difference is that whereas the latter was introduced to repair the city after a war, the former has to prepare for a population expected to increase by 700,000 – the equivalent of a city the size of Leeds – by the year 2016. Central to this vision will be the problem that the Abercrombie plan attempted to conquer: those 'industrial working-class areas' such as Southwark and Bermondsey, which in the new plan have become 'areas of opportunity'. The mayor has talked of a social inclusivity 'to give all Londoners the opportunity to share in London's future success'. Once again Southwark, the Cinderella of the capital, is being told that she will go to the ball. But this time there might actually be some music to dance to.

Southwark now has Charles Saatchi's collection in the GLC's former home, County Hall, and the Tate Modern. Shakespeare's Globe has been back in business for some time. Within the County of London Plan was one particular idea that never came to fruition, and trailed off after the creation of the Royal Festival Hall and the National Theatre – the development of something like a cultural walkway along the river front. Bankside was to become the hotspot it was during the Elizabethan period. Back then royalty visited frequently, but it also attracted a new breed, a new class – one without the muscle or the old money of the aristocracy, but nevertheless with a considerable amount of spending power. They descended on the southern shore to witness entertainments not generally allowed or found across the river, and amid surroundings in which there were pockets of poverty, and more inns than you could shake a beggar at. The class that inhabited Bankside and Southwark during that high season has features in common with those who migrate or visit nowadays, as that cultural walkway has evolved. 'The ancient hospitality and freedom of the South are emerging once more', wrote Peter Ackroyd in *London: The Biography*.[181] 'In the twenty-first century it will become one of the most vigorous and varied, not to say popular, centres of London life. So the South Bank has been able triumphantly to reassert its past.'

I became aware of the first of the new settlers in the early 1990s. It was an elegant flat in north London; a function where most of the guests were employed in media-related industries. A conversation had moved to the great injustices of the day – from the global to the local and more pressing. John Major's premiership featured heavily on the agenda, but not as heavily as the news that a McDonald's might be opening locally. The son of a circus act was in Number 10, and a clown was making his way to Hampstead High Street.

Very quickly the topic moved from egg McMuffins to egg plants, when a single white female cut in with the news that she had recently bought a home south of the river, in Southwark.

'Walworth, actually . . . the Elephant & Castle.'

One of the key problems with the neighbourhood, she declared, was the lack of choice. Aubergines, in particular. She had been unable to find aubergines in the market, and this was indicative of a general fear of diversity on the part of her neighbours. With hindsight, in the moment that followed I saw the urban working-class white population metaphorically booted as far below stairs as it might have been in the 1890s. 'The street is very white', she moaned. 'Mmmm, some of the neighbourhood is very white.'

It seemed an odd point to mention at a party in which the few black and brown faces present were on the covers of CDs or on more than £40,000 per annum. But anyway – whites. She didn't necessarily want them living next door, or taking up the whole street (seemingly her multiculturalism made her colourless; her class made her superior). And so her mission had begun there. A mission to move the street closer to the millennium, to create diversity, bring about change, introduce choice – in the shape of egg plants.

The market now has aubergines and halal meat among its fare. Borough High Street has Pret A Manger lattes, baklavas, and internet cafés. Within its library, where I began my investigation, others – white, elderly – are immersed in their own explorations. They are bent over aerial photographs of the neighbourhood. Their eyes seek out familiar routes. Fingers follow names through old electoral registers. Noses are pressed against archaic maps of nearby streets.

Two sisters pick names from electoral records from the mid-Fifties. Their voices are monotonal, interchangeable.

'Pierpoint?'

'Yes, she lived on our landing in the flats.'

'Webb?'

'Yep, old Mr and Mrs Webb. Didn't they have a daughter?'

'Yeah, that's right. The father was a tall fella.'

'I found your nan's house in Beckway Street', a mother tells her daughter. 'Where we lived after the war, when I was carrying your brother.'

Her daughter chips in with: 'She wouldn't recognise it round there now.'

'Wait till I tell my sister', a man with bottle-thick glasses, and expanding to capacity a stretchy, short-sleeve shirt that his generation – sixty odd and rising – would once have called a 'Sloppy Joe', confides to a librarian. 'She swore blind our school was pulled down in the 1960s, but I knew it was there until they built the estate.' He has a magnifying glass slotted between his spectacles and a photograph, as though attempting to decipher a hieroglyph. 'Mind you, you can't argue with her. She has to be right. Not as bad as she was though. She was like that at school. But I tell you something for nothing.' He taps the photograph. 'I'd rather be back there than here now.'

There are six of them in all. They are the ones who are left. Downcast, confused, and apparently redundant in a world of Tate Moderns and multiculturalism. In a climate where history's narratives are as varied as the contents of a market, they turn to the certainty of their own experience of the past, and the history of a family, a house, a street. But it is more than a sentimental journey, more than a palliative for the incurable ache of nostalgia, an ailment that, like stiff joints, affects everyone of a certain generation. They look to each other for confirmation, and compare notes. Throughout the afternoon chats break out between all those present; allegiances are formed over the memory of certain streets and buildings and names. There is a spirit of recognition.

Two more are added to the fold: a married couple, a similar age to the others present. She has mastered the microfiche viewer, and sits with a cardigan as a half-shell for her shoulders. Her other half sits at her side, giving directions, helping her to navigate a census form.

Sloppy Joe has become embroiled in a conversation with one of the sisters, when it emerges they knew people who once lived on the same estate. The conversation turns to crime and punishment, and 'the do-gooders that get the troublemakers off'. His voice softens, as though he fears he's under surveillance: 'Like I say, they don't want to know about us and what we think.' He moves the conversation on to the content of a glossy brochure, promoting the borough and selling it to outsiders. The cover is an image of the nearby Tate Modern, highlighted in electric blue and neon, resembling Peter Ackroyd's description of the restored building: a box filled with light. The conversion of Bankside power station into a showcase for, initially, contemporary British artists has played a major part in the current makeover of the area, which has seen the arrival of a new middle class along with lofts and lattes.

'You wouldn't think us English had ever lived here if you

look at this.' He opens it and taps a page, the way he tapped the photograph that kept him occupied.

> Southwark is a highly cosmopolitan area with a rich mixture of communities going back centuries. The borough's proximity to the River Thames led to strong links across the world and by the 15th century Southwark had one of the largest immigrant populations. German, Dutch and Flemish craftspeople excluded by the City of London settled in Southwark . . . immigrants from Ireland took up manual jobs . . . the labour shortage was eased by workers and their families invited from the Caribbean and West Africa . . . communities from China, Cyprus, Vietnam, Somalia, Ethiopia, Bosnia and Croatia . . . just under a third of our population is from an ethnic minority and over a hundred languages are spoken by our children.[182]

'They don't mention us English', Joe says. 'You wouldn't think we'd ever existed would ya?' Joe sees himself as part of a long-established tribe that dominated the urban working class within this area from the beginning of the nineteenth century and earlier. It has been airbrushed from the history of the area as reported in the brochure. But how would it be represented? The white working class have never needed to define themselves or be defined before. It's the story I have tried to tell in this book. But if the story of the urban white working class here and elsewhere is to be erased by multicultural rebranding, or those who cannot look 'at people being proud of being British and white without them necessarily being the enemy', if the white working class are about to die and with no one to salute them, they could not have a better epitaph than the outcome of a recent survey.

This was a contemporary version of those studies carried out by social investigators in the nineteenth century. The British Social Attitudes survey[183] was first introduced in the 1980s, and the latest confirms that in twenty years we have become a much more liberal country, and certainly on the issues of race and culture. Therefore the past that Sloppy Joe and his fellow travellers remember, that their parents witnessed and in which they fought, is very much with us. In short, change and reform continue to be implemented by evolution rather than revolt and upheaval. The tolerant tradition abounds. Meanwhile, as the white working class grows smaller here, and with London at large expected to be dominated by a non-white population – as is now the case in the borough of Newham – by the end of the decade, it will not be possible to brand them as the sole perpetrators of racism. Divisions will appear between other races and cultures in the capital, as surely as many will come together for those currently elusive common principles expected to define good citizenship. Umberto Eco has written of late of how in this new millennium major European cities, and eventually Europe itself, will be a variation on New York, where different cultures coexist and come together on the basis of common laws and a common language, in this instance the lingua franca being English:

> This meeting (or clash) of cultures could lead to bloodshed, and I believe that to a certain extent it will. Such a result cannot be avoided and will last a long time. However, racists ought to be (in theory) a race on the way to extinction . . .
>
> Roman civilisation was a hybrid culture. Racists will say that this is why it fell, but its fall took five hundred years – which strikes me as time enough for us to make plans for the future.[184]

The borough is being cast as the new Soho; its industrial premises transformed into creative agencies, television production companies and design consultants; its residential patches increasingly taken up by those enticed by what local estate agents describe as 'urban edgy'. This part of the southern shore, dominated by Southwark, and referred to at the beginning of the twentieth century as 'the metropolis of Les Miserables', has been christened London South Central. The Millennium Bridge has helped link north and south. The proposal for a footbridge between Bankside and St Paul's that had been on and off the agenda for centuries was finally realised. The patch of land between the glass-dome home of the Greater London Assembly, City Hall, and London Bridge station is beginning to mirror the City opposite, as companies traditionally identified with its golden mile are opting for cheaper premises immediately south of the river. Fields, the estate agent on Borough High Street, which has waited for this gold rush since before Kate Larter walked this street with her baby daughter, can't quite believe their luck. Inside the tiny wooden building, which appears to have changed little since the young Dickens walked this street, an employee informs me: 'Almost everyone that wants to buy here is connected to the media. They want something grungy; something whizzy and whacky. A building that looks a bit shitty on the outside, but inside can be converted into something amazing.'

The Hartley's jam factory where Nell Hall spent a large chunk of her working life has been transformed into apartments. The Oxo tower is a restaurant. Many of the buildings in which Nell lived or worked have been eradicated or transformed. Here, on London Bridge, where commuters glance towards Tower Bridge, hoping for a glimpse of an American illusionist suspended in a glass box in mid-air, the Halls once joined the crowd to watch a man walk on water. Here Nell Hall had her first memory when the Thames was frozen. Down below, the water that once crept past 'as though it were ashamed' may some day soon have less reason to be.

Endnotes

1 Williams, Harry. *South London*, Robert Hale Ltd, 1949.
2 Collins, Norman. *London Belongs to Me*, Fontana Monarch, 1959.
3 Owen, Robert. 'Observations on the effect of the Manufacturing System; with hints for the improvement of those parts of it which are most injurious to health and morals', 1815. *The Long March of Everyman 1750–1960*, Barker, Theo (ed) Penguin, 1978.
4 Cobbett, William. Writing in his 'Political Register', 20 November 1824. *The Long March of Everyman 1750–1960*, Barker, Theo (ed) Penguin, 1978.
5 Thomson, David. *England in the Nineteenth Century (1815–1914)*, Penguin, 1950.
6 Dickens, Charles. From Preface to *Oliver Twist, or the Parish Boy's Progress*, third edition, Chapman and Hill, 1841.
7 Dickens, Charles. *Hard Times*, Wordsworth Editions Ltd, 1995.
8 Miller, Thomas. *Picturesque Sketches of London*, The National Illustrated Library, 1851.
9 Harrison, J. F. C. *The Early Victorians 1832–51*, Panther Books, 1973.
10 Mayhew, Henry. 'The Street-Folk', *London Labour and the London Poor* (Vol 1), Griffin, Bohn & Co., 1861.
11 ibid.
12 Charles Dickens letter to *The Times*, 13 November, 1849.
13 *Southwark Recorder*, 24 August 1889.
14 Greenwood, James. 'With a Night Cabman' from *The Wilds of London* (illustrations by A. Concanen), Chatto & Windus, 1874.
15 ibid.

16 Greenwood, James. 'A Night in the Workhouse'. Reprinted from the *Pall Mall Gazette*, 1866.

17 ibid.

18 Whiteing, Richard. *Mr Sprouts His Opinions*, John Camden Hotten, 1867.

19 Sims, George R. *How the Poor Live*, illustrations by F. Barnard, Chatto & Windus, 1883.

20 ibid.

21 David Pallister article, *Guardian*, 25 February, 1999.

22 Mearns, Andrew (with W. C. Preston). *The Bitter Cry of Outcast London*, James Clarke & Co., 1883.

23 ibid.

24 Booth, General William. *In Darkest England and the Way Out*, International HQ of the Salvation Army, 1890.

25 Greenwood, James. 'Some Secrets of Gypsy Life' from *Low-Life Deeps: An Account of the Strange Fish to be Found There*, illustrations by A. Concanen, Chatto & Windus, 1876.

26 Clarke, Peter. *Hope and Glory: Britain 1900–1990*, Penguin, 1996.

27 Booth, Charles. *Life and Labour of the People of London*, Macmillan & Co., 1902.

28 Pete Curran speaking in 1900. Quote from *The Long March of Everyman 1750–1969*, edited by Theo Barker, André Deutsch, 1978.

29 *The Saturday Review*, 1898.

30 There had previously been a theatre entitled the Newington on this site, where some of Shakespeare's plays had been staged when nearby Bankside was London's theatreland.

31 East, John M. (grandson). *'Neath the Mask*, Allen & Unwin, 1967.

32 Bowers, Robert Woodger. *Sketches of Southwark Old and New*, William Wesley and Son, 1905.

33 Hobsbawm, Eric. *Industry and Empire*, Pelican, 1969.

34 Bowers, Robert Woodger. *Sketches of Southwark Old and New*, William Wesley and Son, 1905.

35 Martin, John. *A Corner of England: A Study of Post-war Changes in a London Slum*, Williams & Norgate, 1932.

36 Booth, Charles. *Inquiry into the Life and Labour of the People of London, Between 1886–1903*, held within the Charles Booth Archive at the London School of Economics.

37 Bell, Quentin. Virginia Woolf quoted in *Virginia Woolf (1882–1912)*, Triad/Granada, 1972.

38 Woolf, Virginia. *A Room of One's Own*, Penguin, 1993.

39 Stead, Francis Herbert. *How Old Age Pensions Began to Be*, Methuen & Co., 1909.

40 *The Daily News Weekly*, 10 March 1900.

41 Besant, Walter. *South London*, Chatto & Windus, 1899.

42 *Surrey Magazine*, 1898.

43 Quoted in *The Long March of Everyman 1750–1960*, Barker, Theo (ed) Penguin, 1978.

44 *Southwark Annual*, 1899.

45 Dickens, Charles. *Hard Times*, Wordsworth Editions Ltd, 1995.

46 Morrison, Arthur. *Tales of Mean Streets*, Methuen & Co., 1912.

47 Morrison, Arthur. *Children of the Jago*, Methuen & Co., 1896.

48 ibid.

49 Findlater, Jane Helen. *Stones from a Glass House*, James Nisbet & Co., 1904.

50 Greenwood, James. 'A Night in the Workhouse'. Reprinted from the *Pall Mall Gazette*, 1866.

51 Brome, Vincent. George Gissing quoted in *Four Realist Novelists*, Longmans, Green & Co., 1965.

52 ibid.

53 Whiteing, Richard. *No. 5 John Street*, Grant Richards, 1899.

54 Maugham, William Somerset. *Liza of Lambeth*, T. F. Unwin, 1897.

55 Ridge, William Pett. *Mord Em'ly*, C. A. Pearson, 1898.

56 ibid.

57 Franklyn, Julian. *The Cockney. A Survey of London Life and Language*, André Deutsch, 1953.

58 Chesterton, G. K. 'Slum Novelists and the Slums' in *Heretics*, Bodley Head, 1905.

59 ibid.

60 Brome, Vincent. George Gissing quoted in *Four Realist Novelists*, Longmans, Green & Co., 1965.

61 Findlater, Jane Helen. *Stones from a Glass House*, James Nisbet & Co., 1904.

62 Paterson, Alexander. *Across the Bridges, or Life by the South London Riverside*, Edward Arnold, 1911.

63 ibid.

64 ibid.

65 Chesterton, G. K. 'Slum Novelists and the Slums' in *Heretics*, Bodley Head, 1905.

66 Paterson, Alexander. *Across the Bridges, or Life by the South London Riverside*, Edward Arnold, 1911.

67 Jephson, Arthur William. *My Work in London*, Sir Isaac Pitman & Sons, 1910.

68 Morrison, Arthur. *Children of the Jago*, Methuen & Co., 1896.

69 ibid.

70 Stead, Francis Herbert. *How Old Age Pensions Began to Be*, Methuen & Co., 1909.

71 ibid.

72 *South London Mail*, 2 April 1898.

73 Paterson, Alexander. *Across the Bridges, or Life by the South London Riverside*, Edward Arnold, 1911.

74 Quote from a Report of the Conference on the Teaching of English in London Elementary Schools, 1909.

75 William, Matthews. *Cockney Past & Present*, Routledge & Kogan Paul, 1972.

76 Paterson, Alexander. *Across the Bridges, or Life by the South London Riverside*, Edward Arnold, 1911.

77 *Daily Express*, 10 August 1912. Quoted in *The Leysdowne Tragedy* by Rex Batten, published by the Friends of Nunhead Cemetery, 1992.

78 From the World War I newspaper and cutting files held at Southwark Local Studies Library.

79 Greenwood, James. 'In London Courts and Alleys' from *In Strange Company; Being the Experiences of a Roving Correspondent*, Henry S. King & Co., 1873.

80 Orford. E. J. (ed.) *The Book of Walworth, Being the Report of the Scheme of Study for the Year 1925*, Browning Hall, 1925.

81 Quoted in the foreword in the survey 'Housing Conditions in the Metropolitan Borough of Southwark' by Irene T. Barclay and Evelyn E. Perry (1929), issued by the Westminster survey group.

82 Paterson, Alexander. *Across the Bridges, or Life by the South London Riverside*, Edward Arnold, 1911.

83 Martin, John. *A Corner of England: A Study of Post-war Changes in a London Slum*, Williams & Norgate, 1932.

84 Barthes, Roland. *Mythologies*, Cape, 1972.

85 Clynes, J. R. *Britain Between the Wars*, C. L. Mowat, 1955.

ENDNOTES

86   Martin, John. *A Corner of England: A Study of Post-war Changes in a London Slum*, Williams & Norgate, 1932.

87   *The New Survey of London Life and Labour* (Dir.: Sir Hubert Llewellyn Smith, for the London School of Economics), King & Son Ltd, 9 vols, 1930–1935.

88   Reith, J. C. W. *Broadcast Over Britain*, Hodder & Stoughton, 1924.

89   Martin, John. *A Corner of England: A Study of Post-war Changes in a London Slum*, Williams & Norgate, 1932.

90   Orwell, George. *The Road to Wigan Pier*, Penguin, 1962.

91   Muggeridge, Malcolm. *The Thirties*, Weidenfeld & Nicolson, 1989.

92   ibid.

93   Orwell, George. *Inside The Whale and Other Essays*, Penguin, 1962.

94   Orwell, George. *The Road to Wigan Pier*, Penguin, 1962.

95   ibid.

96   ibid.

97   Paterson, Alexander. *Across the Bridges, or Life by the South London Riverside*, Edward Arnold, 1911.

98   Massingham, Hugh. *I Took Off My Tie*, William Heinemann, 1936.

99   Whiteing, Richard. *No. 5 John Street*, Grant Richards, 1899.

100 Massingham, Hugh. *I Took Off My Tie*, William Heinemann, 1936.

101 ibid.

102 ibid.

103 Fremlin, Celia. *The Seven Chars of Chelsea*, Methuen & Co., 1940.

104 Mitford, Jessica. *Hons and Rebels*, Gollancz, 1960.

105 ibid.

106 ibid.

107 ibid.

108 ibid.

109 ibid.

110 Muggeridge, Malcolm. *The Thirties*, Weidenfeld & Nicolson, 1989.

111 Orwell, George. *The Road to Wigan Pier*, Penguin, 1962.

112 Massingham, Hugh. *I Took Off My Tie*, William Heinemann, 1936.

113 Mitford, Jessica. *Hons and Rebels*, Gollancz, 1960.

114 *Daily Worker*, 4 October 1937.

115 Massingham, Hugh. *I Took Off My Tie*, William Heinemann, 1936.

116 Orwell, George. *The Lion and the Unicorn* (Part III 'The English Revolution'), Secker and Warburg, 1941.

117 Orwell, George. *The Road to Wigan Pier*, Penguin, 1962.

118 Orwell, George. *The Lion and the Unicorn* (Part III 'The English Revolution'), Secker and Warburg, 1941.

119 Franklyn, Julian. *The Cockney. A Survey of London Life and Language*, André Deutsch, 1953.

120 Collins, Norman. *London Belongs to Me*, Fontana Monarch, 1959.

121 Lewey, Frank R. *Cockney Campaign*, Paul Stanley & Co., 1944.

122 The County of London Plan, prepared by J. H. Forshaw and Patrick Abercrombie, Macmillan & Co. 1943.

123 ibid.

124 Williams, Harry. *South London*, Robert Hale Ltd, 1949.

125 The County of London Plan, prepared by J. H. Forshaw and Patrick Abercrombie, Macmillan & Co. 1943.

126 *Picture Post*, 8 January 1949.

127 The County of London Plan, prepared by J. H. Forshaw and Patrick Abercrombie, Macmillan & Co. 1943.

128 Collins, Norman. *London Belongs to Me*, Fontana Monarch, 1959.

129 Bracewell, Michael. *England is Mine*, HarperCollins, 1997.

130 *Daily Express*, 19 December 1962.

131 Hoggart, Richard. *The Uses of Literacy*, Penguin, 1990.

132 ibid.

133 Hobsbawm, E. J. *Industry and Empire*, Pelican, 1969.

134 Potter, Dennis. *The Changing Forest*, Minerva, 1996.

135 Hill, John. *Sex, Class & Realism: British Cinema 1956–1963*, BFI Books, 1986.

136 Barstow, Stan. *A Kind of Loving*, Michael Joseph, 1960.

137 From the Stuart Hall essay 'Between Two Worlds' in *The Long March of Everyman 1750–1960*, Barker, Theo (ed) Penguin, 1978.

138 ibid.

139 From Adrian Henri's introduction to the Virago edition of *Up the Junction* by Nell Dunn, 1990.

ENDNOTES

140 Potter, Dennis. *The Changing Forest*, Minerva, 1996.

141 ibid.

142 Thomson, David. *England in the Twentieth Century (1914–63)*, Pelican, 1965.

143 Merriot, Oliver. *The Property Boom*, Hamish Hamilton, 1967.

144 *Municipal Journal*, 15 May 1987.

145 Potter, Dennis. *The Changing Forest*, Minerva, 1996.

146 Booker, Christopher. *The Neophiliacs: The Revolution in English Life in the Fifties and Sixties*, Pimlico, 1992.

147 ibid.

148 Macinnes, Colin. 'A Short Guide For Jumbles (to the Life of their Coloured Brethren in England)', from *England, Half English*, Macgibbon & Kee, 1961.

149 Bourke, Joanna. *Working-Class Cultures in Britain 1890–1960*, Routledge, 1993.

150 From the newspaper cuttings held at Southwark Local Studies Library.

151 Bob Rowthorn in his essay 'Migration Limits', *Prospect*, February 2003.

152 Clarke, Peter. *Hope and Glory, Britain 1900–1990*, Penguin, 1996.

153 Bond, Edward. *Saved*, Methuen & Co., 2000.

154 Dunn, Nell. *Up the Junction*, Virago Press, 1990.

155 Clarke, Peter. *Hope and Glory, Britain 1900–1990*, Penguin, 1996.

156 Chesterton, G. K. From the essay 'Slum Novelists and the Slums', in *Heretics*, Bodley Head, 1905.

157 Hoggart, Richard. *The Uses of Literacy*, Penguin, 1990.

158 Polly Toynbee, *Guardian*, 20 April 2001.

159 Wolfe, Tom. 'Funky Chic' in *Mauve Gloves & Madmen, Clutter & Vine*, Picador, 1990.

160 Mark Steel, *Independent*, 20 November 1998.

161 'The New Racism' by Nicholas Farrell, in the *Spectator*, 31 May 1997.

162 From the column entitled 'A Nasty Taste in the Mouth' by Julie Burchill, *Guardian*, 5 May 2001.

163 Berridge, Kate. *Vigor Mortis: The End of the Death Taboo*, Profile, 2001.

164 Burn, Gordon. *Fullalove*, Secker & Warburg, 1995.

165 David Hare quoted in the *Guardian*, 20 January 1999.

166 *Guardian*, July 1998.

167 Bailhache, Jean. *Le Secret Anglais*, Quality Press Ltd, 1948.

168 Billy Bragg interviewed in the *Independent*, 15 February 2002.

169 Orwell, George. 'England Your England' in *Inside the Whale and Other Essays*, Penguin, 1962.

170 Matthew Taylor article 'Consenting Apartheid', *Guardian*, 4 December 2001.

171 Mayhew, Henry. 'The Street-Folk', *London Labour and the London Poor* (Vol 1), Griffin, Bohn & Co., 1861.

172 From the column entitled 'A Nasty Taste in the Mouth' by Julie Burchill, *Guardian*, 5 May 2001.

173 Darcus Howe interviewed by Euan Ferguson in the *Observer*, 9 January 2000.

174 Jamie Wilson and Vivek Chaudhary in the *Guardian*, 25 February 1999.

175 From the David Ward article entitled 'MP accused of pandering to racists', *Guardian*, 4 February 2003.

176 Yasmin Alibhai-Brown in the *Daily Mail*, 4 February 2003.

177 From the Lola Young article 'Britain's Hidden History', *Guardian*, 30 October 2001.

178 Wolfe, Tom. From the essay 'Tiny Mummies! The True Story of the Ruler of 43rd Street's Land of the Walking Dead', in *Hooking Up*, Jonathan Cape, 2000.

179 Gurbux Singh quote, from *Independent on Sunday*, 16 December 2001.

180 'Emerging Framework Principles, Elephant & Castle', produced by London Borough of Southwark 2002.

181 Ackroyd, Peter. *London: The Biography*, Vintage, 2001.

182 Southwark Council's 'Welcome to Southwark', Burrows Communications Ltd.

183 Reported in a *Guardian* leader entitled 'This Liberal Land', 5 December 2002.

184 Eco, Umberto. From 'Migration, Tolerance, and the Intolerable' in *Five Moral Pieces*, Vintage, 2002.